Will Hedman
4015 164th St. SW, Apt. 206
Lynnwood, WA 98087

MW00653587

COUNTRY SCHOOL
MEMORIES

COUNTRY SCHOOL MEMORIES

Designed and Compiled by
Bonnie Hughes Falk

Illustrated by
Nancy Delage Huber

Ninth Printing, July 1998

Published by Skandisk, Inc.
6667 West Old Shakopee Road, Suite #109
Bloomington, MN 55438

Library of Congress Catalog Card Number:
86-091104

ISBN: 1-57534-032-1

Books and music published by Skandisk, Inc. are available through *The
Tomten Catalog*, which offers exemplary children's books, Scandinavian
literature and music, gifts, and other contemporary books.
612-829-8998, 1-800-468-2424
e-mail: tomten@tomten-skandisk.com

Printed in the United States of America

To Mother and Dad,
both of whom attended
a country school.

CONTENTS

INTRODUCTION

- *The aroma of a one-room schoolhouse on a crisp winter morning, with the stove glowing red hot*
- *The smell of wet mittens drying on the wood-burning stove*
- *The desks with the inkwell in the right-hand corner*
- *The cold treks to the "little house" out back*
- *The "everyone share" drinking dippers*
- *The "syrup pail" lunches*
- *The cry of "Anti Over"*

Memories — that's what this book is all about. It is a collection of "Country School Memories" from individuals who experienced the one-room school as a teacher or pupil.

The schoolhouse was the center of the rural community for many years — woven into the lives of all it touched. A special kind of education was provided there, and the character-building principles taught and learned linger on in the memories of all it served.

I felt the one-room school was too much a part of our heritage to be forgotten, so I contacted individuals throughout Minnesota and neighboring states and asked them to send me recollections of their country school days. From the many delightful letters I received, I chose excerpts depicting various aspects of country school life. My only regret is that due to space and duplication of material, I was unable to use all of the information I received. The names of the contributors, along with their country school involvement, are listed in the Acknowledgments in the back of the book.

I hope this book will recreate the flavor of the one-room school and the rural communities it served, and that you will enjoy reliving memories from the past.

Bonnie Hughes Falk

THE ONE-ROOM
SCHOOLHOUSE

THE ONE-ROOM SCHOOLHOUSE

I started first grade in 1917 in a typical country school. Like all country schools (which seem to have all used the same plans), it had one room, with three windows on each side which let in all the light we had. There was nothing but the sun for illumination, and on gloomy days we couldn't study. Each school had a cloakroom in front and a coal shed in the back. There was some variation here. Some had both in front, and occasionally the school had a shed separate from the schoolhouse, which made the teacher's work harder. Each school had a stove. In my first school this was in the back. Children in the front rows were often cold and those near the stove got too warm. I remember we huddled near the stove on very cold days.

Most schools had a teacher's desk, a set of maps, a globe that was suspended from the ceiling, and pictures of Washington and Lincoln. They also had a pail and a dipper for water, a wash basin, a coal pail, and a broom and sweeping compound to use on the floor (to keep the dust down). Sweeping was made more difficult because the floors were made of rough boards. The desks were nailed to long boards so that the children couldn't move them around freely. Thank goodness that idea didn't last long because we had to move the whole row in order to sweep.

Times were hard in 1917 and on through the Depression. Our mothers saved every bit of paper that came into the house that had a plain back. These sheets were sewn together at the tops and used for tablets. Only the more well-to-do parents were able to buy store-bought tablets. We all had penny pencils; some of us had slates. They were noisy, but they saved on paper. Money was scarce, so the poor teacher didn't have much to work with either.

Bathroom facilities were primitive — little houses behind the schoolhouse, at least fifty feet apart. These were poorly constructed but served their purpose. I only taught in one school with indoor "restrooms," and they were not too satisfactory, as they were chemical toilets — no running water.
(Dorothea Thompson)

District 11 looked much like other schools scattered across the prairies during the period of World War I — a white frame building with a bell tower. The location was ideal — right between two lakes.

3

What else in Minnesota! The lake on the east side was the larger and also nearer the school. So here we dabbled in the springtime and slid down the snowy embankments and halfway across the lake in the winter.

Having an enrollment of forty pupils, we needed at least twenty double seats. It was of prime importance to get the partner you wanted for a deskmate. The size of the desk mattered very little. If it was a little small for you, it might be just right for your deskmate.
(Ingeborg Bolstad)

All of the buildings that I taught in were frame, except one which was stucco. They were cold in winter, hot in summer, and often had no screens or storm windows. Floors of wood were hard to keep up, but sweeping compound helped. Much scrubbing was required in muddy weather. Shades were in the middle of the windows, so they pulled both up and down. Lamps hung on the walls. There was no electricity. Dark days were good times for drill. At least one cloakroom was provided; in larger buildings there were two. A wash basin, pitcher for hand pouring, and a method of getting a drink was needed. We went from the common dipper, to cups from home, to paper cups, to the bubbler fountain.
(Arlie M. Klimes)

In our schoolyard there was a fairly large, grassy area with some trees in one corner. We had outdoor toilets until the building was remodeled, and then we had indoor "chemical" ones. Neither type was very "fragrant." There was a well and hand-operated pump on the east side. I recall the big round stove, which was protected by a metal sheath imprinted with scroll-like designs. We stood there to warm up after outside recess. There were always mittens, with their woolly smell, drying near the stove. There was a fence all around the yard. Later, remodeling added a basement and a kitchen.
(N. Wyelene Fredericksen)

The school building consisted of one room and an entry or hall. The school I attended as a student had a big jacket stove in the front corner of the room, a teacher's desk, wall maps, library shelves with glass front doors, a globe which hung from the ceiling on a pulley, blackboards on the walls all around the room, bulletin boards above the blackboards, and a water cooler and basin in the corner. The students each had their own cups in their desks. There were outdoor privies.

A big bell was in the belfry, with a rope to ring the bell hanging in the schoolrom. It was tempting to some children to pull that rope. When I was the teacher, I made it a rule that whenever that bell was rung, it was school time. So when someone ran by and pulled it during playtime, we all had to come in. Just once was enough and it wasn't touched again.
(Margaret Thompson Cimenski)

The school building was one large room, with an enclosed entry (too cold to be used during the winter months) and a porch. There was also a coal shed attached to the main room, as there was a coal stove near the center of the room which heated the building. There were about four windows on each side of the schoolroom, pictures of George Washington and Abraham Lincoln in the front of the room, and maps and a globe. Water had to be brought from home. One of the families would bring it in a big water can and get a small fee for hauling it. The water was placed in a big crock jar with a spigot and used for drinking, as well as for washing hands.
(Mary D. Thompson)

I had cousins on a farm near Spencer, Iowa, and they went to a country school. I visited them there while I was in the primary grades, and I was fascinated. Just a little old tumbling down school, with long seats that held two or more pupils. You always had a deskmate. There were noon lunches in tin pails, with covers to keep out the flies, etc. — like a picnic. I loved it and wanted to go to that school. Memories of that school always stayed with me.
(Elma Summers)

School district 55 was located ten miles southeast of Waseca. The building was very small, with just two windows on each side and a little entry. There was a square trapdoor in the ceiling leading to a small garret or attic. A first grader of the 1900 school year said his teacher threatened to put him up there if he would not be quiet. Needless to say, he never was put up there.
(Ruth V. Esping)

In the early years in country schools, there were no lights in the buildings; then kerosene bracket lamps were hung on the walls; then the Aladdin Wall Lamp with its bright light; and much later, electric lights. Each day a pail of water was carried from the neighbor's place to the school, sometimes by one of the older boys. The pupils used the one dipper from the water pail. Later, a water fountain with a faucet was used, and each child used his own cup.

All older school buildings were cold. The first heating stove was a square wood-burning box stove. Early in the morning on cold days the children sat around the stove studying. It was too cold in the back of the room. Later on, a circulating coal-burning furnace was installed. At one time heavy paper was put around the base of the school building and then banked with manure to help keep the cold out.
(Forrest and Ethelyn McKinley)

Some of my schools had indoor chemical toilets and oil burners. Water for drinking was carried from the well of a nearby farm, or I brought it from home. When the coal was stored in the shed, the locks would freeze from drips off the roof, so I kept salt water under the stove to thaw it out. Once, the coal was in the basement and there was about three feet of water down there. I was supposed to walk a plank from the steps to the coal. I finally refused because if I hit my head and fell, I might drown!
(Emily Sedlacek)

Winter was the hardest time in the country school. More than once the teacher didn't arrive until shortly before the students, so there was often no heat in the school. Since there was no insulation in the building, it would get very cold. We often sat around the stove until ten o'clock before starting classes. Ink would freeze in the inkwells and our lunches would freeze in the dinner pails on the shelves.
(Alice M. Jenkins)

We lived in North Dakota in the early 1900s. My three older sisters went to a sod schoolhouse. The walls of the building were very thick. The roof had a few green plants growing from it. One day I visited school. We four sisters all rode to school on one pony. Two sat behind the saddle, and Pearl, the oldest, drove the pony, with me on her lap holding onto the pommel. The distance was nearly two miles.

I remember being carried in the schoolroom by a nice teacher. She gave me a book to read and put me on the window ledge. Due to the thick walls, there was a lovely, big place to read. The floor was of wood and the sod walls were coated with a green color. A

stove in the corner of the room kept all of us warm. By the time I started school, a new wooden building replaced the sod building. This was approximately 1914 or 1915.
(Sally L. Ose)

Our schoolhouse was a wood frame building with windows on both sides — east and west. A round oak stove heated the building. We had outside privies, one for the boys and one for the girls. We used old catalogs instead of toilet paper!

In later years the schoolhouse was raised up and a basement was put under it. Two chemical toilets were added to the main floor, plus an entrance and a place to hang our coats. A small library was also added, with a garage for the teacher's car below it. In the basement, a kitchen was at one end, with a furnace, furnace room, and coal room at the other end. Electricity was also installed at that time. The new addition was used for community meetings, like Farm Bureau and 4-H, and miscellaneous parties.
(Elsie S. Fredericksen Williams)

The country school I attended was in a little town consisting of one store, which included the post office. The owners lived in the rear of the store. There were six more homes, three elevators, and the schoolhouse. It was a large one-room school, and about thirty pupils attended.

I was really too young to start school when I did, but my brother (two years older) was too afraid to go alone, so I went with him. When mother withdrew me, as Jack became acquainted, the teacher wrote to her saying that I was one of the better students and she would like to have me stay. Therefore, my brother and I remained in the same grade for the next eight years.
(Ruby Vickers)

Our schoolhouse was one room, with a lean-to for a coal bin and a cloakroom (unheated). There was a four-stall barn for horses. There were also two outbuildings labeled "boys" and "girls." One wall in the schoolroom was covered with blackboards and there was a case of roll-down maps. And as long as I can remember, there were half-worn-out erasers, and it was a special privilege to stay after school to clean them. There was also a teacher's desk, recitation bench (which didn't have to be large because enrollment was never over fourteen), a school clock, a picture of George Washington, a shelf with a large

7

unabridged dictionary, and a picture of Sacajawea (a must in North Dakota schools). Our library was one tall bookcase. There was a table which held the water cooler, a covered Red Wing jar with a spigot on one side. Our lunch pails were empty syrup pails. There was no well so one of the big kids had to carry water from home. A few had fancy metal cups. The rest of us made cups by folding a piece of tablet paper. You had to drink fast because tablet paper soaked up quickly! There was a large stove, on which wet mittens always hung in the winter; there was always the smell of drying (or scorching) wool. Teachers had to learn to fire the blast with lignite, a smoky, sooty coal mined in western North Dakota. One had to strike a delicate balance between a fire that was too low and would go out overnight, a fire that was too hot and would burn out overnight, or a fire that was just right and properly banked so just a good shaking would get it going the next day.

For equipment we had big fat tablets with red covers (with a big 5 or 10 on them because that was what they cost), penny pencils of unpainted cedar that had no metal cuff to hold the eraser, inkwells in the desks, pen points that always seemed to scratch, and a wind-up phonograph (very cultural).

One of the things I remember best was the flag. It was special to all of us. The school day started with the pledge to the flag. It was a special privilege to put up the flag in the morning. At the first drop of rain on the window, hands were raised and waved frantically, with the cry of, "Teacher, teacher, it's raining." Teacher would immediately send someone out to take down the flag. It was *never* allowed to stay out in a storm, and I still cringe when I see flags drooping, neglected in the rain.
(Mae F. Hardin)

District 73, the Hill Billy School, stood small but sedate, surrounded on three sides by grain fields and on the south side by hilly pastures. A small graveled road meandered past the school, sweeping gently past to join the larger roads on either the east or the west end. I was fortunate to be the teacher of this little prairie school for three wonderful years.

Our light was provided by wall lamps with shining reflectors hung by brackets above the blackboards, thereby making four on each side of the room. This lamp light was frequently necessary during stormy or short winter days. How I would love to have one of those lamps now!

8

Our bathroom facilities consisted of a boys' and a girls' toilet built on either side of the big coal shed. There was a gray enameled wash basin, with a red bar of Lifebuoy soap beside it, standing on a small wooden stand in one corner of the schoolroom.

Water was carried by pails to fill the large crock fountain that stood just inside the schoolroom. This fountain had to be carefully drained each evening during cold weather; otherwise, the freezing water would cause it to crack. I was most thankful this never happened during my years at the school. I can well imagine the stir that would have been created had it been necessary to ask the school board to buy a new water fountain!

We were fortunate to have a case of large maps that could be pulled down when needed or rolled up when not in use. There was also a bookcase with a glass front that held perhaps as many as one hundred books. Lucky were the children whose parents took them to a public library. To be honest, I know of only one family who made use of the public library, so the children were very limited in their reading material.

The smallest desks were on one side of the room, the middle-sized desks in the middle of the room, and the large double desks on the outside. Our school wasn't very large — perhaps an average of fifteen or sixteen students in one year. Our smaller school, with all grades in one room, gave us the opportunity to give a lot of personal attention to each child. We knew our students very well because of the small classes.

The Sunday afternoon before opening day, I had the exciting task of making the schoolroom attractive by placing a jar of fall bittersweet on the bookcase, with a cluster of fall leaves placed casually beside it; then going about the room tacking up pictures cut from magazines. All teachers were especially fond of the homey Norman Rockwell pictures to be found on the cover of *The Saturday Evening Post*. These pictures mounted on bright pages of construction paper were highly prized for decorating the schoolroom. My last chore before leaving for my boarding place was to polish the little hand bell with my freshly ironed handkerchief, and to place it in a prominent spot on my newly acquired desk.

(Margaret Seeger Hedlund)

THE
LONG
WALK

THE LONG WALK

There were very few days when we didn't walk the two miles to and from school. When my brother got older, he made a "stoneboat," as it was called, and his pony, Bud, pulled it to take us to school when it was extremely cold. To keep warm we were made to wear long-legged underwear, which I always rolled up after arriving at school. It was a bit of a battle to get us to wear it, and there was always an argument to get my brother Sonny to wear something on his head.

I clearly remember the fear we often had of a large bull when we were walking to school. He seemed to know how afraid of him we were. He would paw the dirt and beller. We had heard that wearing red might anger him, so anything red was hidden. Many times we went way out of our way to avoid him. I can remember even crawling in the ditch to get past him.
(Mae Hanson Hughes Kjos)

The country school we attended was about one mile from our home. It became a long walk when it was cold. We were dressed well in the winter, and we were strong and had good legs then. Instead of coming to get us with horses if the weather was bad, my dad would walk across the field to meet us.

In the spring and fall the walks were fun. Several families walked together. In those days wild flowers grew abundantly along the road. All the huge machinery of today hadn't ruined the natural beauty of the countryside. Lots of woods were around our school, and we played there during recess. In the fall there were chokecherries and hazelnuts, which were fun to hunt and eat.
(Ada Ronnei Pederson)

My family lived two miles from school. My dad and near neighbors often gave us rides. We did not have a car until I was in the third or fourth grade, so the trips were made with horses. In the winter I remember the big bobsled, with straw in the bottom and blankets galore to keep us warm.

In the spring and fall when we walked to and from school, we were frightened of cows, and especially the bulls, which were in pastures along the way. Someone had told us that if we paid no

attention to them they would not bother us, so we would walk past them with our heads down, looking at the ground.
(Selma Anderson Hughes)

The years I attended a rural school as a student, we walked one and one-half miles each morning and afternoon, regardless of the weather. I loved school and never wanted to miss a day.

As we got older, we were required to do the breakfast dishes before leaving for school. My sister and I then would have to hurry. We'd run between two telephone poles, walk between the next two, and would arrive on the school ground many times as the last bell was ringing.
(Margaret Thompson Cimenski)

I remember walking to country school when it was quite cold. My brother and I had to walk one and one-half miles. One morning, even though I wore knitted wool mittens, my hands were really cold and I let the teacher know it. Then a boy took me out to the well and pumped C-O-L-D water on my hands! Eventually, they warmed up.

On cold, cold stormy days in the winter, my grandfather came to the school to get us. He had a medium-sized sled, pulled by a horse. He put a heavy blanket over me for the ride home.
(Orline Golden Foelschow)

One morning as I was walking to school, I heard a bull roaring. He was coming along the side road. If I quickened my pace, he did likewise. I saw I wouldn't be able to make it to the school, so I jumped the fence of a neighbor who lived close by. The bull came way up to the fence where I had jumped. By that time the neighbor was there to help me. I had never been able to jump a fence before and I haven't since! I guess panic got the best of me. The bull was sold the next day and I watched him go!
(Selma O. Sanvik)

Walking two and one-half miles to school involved many interesting experiences. Seeing the abundant violets and Dutchman's breeches on the side of the hill was always a thrill. While cutting across farmers' fields, the boys would tell us that a bull was coming after us. This caused us to run great distances to get ahead of the bull, which I never remember seeing.
(Margaret Jenkins)

In the spring and fall when the weather was nice, we walked the two and one-half miles to and from school each day. Sometimes we would get a ride with farmers from the area who came to the creamery in Cambria. In the winter parents would take turns transporting us to school. The roads weren't open after a snowstorm for two or three days sometimes, and we would go to school in a horse-drawn sleigh. It was fun to go in the sleigh, but it was also cold. My mother would heat bricks in the oven and wrap them in paper and cloth to help keep our feet warm.
(Alice M. Jenkins)

I boarded at a home one-fourth mile from the school, and even on the coldest days I walked. It was in the days before women wore slacks, and I would wrap newspaper under my hose to keep my legs from freezing. The years were 1927 - 1930.
(Ruby Vickers)

As far as walking to and from school, my experiences weren't all that enjoyable. I walked as much as three and one-half miles when the roads were impassable to cars. My clothing was so bulky that I doubt if I could have lifted my one hundred pounds back into a standing position if I had fallen down! Besides, subzero weather didn't help one iota. I have had both frozen hands and feet.

As a teacher, I enjoyed the enthusiasm of my pupils when they related what they had seen on the way to school. When one lad got his first glasses, he was happy to see that leaves on trees were actually separated. Those walks taught observance of things around us.

Riding back and forth was wonderful. One could roll down the windows and blow the cobwebs out of one's brain. This was my time to be alone — to meditate on the day to come, or to relive the day just past. I could see my day in retrospect, make plans, and become peaceful within myself. It was also very relaxing to drive home, anticipating some family activity before correcting papers.

One experience I had was during World War II, when gas and tires were rationed. No matter how I hoarded the gas, it just would not stretch. So unless someone gave me an unwanted stamp, I walked for a couple of days. A far greater handicap was the tires. One tire was cut and put over the other as a reinforcement. The Texaco station owner got tired of fixing the tires, so he called the ration board and told them that he was putting on four new tires and that they

should send him four stamps. The stamps came, and I am ever grateful to him.
(Arlie M. Klimes)

I taught my own daughter through the eight grades, taking her along to the rural schools. We drove as much as fifteen miles to school. One winter she walked ahead to see how hard the snowbanks were; then if they were hard, I'd drive my Model A Ford Coupe over the top. Because of floods one spring, we drove eighty miles a day to get to a school twelve miles away.
(Emily Sedlacek)

We lived about two miles from school. We walked when it was nice and got a ride in the cold months. Usually it took us a long time to get home from school since we fooled around with the other kids, throwing rocks in the ditches of water, talking, and even playing games. If we were in a hurry to get home, we'd climb the fences and cut through the fields. We had one bike for five of us, so we took turns riding that.
(Marva Rumelhart Ball)

In 1911 when I was six years old, I attended a rural school two miles from my home. On nice days I walked with my older brother, and we joined several other kids along the way. When the weather was rainy or snowy, our dad hitched a team of horses to a lumber wagon or a bobsled and took us. By the time we reached the school, there were at least a dozen kids in the vehicle. Dad was sure he had plenty of horse blankets to cover the noisy kids.

When there was snow on the ground, Dad hitched Old Dan (a pacer) to the cutter, and we drove him to school. My older brother headed Old Dan toward home, and he'd go by himself. One day Old Dan didn't get home when Dad and Mom expected him. They looked up the road and saw him standing beside a telephone pole. For those of you who are unfamiliar with a cutter, the fills are set off center on the cutter so the horse can travel in the track, so you understand why Old Dan was stopped by a telephone pole. Dad tried many times to send Old Dan to school to get us at four o'clock, but Old Dan was a smart horse. When he'd get to the road, he'd turn around and go back to the barn. Since Dad's plan didn't work, it was *he* and Old Dan who came to get us.
(Marjorie Sperry)

We rode to school in a wagon called a "Democrat." My father had built a small shed on the school ground for the horses. I walked to school most of my early days of teaching, through snow, mud, and water. When I started driving, I had many problems driving through snowstorms, rainstorms, etc.
(Eldora Nannestad)

For the first three years, I went to a one-room country school which was located two miles from my home. We had a neighbor girl across the road who was several years older than I, and her father always took her to school with a team and buggy. I got to ride along, but she was sick most of the time so I had to go alone, and two miles seemed like an awfully long way to a six-year-old. In the winter when the weather was bad, I missed a lot of school.

After I finished my schooling, we moved to a farm that had a country school on one corner. During that time the young teacher roomed and boarded at our house. In the spring of the year sometimes the dirt roads were nearly impassable, so I would take the teacher to school on horseback across the fields.
(Harley Oldenborg)

Every pupil, and the teacher, walked to and from school. Buses were non-existent, and very few families owned automobiles. Many of the pupils lived on the south side of the lake (the school was on the north side), and these pupils waited anxiously for the winter freeze so that they could walk across the lake and shorten the distance.
(Ida Posteher Fabyanske)

We recall the fear some children had of a neighbor's dog when they had to go by that farmhouse to and from school. This big dog would seem to hide by the trees, in the tall grass, or in the road ditches. He never barked and you couldn't see him anywhere. Then all at once there he would be, with his nose right down at the children's heels like he was ready to bite. Luckily, he never did. But oh, how he did frighten the children!
(Forrest and Ethelyn McKinley)

I walked to and from school, one mile each way, rain or shine or snow (sometimes knee-deep). It was a fun time to chat with my sisters and brothers while walking to school. I also enjoyed watching the birds and stopping by the pond along the way to watch the frogs

and turtles. I think I enjoy all the beauties of nature so much more having been so close to them in my daily walks to and from school.
(Van Johnson)

Each school district in the southeastern area of South Dakota reached out two and one-half miles in each direction from the schoolhouse — a school every five miles. In those "horse and buggy" days, that was far enough, especially with dirt roads (not even gravel). You went to school on foot, in a buggy, or on horseback. I write of the 1920s.
(Milton S. Johnson)

When I started first grade, my cousin was starting her first year of teaching. Throughout the winter, she lived with us. We were about one and one-half miles from school. Many times in the winter my father took us to school in a horse-drawn cutter, complete with heavy robes and foot warmer, with hot coals in it to keep our feet warm.

Most of the students walked to school, except for one family I recall who lived about three miles from school. They had a horse-drawn cart, in which they rode to school. Many times we would meet them on the corner and get a ride with them.

On our way to school we passed a gravel pit that had water in it. Once this froze over in the fall, we would often stop there and play on our way home. My birthday was November 17, and of course that was one of the days the kids chose to stop and play. I knew if I went down on the ice, I would surely get a "birthday spanking," so I decided I would wait in the cart. It seemed like they were having so much fun and were playing longer than usual, so I finally gave in and went down to play, too. As soon as I got down on the ice, I got my "birthday spanking." They grabbed me by my arms and feet and bounced my bottom on the ice, once for each year, of course.
(Deloris Delage)

In the wintertime nearly all kids, both boys and girls, had their own skis; very few walked to school. We would line the skis up in the schoolhouse, and they would almost fill a whole wall. At recess and noon hour we would run to a little hill just east of Magnuson's driveway, place several sets of skis together, and then sit down on them and slide down the hill. After the path hardened, we sometimes made it all the way to the creek. Then we had to pick up the skis and carry them back to the top of the hill for another try.
(Holger O. Warner)

We got to school by walking a mile or so. The road was a typical gravel road — hot, dusty, muddy, icy, or cold. We were cautioned by Mom not to take rides with anyone, so the day we were offered a ride home by a neighbor, I stuck to my guns and refused. This meant my brothers and sister had to stay with me and continue the long walk home. After we got home, Mom said it was okay to accept a ride if we knew the person. Why hadn't she told me that in the first place?

We would sometimes lay an old purse, with a long string attached, on the road — carefully covering the string with gravel. We'd then take the end of the string and hide in the tall grass until a car came along. When the car stopped, my brother would yank the string hard; then we'd all laugh and run like the dickens!
(Jerrie Steinwall Ahrens)

I walked to school most of the time, but some of the students rode horses. My dad took me to school the first day with a team of mules. We lived one mile west through the field. I knew no one. My teacher gave me a picture of a goose to color. I told my dad I was going to color the feet black, like it had been in the mud. When I looked up, my dad was gone! I cried most of the day.
(Hazel Hubbart Parquet)

I walked about one-half mile to and from school. Sometimes the snow was over knee-high. On the way home one day, I froze all ten fingers. This was very painful when they thawed out. Naturally, all the skin peeled off.
(Signe Haraldson)

We lived about two miles from the schoolhouse and often walked home in nice weather, but my mother or dad usually took us in the morning with the Model T Ford.

One time we had a cart, and we hitched up a horse to take us to school. However, the horse usually got away and ran home ahead, so that didn't work out very well.
(Mary D. Thompson)

One night there was a snowstorm, during which huge snowdrifts accumulated. The hired man took me to school the next morning by sled. When we were about one-half mile from the school, the horses refused to go any farther. I decided to walk the rest of the

way, not realizing how deep the snow was. With every step, I'd sink to my knees. I was so sure that I wouldn't make it that I yelled and yelled, hoping someone would hear me. I finally made it to the schoolhouse, but I had frozen my ankles along the way.
(Selma O. Sanvik)

The weather had warmed up and the road was very muddy as I walked the mile to school one March morning. Several young men came along in a farm wagon. Very graciously, they offered me a ride. My boots were muddy, and when I attempted to climb into the wagon, I fell into the mud. The fellows burst into laughter. I stood up and told them they weren't gentlemen and proceeded to give them a lecture on manners. Needless to say, they then jumped out of the wagon and helped me in.
(Edith O. Chaffer)

I walked a mile and a half to school each morning and evening — not too bad a walk if the weather was nice, but this could be an unending distance if it were raining or storming.

I well recall one particular evening when I got a call telling me that there was a bad storm brewing. I hastily put on my warm clothing and began my walk home. Snowflakes were swirling wildly about as I hurried on my way. About halfway home, the storm had become so bad that I could not see the familiar landmarks. I stumbled along blindly, becoming more frightened each minute. Suddenly, I became aware of the field of corn shocks that was at the side of the path I followed across the fields. Now I knew I was on the right path and hurried as fast as possible, nearly losing my breath because of the strong wind. Then the big red barn came into view — perhaps ten feet from me. What a grateful feeling of both surprise and relief overcame me. Yes, I got quite a lecture on the dangers of staying so late at the schoolhouse, and also for not watching the winter weather more closely.
(Margaret Seeger Hedlund)

THE SCHOOL DAY BEGINS

THE SCHOOL DAY BEGINS

The education in a country school was broad and comparatively good. A sense of independence in studying was achieved. "On your honor" meant something if you were to have privileges. You achieved more by being free to move around and get things when needed, not having to wait. All could learn from listening to other classes. If you missed something, you had another chance to pick it up. You had an idea of what the next year would bring. In some ways a rural school teacher was a tutor. A teacher learned to stagger classes and to hold several at one time by doing board work, written guide sheets, and oral work at the same time. There were spelling contests at the school, county, state, and interstate level. It was an honor to be able to take part.

As a teacher, I required at least one book report a period. Schools exchanged books, pupils had library cards in a nearby town, whole schools drove in to a library to get books to keep for a month, and we could get twenty-five books from the traveling library. Pupils recommended books to each other and also exchanged books. They really read quite broadly.
(Arlie M. Klimes)

What I liked so much about country school teaching was that I could arrange things as I liked. It was tutoring, not teaching. Each child went as fast as he could; no moving them along just because it was the next year. Some went faster than others, and the slow ones eventually caught up. I firmly believe that all subjects should be taught in levels, with a test to see if one is ready for the next level.
(Elma Summers)

Children were sent to school whenever the parents decided they were ready. The teacher passed them on according to their ability, so children started anywhere between the ages of four and seven and graduated anywhere between eleven and fifteen.

Having one teacher for all the grades meant that time in class was very limited, so we always had a lot of homework. Consequently, I believe the parents became more involved than those of today. Also, what I consider to have been a decided advantage was that pupils were always able to review what they had studied, since they were

exposed to the same things year after year. If a pupil couldn't master fractions or decimals in his own class, he could always refresh his memory the following year with the next class.
(Ida Posteher Fabyanske)

The education in a one-room school was good, I thought, because you heard what everybody else was studying, so you were pretty smart by the time you went through the eight grades.

I remember when we got a wind-up phonograph and some good records, so we had our own "music appreciation" hour. We had to be able to recognize the piece, giving its name and composer. The same with picture study. We would be expected to know the name of the picture and its artist. We also had penmanship classes, learning to write by the Palmer method.
(Mary D. Thompson)

Most classes were very small, with only one or two in a class. Older children helped the younger ones. Some studied while others recited, and it all seemed to come out right. They learned a lot by just listening.

When I was in the first grade we got a lot of busy work, which was exactly that. The teacher put numbers on our desks with chalk, and we outlined them with corn. At recess time she swept them all into a box. Sewing cards were better because we could take them home.

In the early 1900s we had many newcomers, mostly from Norway or Germany, who came to school to learn English. They were often young men. Sometimes the pupils were nearly as old as the teacher, as the boys had to help at home and only attended in the winter months. Some schools only ran eight months so the boys would be home for spring work.
(Dorothea Thompson)

Every morning we had opening exercises, which consisted of singing, reciting proverbs, or the teacher reading from a library book. We had a library from which we chose books to read. Some were read over and over again.

The size of the classes varied. Sometimes you wouldn't have any pupils in a particular grade. If all classes were filled, you'd maybe have only ten minutes for a class. The most pressure was to try and teach the seventh and eighth graders the right things, as they had to have a mark of 75 on the final exams. Subjects taught were history, geography, language, math, writing, art, and sometimes science.

Friday afternoons were used for art. The girls would sew and the boys did what we called small carpentry work. We also did drawing and painting. We always made a gift for the moms and dads for Christmas.

I think the country schools were a special part of education. The little ones learned from the older ones. No matter what class you were conducting, the rest could listen in.
(Selma O. Sanvik)

Our subjects included reading, writing, the Palmer method of penmanship (which was stressed), spelling (lots of words that we had to learn or else!), arithmetic, history (mostly American), geography, language, and on Friday afternoons we had art. Each grade individually came to the front of the room for recitation. The pupils in the other grades were to study or listen to the class that was being conducted. However, during that time some pupils might throw spitballs or paper airplanes, pass notes to their friends, or maybe even put chalk dust on someone's face or in their hair!
(Elsie S. Fredericksen Williams)

We had reading, penmanship, music, arithmetic, language and grammar, history, geography, physiology, and art. I read most of the books in the library many times and I got many certificates from the county office for library reading.

A county superintendent came a couple times during the year to check supplies, conditions of the school, and the students. We had to take State Board Examinations in the eighth grade. They took turns giving them in the neighboring schools several miles away. We always walked the distance to take the tests. Mom usually made a special lunch for us for the event. I can remember mincemeat pie was a favorite treat, along with some special fruit, which made the long trek more enjoyable.
(Ada Ronnei Pederson)

We always had a so-called monitor each week. The hand bell was rung by one of the students. The day started by pledging allegiance to the flag, and the teacher always read one chapter from one of the classics.

A lot of our work in reading was memorizing, and a lot of it stayed with you through the years. We had to draw maps of all the con-

tinents, put in all the countries, and know the capitals. Each class went to the bench in front for recitation.
(Lucille Siefkes)

Subjects taught were reading, history, geography, civics, language, spelling, arithmetic, and science. We had penmanship once a week and also art. Penmanship papers were sent in to the county superintendent's office and the best ones got certificates. We had Y.C.L. (Young Citizens' League) days once a year and the best art, penmanship papers, and booklets were sent in. We also had spelling contests and the best spellers went on.
(Marva Rumelhart Ball)

The first book I remember learning to read was *The Sunbonnet Babies*. When I began selecting library books to read I remember I liked biographies and autobiographies, and I still do.

I have often felt that my elementary teachers in country school did a very good job teaching the math processes. We practiced and practiced for speed and accuracy in addition, subtraction, multiplication, and division. We worked on spelling, too. Spelldowns were common practice.

To graduate from the eighth grade, students had to pass State Exams. We spent weeks and weeks studying old examination questions. All our grades on report cards, tests, and papers were written in percentages, with 75 as a necessary grade for passing.
(Selma Anderson Hughes)

Friday afternoons were the only times we had music or art. Music included singing from *The Golden Book of Songs* (Old Black Joe, Yankee Doodle, Battle Hymn of the Republic, etc.).

We had a lot of spare time before the teacher called us to the front of the room to recite. I spent much of that time completing a booklet, writing stories out of encyclopedias, and copying jokes out of magazines.
(Margaret Jenkins)

No two children were allowed out of their seats at any one time. The children raised their hand, pointing one finger if they wanted to go to the toilet, two fingers if they wanted to sharpen their pencil, three fingers if they wanted to speak to another pupil, four fingers if they wanted to use the dictionary, and their whole hand if they

wanted to contact the teacher. That way the teacher could look up from a class in progress and know what the child wanted to do, nodding her head if permission was given, and not disturbing the class.
(Ruby Vickers)

The smartest high school students always came from the rural schools. They were especially smart in reading and spelling. Phonics was always an important part of education for all beginners in our school days. Later, when we were teachers, we were all good readers and spellers. Today, in so many grade schools, phonics and other good aids are not taught to beginners, resulting in a generation of such poor readers and spellers.
(Carol Johnston Jeddeloh)

All my eight years of elementary education were in a rural school, and I have never felt that my education was neglected because of it. Since all classes were in one room, younger and older pupils benefited from listening to other classes. Classes were not restricted to the 3 R's. I remember having a man teacher who taught cooking, sewing, manual training, and crafts. I still have a laundry bag that I made in the seventh grade — over seventy years ago.

Country children were shy and sometimes ridiculed by "town kids" when they started high school, but teachers were ready with praise. They said "country kids" were better disciplined, had more respect, and had no trouble keeping up scholastically.
(Mabel Winter)

To graduate from eighth grade you had to take State Board Examinations that were really some humdingers. Some of the answers to those questions I, the teacher, didn't even know!
(Helen C. Williams)

It was customary to have Friday afternoons reserved for such special activities as art and industrial arts. There definitely was a male/female division for such projects, but there was some overlapping. I had a strong interest in art, so these were "red letter days" for me. We "published" a school newspaper, actually one copy only, which was sent home from family to family. I remember doing covers and illustrations for it. I even recall doing a picture of the students around the wiener roast bonfire and trying to dress them up in their usual jackets and sweaters. The wiener roast was a treat for raking the schoolyard.

State Board Examinations were the dread of every eighth grader because the exams had to be passed before getting one's eighth grade certificate. It was possible to take the exams over again, and I think some of the seventh graders tried them also. We had study booklets with sample State Board questions, and we labored over them in preparation for the exams.
(N. Wyelene Fredericksen)

During World War I, schools taught crocheting, knitting, and tatting. Many students knitted squares from wool yarn, khaki-colored, later to be put into blankets for the soldiers.
(Forrest and Ethelyn McKinley)

In addition to the traditional thread of mastery of facts and skills in the subject areas being a "must," emphasis was also placed on developing a pupil's potential for self-discovery. As a result, activities such as science experiments, making graphs, charts, posters, booklets, or other projects to enrich learning were encouraged. These items made up the room displays at completion time and were entered in the Waseca County Fair at the end of the year. Prize money, whether it was $1 or 50¢, was a welcome income for these students. Likewise, it served as an incentive to develop original ideas in the future.
(Hannah Lambert)

The school superintendent came once a year. I remember the teacher getting things cleaned up and giving us more assignments. The superintendent would come and sit by the teacher's desk and stare at us kids all day. We were all afraid of her because of the warnings we got and because she looked so stern.
(Diann Lundeby Wilson)

Eighth grade graduation was a big day. For our final tests we had to go to a town school, and for the graduation we went to a big church about fifteen miles from home. After the eighth grade, most kids stayed and helped on the farm. Many couldn't afford to go to high school.
(Ella Bieberdorf)

School attendance was very important, and striving for perfect attendance was stressed. I still have an Attendance Certificate (part of a book of Friendship Verses) which I received for perfect attendance the entire school year of 1949.
(Norma Hughes Schlichter)

Having taught for thirteen years in the rural schools of Blue Earth County from 1931-1945, I look back and try to evaluate the niche into which the "Little Red Schoolhouse" fit in our society. These were rural communities, and many of the children felt their education was complete after the eighth grade. I know it was impossible to add many frills, but believe me, if capable, they learned the basic 3 R's. I knew each parent and that helped to solve many problems in learning, as well as discipline. I firmly believe that with the closing of our rural schools (small schools), we have lost the last stronghold of our democracy.
(Frances Crook Olson)

I am one of those people who feel we lost something very vital to children's development when we disposed of the rural schools. Now we continually combine/pair schools until the kids will be simply numbers, not individuals. To counteract that "progress," we have to hire child psychologists/counselors so the children can experience a one-on-one relationship.
(Alice L. Soffa)

I, for one, think that we were "sold a false bill of goods" with the big idea to "haul them all into town, have a big school, and you will automatically have better education." We could read and write, spell, and figure when we graduated, and I think we got a good eighth-grade-level education. We were taught the real basics. When the other classes were called forward to recite, the rest of us "listened in," resulting in a lot of "cross-fertilization." When we got to the upper grades, we had been there before. And when you learn spelling at fifteen words a day for several years, you don't misspell many words. And when you learn the multiplication tables with your mother breathing down your neck, and when you memorize Longfellow and Whittier and can reel some of it off fifty years later — well, the "Little Red Schoolhouse" did its job well and was a factor in both education and rural social life. The dismal reports nowadays of being unable to read, write, figure, and spell are quite an indictment of our large educational factories of today. We can't go back; I'm not suggesting it. But we have to get better.
(Milton S. Johnson)

THE "SCHOOLMARM"

THE "SCHOOLMARM"

I began teaching in District 45 in Pope County in September 1923. I had received my first grade teaching certificate from St. Cloud Teachers' College. I taught all the grades from the first to the eighth and I had twenty-one pupils. I stayed with a nearby family during the week and paid out $20 a month for room and board. I learned to like tomatoes while staying there, as I got tomato sauce at every evening meal!

In school I was the janitor as well as the teacher. I swept the room, using a lot of sweeping compound. Two women in the district washed the windows and floor once a month. It was hard to keep the schoolhouse warm, but when it was very cold, I would put into the stove two buckets of hard coal, staying to see that it would burn and keep fire all night. There were lots of ashes to carry out. I was always at the school early in the morning, so I took out the ashes before any pupils arrived at school. The outhouses also gave me lots of work after a snowstorm. There would be drifts to walk through and then if the doors had been blown open by the wind, snow often drifted in.

My salary was different through the years. The lowest I was paid was $50 and the highest was $400 a month. I enjoyed teaching in the rural schools. I taught for twenty-five years and have many happy memories. I was lucky to have had very nice pupils
(Agnes Brenden)

As teacher I was also the school nurse, disciplinarian, psychologist, janitor, arbitrator, and more, besides teaching, and I was only a couple years older than some of the pupils. As a teacher I remember preparing the orders for supplies and hoping the board wouldn't think I was extravagant or lazy if I felt I needed workbooks.
(Alice L. Soffa)

I graduated from high school at Clarkfield, Minnesota, at the age of sixteen. I went on to take another year of really intensive training for teaching in a rural school in the High School Training Department. I graduated in 1924; there were eleven girls in my class. I was not granted a first grade certificate upon graduation, however, because of my age. As soon as my eighteenth birthday rolled around, I was fully accredited.

33

My first school was near Minneota in Yellow Medicine County. The oldest students were almost as old as I was. I had never attended a rural school, so teaching in one was a whole new ball game for me. I walked back and forth to school on the coldest and snowiest days, often to find that the old stove had gone out overnight. What I knew about stoking a fire you could stick in your eye and you wouldn't feel it! Often you fired only with wood, even overnight.

After teaching three years in Yellow Medicine County, I attended Mankato State Teachers' College, as it was called then, and received a lifetime certificate to teach in town schools. While there I developed an interest in working with the rural department of the college. They would send groups of two, three, or even four at a time out to do their practice teaching for six-week periods. Then you got a new batch. Here I might say that I was getting $70 a month from the school district and an added $10 a month from the college. As I look back, I wonder how I ever did all that work — thirty-five kids in all eight grades — and those practice teachers, some of whom were real "greenhorns." Those were the days! I think of teachers nowadays with their top wages and aides to help with their work, and still they strike for more. Maybe if they'd lived through times like I did, they'd think twice.
(Helen C. Williams)

I started teaching in 1931. During the Depression years teachers were poorly paid. Salaries of $25 and $35 were common. However, I don't remember getting less than $75. (Compare that to what teachers get a month now.) At times there were so many teachers for every job that they underbid each other. Of course the school boards, which were also hard up, would hire the lowest bidder. School boards had a different code of ethics.

After you had a job, getting paid could be a hassle. School boards were short of money, and teachers were often given orders instead of checks. These had to be signed by all three board members. We picked it up from the treasurer, took it to the clerk, and then to the chairman. Often they weren't home and we'd have to go back. No one ever thought of taking it to the teacher. That would make it too easy for her; teachers had to earn their salaries!
(Dorothea Thompson)

I didn't get a chance to teach in a rural school until the Second World War — the 1940s. I graduated from Mankato State and taught social studies and English in junior high school until I was married

in 1920. Then no more teaching until I saw an ad in the *Free Press* — "Rural school teachers needed. Please would any retired teacher come to our assistance and take a school for a few months until the war is over and the regular teachers are back?" Well, I jumped at the chance. The first school I got was the brick school in Butternut and I had eight pupils. I loved it.
(Elma Summers)

My salary the first year I taught (1932) was $70 a month. I paid $14 a month for board and room. A quote from my contract stated, "Miss Anderson agrees to do all janitor work, with the exception of scrubbing the floors and woodwork and the washing of windows." I learned how to get the fire going on Monday mornings and then to fix it at night so there would still be coals to get it going easily the next morning. We had coal for fuel.
(Selma Anderson Hughes)

I had several surprises when I began teaching in a country school, since I had never gone to one or even been in one before I began teaching. Can you imagine that? Surprise Number One — I went to the board and told them I could find no teachers' textbooks. I had no idea that the teacher used the pupils' books! However, the board bought me a whole new set of needed books. How nice! Surprise Number Two — I was used to water fountains at our consolidated school. I soon learned from the children that each morning water was carried in from a pump and put into a so-called water cooler. As far as I'm concerned, it really never kept the water cool. The pupils always took care of the water voluntarily each morning; they were so good about it. Surprise Number Three — no piano! We sang with a phonograph and learned many songs from records. The board bought us a second-hand piano at semester time. And of course — the outside toilet! I always laughed to myself at how many needed to "leave the room" on beautiful days and when it was very, very cold, no one seemed to leave. Strange, huh?
(Clara G. Hagedorn)

I attended Mankato Teachers' College and graduated from the Junior High Department in 1926. At the time of my graduation, teaching positions in Blue Earth County were difficult to obtain, as teachers were holding on to their positions. New graduates were going out into country schools whenever openings could be found,

rather than risk having no position at all. So in September 1926, I found myself in the South Lincoln School, with thirty youngsters from ages six to fourteen, and all eight grades! I'd never had a day of primary or intermediate training, and it was an entirely new world to me. I tried to bring in new ideas and came to enjoy the work. Some tell me that I was their favorite teacher.
(Reba Clark Meixell)

In rural schools we were not only teachers, but janitors and firemen as well. None of us would trade our experiences and memories of the schools. We attempted to keep the school in top condition at all times, fearing the visit of the county superintendent, who would drop in unexpectedly. I think the country schools contributed their part ably in the education system and we can be proud of all of them.
(Clara Anderson)

My sister taught in country schools for over twenty years. I remember the first check she received from teaching. The banker hesitated giving her the money when she wanted to cash it, as he thought she looked too young to be a teacher.
(Mabel Barsness)

The country school teacher started the wood fires each morning and kept the schoolroom clean and in order. At times she got extra help from the pupils. Often they erased and washed the blackboards and had the job of taking the erasers outside and pounding them together to get the chalk dust out. A well-liked teacher probably received a lot of good help!

One teacher planned a nice surprise for her pupils. This was back in the years when the school had a hard-coal heating furnace. When the coals were red hot, the furnace door was opened; then, using a long-handled screen corn popper, the popper was held over the coals, shaking it until all the corn was popped. The students helped, too, and all enjoyed that popcorn treat. This was one fun day that took place on a Friday, after the last recess. Often there were games and other special events which were planned by the teacher for Fridays.
(Forrest and Ethelyn McKinley)

After high school graduation in 1940, I attended Northern State Teachers' College in Aberdeen, South Dakota, for one year, and I received a certificate to teach in a rural school. I taught in the very school where I had been a student for four years. I drove my brothers' Model A Coupe back and forth to school (three and one-half miles one way) and stayed at home with my parents. I paid my brothers a very small amount for the use of the car and gas. I didn't pay my folks anything, but I worked in the house.

My wages the first year (fall of 1941) were $65 a month. I carried the water (for which I received $3 a month) in a large water can. My second and last year of teaching I received $80 a month — quite a raise! The school now had an oil burner, so I didn't have to build fires.

(Mary D. Thompson)

After high school I took a year of Normal Training (as it was called). This entitled me to teach in the rural schools. I taught in several districts. We began the school day at nine o'clock. We had a fifteen-minute recess in the forenoon. Then everyone would peek into his or her lunch bucket for a snack before playtime. At noon we had an hour break. During the winter we sometimes shortened that to half an hour. In the afternoon we had another fifteen-minute recess. If there was anything left in the lunch pail, it was a delightful find. School closed at four o'clock. I always played games with the children at recess time. We were like one happy family.

During the winter it was hard to keep the room warm at times. I had a furnace in one school, but usually it was the big jacket stove. In the evening the fire had to be banked, with the hope that some coals would still be alive in the morning so I wouldn't have to start from scratch. I usually carried matches, as at one school the padlock for the entrance door would freeze, so I would have to thaw it out.

(Selma O. Sanvik)

I vividly remember having to build fires. I had to learn fast. I used corn cobs to start the fire; coal was used for heating. During cold weather in the winter, I learned with good success how to bank the coals with ashes so the fire would remain overnight. Pretty nice to come to a schoolroom with some heat; then I could get the fire going quite easily with the HOT coals. With coal, one must always burn off the gases before closing the drafts and dampers. We had to think of the fire hazards, too, leaving a building unattended for fourteen hours or so.

(Orline Golden Foelschow)

I started teaching after four years of high school, plus one regular term and a summer session at Moorhead Teachers' College. Later I attended many summer sessions at Bemidji and one year at Gustavus. I taught for nineteen years, all in rural schools in Traverse County. There were hardships — like walking to school on a cold Monday morning and finding the room temperature at zero degrees. There were no telephones or indoor toilets. We suffered through the Depression years, as did other folks. One year I taught for $50 a month, and some of that went for books and supplies for the school. I paid $18 a month for board and room.
(Mabel Winter)

One thing that was very apparent when a new teacher came into the school district was the race as to which one of the local boys would get the first date and, hopefully, marry the girl. It's surprising to find how many teachers remained in the community because of this fact. My first experience at the age of eighteen was no exception.

The Palmer Store near District 10 was a gathering place for the local boys during their off hours. Card playing provided them with many hours of fun. There must have been some monetary investment and remuneration, as I found one of the local fellows the frequent winner of a box of chocolates. He would bring this box of chocolates to the school and then offer to give me a ride to my boarding place. In spite of his good intentions, I never dated him.

However, there was a certain Waseca basketball player whom I dated occasionally. He and his friend would come out into the country and pick up my girlfriend, and we'd be back in time for the boys to play the game. One particular afternoon this basketball player called to say he'd pick me up at six-thirty. The Palmer Store was on the same party line as the school. Evidently, there had been some "rubbering" at the store, since the aforementioned "candy bearer" came to the school when it was time to take me home and literally kidnapped me by taking me all the way to Mankato and not bringing me home until eleven o'clock. This caused a few anxious moments for my date, as well as for the boarding house.

Three weeks later, I was met by the sheriff and his deputy as I came to school one morning. It seems that this persistent fellow had sold mortgaged property and had skipped the country. His mother had told the sheriff that he had been seeing the "School Marm" and

was sure I knew where he was. I wasn't even aware that he was missing or gone!
(Hannah Burtness)

My first priority after receiving my teaching certificate was to "get a school," as we said. It meant writing stilted letters of application, stating one's qualifications. I felt ill at ease doing this. We hadn't been taught to think highly of ourselves, but out of necessity I had to do this now. I recall the day I went to call on the three board members, each in his own house. This was my first year. When I drove into the clerk's yard, I met a classmate driving out. I was the third applicant that day. I was hired for the school, a seven-month school, at $75 a month. Was I glad! I had a school! The first week there I wonder if I slept a night through. There was so much to do and I was so nervous.
(Sophie C. Vold Hauge)

School board members were indispensable to a rural teacher because they so unselfishly gave of their time to help with reports, to order supplies or books, set up the school calendar, put up the stage, mow the lawn, fix the furnace, pull the teacher out of a snowbank, or help in other emergencies. The wives were also invaluable in getting the school ready for fall opening by supervising the cleaning and putting up clean curtains, or even making new ones.
(Dorothy Powell)

When I began teaching, I had six weeks of college training and two hours credit from an extension course. I received $80 a month most of the time, once receiving $90 and another time $110 a month.

On the first day of school one year, the wife of one of the school directors was very gracious to me. She told me she had cleaned the school and worked hard at it. She said she didn't disturb the teacher's desk because she thought I'd prefer to clean it. When I opened the desk drawer, out jumped a mouse! The children broke into laughter. Several of the boys gave chase and killed it. The children said that was nothing; all their teachers had mouse trouble. One used to stand on her chair while the boys chased and killed the mice. I laid in a supply of traps and soon had control.

One morning I came to school and saw that a mouse had gotten caught by its tail and was running around the room dragging the trap. I couldn't stand handling mice, so when a boy walked by my school

on his way to catch a ride to high school, I asked him to come in and do away with the mouse. He did so, with a laugh that he tried to hide.
(Edith O. Chaffer)

In one school I had fourteen students — all grades. It was rationing time then, and I had gotten a 1935 Ford from my brother. It was two miles around the road to school, and the parents gave me gas to drive if I'd take their children. I picked up four families — seven children.

I remember well having only two days of school during the month of February and the first two weeks of March one year, as all but two of the pupils had the whooping cough. We didn't have to make up the days, but we had longer assignments.
(Hazel Hubbart Parquet)

Several of the teachers stayed at our home while they were teaching. We really enjoyed having them. Our mother enjoyed cooking and baking, and she made especially good things for the evening meal. She would set the table in the kitchen for the family. The table in the dining room was set for the teacher, and one of us girls took turns eating with her. We really looked forward to our turn.

The teacher's room, I'm sure, was not too warm, but every morning our mother would send one of us upstairs with a pitcher of hot water for washing. There wasn't any running water, hot or cold, or any indoor bathroom facilities in those days on the farm. A white enameled pail, called a slop jar, was used for waste water, and a big white wash bowl and pitcher of water, with towels and soap, were provided in the teacher's room.

The teacher walked to school, and from experience I know the schoolroom was pretty cold when she got there. Usually it was comfortable enough by the time the pupils arrived. Most of the teachers we had came from a distance, so they stayed weekends, too, and they went home only for holidays. We had many enjoyable times with the teachers who stayed in our home.
(Ada Ronnei Pederson)

We would have the teacher over for a meal every once in a while. Some kids would be jealous if they knew the teacher had been to our house for supper. One teacher had her own car, a Model A Coupe, but usually they did not own a car. I remember my first grade teacher

because she had such outstanding blood veins in her hands! Another teacher I had for third and fourth grade was a good teacher and a nice person, but I remember best her chunky beads and how she had a different pair for every dress. I was a good student and I guess I liked all of my teachers because they treated me well.
(Mary D. Thompson)

My grandfather was treasurer of the school board, and I felt extremely important when I was allowed to carry the teacher's monthly salary envelope (sealed, of course) to school. School board members were highly respected, and pupils were instructed by the teacher to be on their best behavior when a board member paid the school a visit.
(Ida Posteher Fabyanske)

My teaching career started in 1934 at the age of nineteen years, after one year of teacher's training. Having attended a rural school for eight years helped immensely. I taught in the rural schools, grade one through grade eight — then later, grade one through grade six — for twenty years. One school I taught in I had only seven students, another had twenty-five, and in one school I had forty some students in all eight grades, with twelve students in grade one. That was a challenge, but very rewarding. During this time I took "off campus" college courses and attended St. Cloud State College during summer sessions and night classes, finally getting my four-year degree. My beginning salary in 1934 was $45 a month for only nine months. The salary gradually increased each year, but not enough for me to be able to take off a year or two to attend college.

Each year we had what was called the "Teachers' Institute." This was held in the court house, and each rural teacher attended. There were workshops led by people from the State Department of Education, where new ideas and innovations were brought to us. Also, ideas were exchanged between teachers. This was very helpful and enjoyable. At one of these I remember writing down all the different jobs a rural teacher had — teacher, mother, nurse, custodian, lawyer, policeman, and counselor. Quite a responsibility!
(Margaret Thompson Cimenski)

For grades one through seven I attended school in town. Then they were going to charge $3 a month tuition for each child, so my dad said we had to go to the country school in our district. The teacher

I had that year was pregnant and not feeling too well, so she let me do a lot of the teaching of the younger children. Of course I thought that was great and it is probably the reason I decided to go to Mankato Teachers' College, as it was called then. I graduated from there with a certificate to teach lower elementary and in rural schools.

One of the boys I had in seventh grade later on married my youngest sister. I was glad to have him in school, as he carried in the wood for the old stove. He also filled the water pail when needed. It is funny people weren't sick more, as we all drank out of the same dipper.
(Viola Burnett Campbell)

As a teacher in a one-room country school, I spent four of the happiest years of my life. I taught in the same school all four years. The average number of pupils was twenty-two, and I had all eight grades inclusive. It was necessary to build the fire after I arrived at the school. I did all the janitor work also. There was no running water or telephone. I was one of the better-paid teachers, as my salary was $110 a month. The year I left, the teacher's salary was dropped to $65 a month. No married teachers were allowed.
(Ruby Vickers)

While attending high school, the thought often came to me that I would like to be a school teacher. In 1918, my dream came true when I graduated from high school and a year of teacher's training. The first school I taught in was in the western part of Pope County. My salary was $70 a month, which to me was indeed a large sum. I paid $18 or $20 for room and board.

The first day of school I did not know exactly what to expect, but I learned fast. When I came to school the first morning, one of the school board members was there to show me around — especially the heating system and how to take out the ashes from the big stove. I quickly learned that there was much more to rural school teaching than just teaching subjects!

Before classes started in the mornings, we always enjoyed singing songs. After study periods of reading, writing, spelling, and phonics, classes were called to the front to recite. Of course we also had spelling bees; how proud the children were when they went to the head of the class. The children were all so lovely, and it was truly a pleasure to work with such fine boys and girls.
(Olive Barsness)

I taught in rural schools from 1917 to 1923. At my first job I earned $60 a month. I taught all eight grades — twenty pupils. A few happenings stand out in my memory: the barn owl that got inside the schoolhouse and perched on our Christmas tree; the nest of newborn baby mice that I found in my desk one morning; the small daughter of a Russian family who spent her first year just "listening," since I knew no Russian and she knew no English; the boy we lost from diphtheria before anyone suspected, and the quarantine that followed; and the horrible black measles I caught the last week of school.

I also remember the time a wagon load of gypsies parked near the school. After morning recess, we discovered that one little first grader was missing. I was beside myself with fear that she'd been kidnapped by the gypsies, but we eventually found her under a table in the basement, crying because someone had hurt her feelings.
(Blanche Lindholm Johnson)

During my teaching years, I boarded with a family in the district, which was the custom at that time. At each of my boarding homes I paid $15 a month. This does seem cheap, doesn't it? But then one must consider that my salary the first year was $55 a month and I believe the last two years it was $60. These wages were very average or could perhaps even be called "good" for the years of my teaching.

Dad took me to my boarding place on Sunday afternoons and returned for me on Fridays after school. The trip to get me was a big event in the life of my family. Usually Dad was accompanied by my mother, sisters, and brother, so they could enjoy the ride and have a chance to visit. This trip was perhaps the longest one our car made, my school being about fourteen miles south of Glenwood. To reimburse Dad for the time and the wear and tear on the car, I would buy tires when necessary and help out with the gas bills. Also, with a regular paycheck coming in, there were many things I could buy for my family.

During cold weather Dad would go to the schoolhouse with me on Sundays to help split the chunks of wood into kindling or help me pile the larger chunks in neat rows at the side of the entryway. There was a large coal and wood shed in back of the school. I became quite adept at making the fire in the big jacketed stove and also mastered the art of banking the fire before going home in the evening, thereby assuring me of some heat when arriving in the morning. Banking was done by putting a pail of coal carefully over the red hot coals that were burning low in the firebox, and then placing a layer of ashes from the ash pan over the top of the new coal I had just put into the stove. It was most important to make a "breathing hole" in the top of the banked fire or else the fire could smoke or perhaps even explode in one big damaging puff.

Teachers were always invited overnight to each house at least once during the school year. How proud the children were to say, "Teacher came to our house last night."

My three years of being "Schoolmarm" of District 73 have left many pleasant memories in my mind. You might ask, "Would you do it over again?" My answer would be, "I certainly would!"
(Margaret Seeger Hedlund)

THOSE "SYRUP PAIL" LUNCHES

THOSE "SYRUP PAIL" LUNCHES

Lunches were brought from home. Each child had a pail of some sort for his lunch, usually a syrup pail. Some lunches might consist of cold pancakes. Some children I knew had lard on their bread in place of butter. Sometimes there might be a treat. Mothers sent the best they had. There were no hot lunches or milk breaks in those days, although sometimes things might be heated on top of the stove. I can remember baking potatoes in one furnace.
(Dorothea Thompson)

We brought our noon meal in some kind of a pail or lunch box, and it usually consisted of sandwiches (maybe even salmon!), fruit, and a dessert (usually cookies). My mother used to "start" our oranges for us when we were little — by cutting off the stem top, and around the edges she made slits so we could peel off the quarters.

One funny little thing I recall is my friend eating a cookie while she was writing on the board with chalk and getting mixed up and trying to take a bite of the chalk instead of the cookie. We giggled over that.

An innovation was when the mothers decided to have hot lunches during cold weather. Each family took turns serving one day. I recall with embarrassment one family bringing bean soup, and we all got the silly notion that it had worms in it, when what we really saw was the embryo of the bean seed!
(N. Wyelene Fredericksen)

Our lunch buckets were kept in the cloakroom, except in real cold weather, when they were put by the stove so the food would be thawed out by noon.
(Lucille Siefkes)

We got up early in the morning to prepare our lunch for school. That lunch usually consisted of a couple slices of buttered bread, meat of some kind, or maybe some homemade apple butter, and either an apple or an orange. At noon time our lunches were cold, so a kind teacher let us toast our sandwiches in the large heater stove. We sharpened a lath, which teachers used in those days to start the fire when they came to school in the morning, and stuck the sharpened

47

lath into our sandwiches and held them over the nice red hot coals.
(Elizabeth Juhl)

Our school lunches consisted of sandwiches from home. If we were lucky, we might have cookies or cake, and maybe an apple or an orange. We thought it was a real treat if we had "boughten" bread, which meant we bought it at the store or bakery! Our mother made delicious homemade bread at least three or four times a week, but of course kids like something different once in a while. If we were lucky, we might have a thermos bottle and bring cocoa, but sometimes the teacher made cocoa on top of the heater, too. Lunches were pretty monotonous, but we survived. Some of the kids who were really poor only had lard on their bread! We always had homemade butter because my dad and brothers milked cows, and we had our own milk and cream. Homemade bologna in the winter was also a treat.

When I was teaching, we often would bake potatoes on top of the stove, or one of the mothers might make a rice or bean dish (with surplus commodities), and we'd reheat it on top of the stove.
(Mary D. Thompson)

Lunch time was like a family time in the rural school. Each student brought his lunch in a pail of some sort. When I was a student, we used syrup pails and envied those who had "real" lunch boxes.

When I taught, most of the students had lunch boxes, except some of the boys who didn't want to be bothered and brought theirs in sacks. We all sat at our desks and ate together. This was a learning time, too, as we discussed good manners, etc. I asked them to sit quietly at least ten minutes. Then those who were finished were dismissed for play.
(Margaret Thompson Cimenski)

Lunches were provided in various ways. Pails were used as containers. There was often bartering of food. One girl had only a pancake at times. Jars of food were placed in warm water on top of the stove. In very cold weather mothers took turns bringing hot food, enough for all. One could bake a potato in the ashes.
(Arlie M. Klimes)

We always carried a cold lunch. A popular menu was a peanut butter and jelly sandwich, with a piece of fruit and some cookies

or a bar for dessert. When the weather was warm, we could go outside to eat our lunch. After we finished our lunch, we usually had
time for a short softball game before we had to go in for classes again.
(Van Johnson)

There was no hot lunch program available when I went to school.
We carried our lunches from home, probably something like this:
homemade bread, mayonnaise, leftover roast beef or egg salad, cheese
on Fridays, maybe head cheese, a home-canned pickle, an orange
or banana or apple, and once in a while, a powdered sugar doughnut.
Now those doughnuts were good "trading" material!

In the colder weather the older girls in the room helped the teacher
make hot chocolate for lunch time. I remember my sister always
helped. Sometimes I helped pass out the crockery — white farmer
coffee cups. Oh, the smell of that chocolate still sweetens the memory!
I think there might have been a charge of three cents.

Our lunches were wrapped in newspaper (food was individually
wrapped in wax paper) and then tied with string. The smell of food
and newspaper is quite delightful yet. Special times of the year we
were given free samples of "mentholatum" in a very small, flat tin
(it smelled so healthy), and a talk on germs. The pictures were
interesting; you didn't get to see germs very often!
(Jerrie Steinwall Ahrens)

We would bring our lunch in a half-gallon syrup pail. We had
sandwiches, sometimes a hard-boiled egg, and some cookies or cake.
A piece of pie was a real treat. We had plenty of apples from our
large orchard, so we had fruit the year round. An orange or a banana
was a special treat.
(Ada Ronnei Pederson)

I remember heating a jar of food in a shallow pan of water for
noon lunch, or baking a potato on the ledge inside the furnace. Bump
the potato and the hot lunch burned to a crisp! We carved our initials
on the potato so we got our own.
(Alice L. Soffa)

All the children carried their lunches from home in a tin Karo
syrup pail. If more than one child from a family was going to school,
they used the gallon size. Lunch was basically a syrup or jelly
sandwich. We seldom had meat sandwiches and very little fruit,

mostly at Christmas time. We seldom had dessert unless we had celebrated a birthday or other special event. No one carried milk. We drank water which was pumped from outdoors and then put into a fountain in the school entryway.
(Lucina E. Valento)

Regarding the noon lunches, the teacher lived close enough so that she could go home, as did a number of the pupils. Most of us, however, brought our lunches from home, wrapped in yesterday's newspaper and tied with grocery string. Lunch bags were not yet available, and no one would have considered "buying" a paper bag to be used once and thrown away. We seldom had anything to drink with our lunches, as thermos bottles were fairly new and "too expensive" for kids.

There was no behavior problem during the teacher's noon-hour absence, since she always appointed a "monitor" who was instructed to write down the names of pupils who misbehaved. The usual punishment was to write the multiplication tables, either on the blackboard or on paper, during the following recess period. Needless to say, by the time we all got out of the eighth grade we were very good at multiplication!
(Ida Posteher Fabyanske)

The years when there was a Mothers' Club that provided noon lunches were special. Each mother would take a turn bringing hot lunch for everyone in the school. We all eagerly waited to see what was going to be brought each day.
(Norma Hughes Schlichter)

IT'S
RECESS
TIME

IT'S RECESS TIME

(There are several variations in spelling and word structure for some of the games listed in this chapter. For consistency, I have chosen the most common usage.)

Funny, I never remember hearing anyone say, "There's nothing to do" at playtime in the little school on the prairie, even though there was no fancy playground equipment (slides, jungle gyms, or merry-go-rounds); only a pair of sturdy hand-built swings. We enjoyed them and we certainly learned to share. But we didn't always swing. Sometimes in the spring one of the boys would try a little baseball, but with an enrollment of never more than fourteen children, and of course some of them first and second graders, this was never terribly successful. We played "Hide and Seek" sometimes, too, but with a choice of only four places to hide — behind the schoolhouse, the barn, or the "boys," or "girls" — this often got dull in a hurry.

There were, of course, games familiar to children growing up everywhere — "Pump Pump Pullaway," "Tag," "Statue," "Poison Tag," and "Duck Duck Gray Duck." One of our favorites was "Anti Over." We divided into two teams and one went on each side of the schoolhouse. One team would throw the ball and yell "Anti Over." If it didn't go over, you had to yell "Pig's Tail" and try again. If it went over and lit on the ground, their team had to try throwing it over. If someone caught it, they could come dashing around to the other side. Anyone from the opposite team whom they could touch with the ball had to join their team. The game ended when one team had all the players or when the bell rang. Another favorite was "Cops and Robbers," where everyone dashed wildly around the playground either chasing or being chased. If you were caught, you were locked in the woodshed, but if the jailer forgot to say "Tick-tock-double-lock" when you were shut in, then it was perfectly legal for you to escape.
(Mae F. Hardin)

The boys would run outdoors at noon hour and recess yelling, "Batter up, pitcher, catcher, first baseman," telling what position they would play in a game of "work-up." Softball was a game everyone played and became very skilled at.

Other games were "Hide and Seek," "Tin Can" (a version of "Hide and Seek"), "Anti Over" (throwing a ball over the school, with the other side trying to catch the ball before it bounded), "Last Couple Out," "Prisoners' Base," "Pump Pump Pullaway," "Lemonade," and "Fox and Goose" (in the snow). The games required almost no equipment or teacher planning.
(Margaret Jenkins)

Recess was spent with everybody playing together — maybe "Softball," "Captain May I?," "Hide and Seek," or "Tag." Some days we just played on the swings. Once in a while we'd sneak down to a bridge (about one-fourth mile away) where there was a stream, and we'd pretend we wouldn't hear the bell.

In the winter when it was cold, we would play games inside or in the basement. We also played on an ice pond and had snowball fights across the road. Each side had a ditch, and if you hit someone on the other side, they had to come to your ditch. The object was to get everyone on one side.
(Marva Rumelhart Ball)

When it was too cold to play outside in the winter, we would play cards (whist) at recess. Other recess activities were circle games, "Hide and Seek," "Pump Pump Pullaway," and "Anti Over," which was played over the shed in back of the school. The shed was there to house the horses that were sometimes ridden to school by some of the students.
(Deloris Delage)

.Our school had a hill behind the barn where we could slide on our sleds in the winter. There was a slough at the bottom of the hill which froze over and made a nice long ride on the sled. During nice weather we played other outdoor games, such as "Captain May I?," "Pump Pump Pullaway," "Baseball," "Hopscotch," "Fox and Goose" (a game played in the snow, with paths in a circle and dissecting lines), and many other games. We also had a teeter-totter, swings, a slide and a merry-go-round, so we didn't lack for things to do.

Of course in the spring we played marbles, too. A beautiful glass marble was hard to come by, and most of our marbles were the smaller clay ones, known as "commies" (for common, I suppose). Sometimes you might be lucky and have a steel one.
(Mary D. Thompson)

At recess time we played jacks, marbles, jump rope, and ball. My brother was good at marbles; he had a lot of them. Some were called "cat eyes," "aggies," "steelies," and of course his "shooter." Mom would make little leather pouches to carry them in. Jump ropes were clotheslines, and some were real long. There was a girl at each end, and you had to be good to play with those older girls. Most of the time you did your jumping individually, but remember, not too much or the shoes might give out!

Also, there was a stream nearby, and we could pick spring flowers or clover and make wreaths and crowns for each other, or hold dandelions under each other's chin to see if you liked butter. If there's a yellow reflection on the underside of your chin, you do like butter.
(Jerrie Steinwall Ahrens)

We had a skating rink about one-fourth mile from the schoolhouse. At noon hour we could run there and do a little sliding around, as very few of us had skates. My brother and I usually walked home across the frozen pond, but we walked across it one too many times. CRACK! CRACK! And we were both in the cold water and ice. We walked home, about a mile, as fast as possible and put dry, warm clothes on. Surprisingly, neither of us even got a cold after that encounter.

After the frost went out of the ground in the spring, the big boys got us to help drown out gophers at recess and noon hour. The boys got old pails out of the woodshed. Some of us had to pump the water, others carried the pails of water to pour down the gopher hole, and the big boys stood there with sticks to kill the gopher when it came out.
(Orline Golden Foelschow)

One activity we had was chasing gophers. These nasty little rodents were very destructive to crops, and multiplied so rapidly that they were more than a nuisance. It didn't matter what game we were playing; if someone spied a gopher, it took immediate priority over any other activity. Away we all flew after it as fast as our legs could carry us. Since they had holes all over where they could pop out of sight almost at will, we were never successful in catching one, but we really tried.
(Mae F. Hardin)

We all played ball in a pasture across the road from the schoolhouse. Girls, as well as boys, played with a hard baseball, as

we all had to play together to have enough for teams. There was a place in that same pasture where an ice pond formed, and we used to skate there. We had clamp-on skates which we fastened directly to our hightop shoes. Warm days developed "rubber ice," which was much fun and not dangerous because the water was very shallow. However, it was very wet, so we had to dry out by the old heater. The gravel pit was to the east, and that provided a very steep place for sliding. It was really very dangerous, so the more daring were the ones who used it most often.
(N. Wyelene Fredericksen)

Toward spring we would have a few thawing days. The potholes in the neighboring fields would fill and then freeze, so for a little while we could go sliding on the ice. Few of us could afford skates, but that didn't stop our fun. This sport sooner or later almost always ended in the same way. Because we loved to slide on the ice, we would try to stretch the season just one day too long, and someone would go through the thin ice. The potholes, for the most part, weren't too deep, so no one was in grave danger. However, whoever it was — sometimes several — got a really icy bath.
(Mae F. Hardin)

We played several games at school. Outdoors we played ball games, "Hide and Seek," "Tag," "Anti Over," and "Pump Pump Pullaway." Inside we played "Fruit Basket Upset," "Guessing Games," "Hide the Thimble," and in the hall we played "Pussy Wants a Corner," "Blind Man's Bluff," and "Drop the Handkerchief." We really had a lot of fun.
(Ada Ronnei Pederson)

Every winter we had our hopscotch tournaments. We drew the hopscotch grids on the floor with chalk. There was only room, by squeezing, for two grids between the seats, so there was one for the big kids and one for the little ones. The competition was really heated. I wonder if any of my contemporaries, sitting tense before a TV during the "Super Bowl," can remember being *just* as excited watching to see whether their favorite player tossed his leather mitten in the right square, or willing him *not* to step on any lines.

Another game we played a lot was "Skip." "It" skipped around the room and tapped someone on the head. This person got up and tried to catch "it" before he reached a circle drawn with chalk on

the floor at the front of the room. If he caught him, he could sit down again. If he didn't, he was "it." The trick, of course, was to *skip*, not run. If you ran, you forfeited, and when you're in a hurry, it isn't always easy to remember to skip, not run. We sometimes played this to help kids thaw out when they came to school in the morning.
(Mae F. Hardin)

Playground equipment in early times was very simple. Our baseball bats often were barrel staves or other discarded boards or sticks. The balls, too, were made at home. Old stockings and sweaters were ripped or cut up and the yarn wound into a solid ball. This was covered with leather from an old boot which had been cut, soaked, and stretched. These balls bounced very well.
(Ruth V. Esping)

Popular recess games were "Run Sheep Run," "Red Rover," "Pump Pump Pullaway," "Duck on a Rock," "Anti Over," "Here Comes the Duke A'Roaming," etc. Weather permitting, there was always a kittenball game in progress.

During the winter months many of the pupils brought sleds to school. This served several purposes — the small children were allowed to ride if big brother or sister was willing to pull; they carried books and lunches; and they were used on the hills during recess time and the noon hour.
(Ida Posteher Fabyanske)

Children (and the teacher) looked forward to recess and noon hour. Many were the games we played. There were many variations of "Tag," "Pump Pump Pullaway," and of course, ball. I was usually chosen last for ball games because I couldn't hit the broad side of a barn!

In winter if we had a creek or a hill nearby, we went skating or sliding, often combining recess and noon hour to have a longer playtime. In the spring we drowned out gophers. On rainy days we played blackboard games or moved back the seats and played circle games. We often had to improvise for play equipment. New things were hard to get, especially if the school board thought it was all "darn foolishment," so the teacher often used her own money to buy bats and balls. One board member thought that we could make our balls and use sticks for bats.
(Dorothea Thompson)

One day some boys brought a one-horse cutter sleigh to school. The box was gone — just the runners with a platform was left. They could sit on the platform and steer it when out sliding. During recess, the teacher (a man) said he could "stand up" and ride down the hill with the boys. The bigger boys sat on the platform, with their feet down so they could steer it. The road had a curve, with trees across the road. They would turn up the road to the left and then would continue to the end of their regular run. This time, however, the boys turned the cutter into the trees and jumped off, leaving the teacher sailing on through the air and into the trees. The teacher never said a harsh word to any of them, but he never rode the cutter with them again either!
(Forrest and Ethelyn McKinley)

One always sees lovely pictures of children building snowmen with funny hats and carrot noses, but there was something about the powdery wind-blown snow in North Dakota which just wouldn't pack right, so we never made snowmen in the winter. On the rare winter days when it was decent to go out, we had to play something active to keep warm. Sometimes it was just "Tag," or if there was a fresh snowfall, we would make a big "pie" in the snow. When the drifts got high, some would bring sleds and slide down their steep sides. These were the only "hills" we had in that flat country.

Of course, much of the time it was just too blue cold to play outside. Anyone who had walked over a mile to school, and maybe frozen a nose or cheek, wasn't all that eager to go out at noon, since they faced the same trip home. And recess was just too short anyway to get all bundled up with all the scarves, mittens, boots, etc., and then take them all off again. Besides, they might not be dried out from when you came in the morning. So when it was bitter cold we stayed in, which limited our activity, to say the least. I'm sure on those days the teacher thought she had a lot more than fourteen pupils!
(Mae F. Hardin)

PROGRAMS, SOCIALS, AND OTHER DIVERSIONS

PROGRAMS, SOCIALS & OTHER DIVERSIONS

A Christmas program was a MUST. We started practicing right after Thanksgiving. We'd hand out the parts to be memorized before Thanksgiving vacation. It was indeed fun to get ready for the "big night." We had to provide a stage, using sheets as curtains. One neighbor would bring a gas lantern for light. Then the last day planks were brought in for extra seating. The fathers were good helpers. The parents brought the lunch and plenty of coffee. When the program and lunch were over, the desks were pushed to the side and the planks were removed. Then, young and old played games and everyone enjoyed themselves.
(Selma O. Sanvik)

The Christmas program was the highlight of the year, rivaled only in importance by the annual school picnic or the visit of the county superintendent. The country school programs were exciting times, both for the child and the parents. Each child always gave a recitation or had a part in a play involving several students. The front of the room was closed off from the admiring audience by an old, much-mended, gray curtain, which was strung by strong wire.

After the program, lunch of hearty meat sandwiches and large pieces of cake was served by the mothers. A bushel basket full of tin cups would be borrowed from an auctioneer for the big celebration at school, and coffee was brought in large gray enamel coffee pots by wives of school board members. The balance of the evening was spent playing games or dancing reels. This part of the evening was much enjoyed by older students and visitors.
(Margaret Seeger Hedlund)

At Christmas you were expected to put on a program for parents and the community. We strung up a curtain across the front of the room, and behind it we tried to have order out of chaos, with all the children, properties, and everything back there. Usually it turned out reasonably well. I always hated all the time it took to practice for those programs because we lost good school time. But it was expected, and often a teacher was judged by the programs she produced.
(Helen C. Williams)

There was always a Christmas program at school put on by the teacher and pupils and attended by nearly everyone. Some programs were given in the afternoon. If the programs were given at night, the families would bring their lanterns and lamps to light up the school building. Along with the program, there was always a lunch. Then we got back into the horse-drawn bobsleigh and headed for home, listening to the ringing of the sleigh bells.
(Forrest and Ethelyn McKinley)

During the Christmas season we spent much of our time practicing for our annual Christmas program. We spent hours cutting out red and green wreaths to use to decorate all the windows. This was always such a happy time. Everyone was in the holiday spirit, and we got to know all of our fellow students so well during this time. All of the students took part in decorating the Christmas tree, which was always placed at the side of the stage, along with a manger scene.

At the end of the program, we had a potluck lunch, which included sandwiches and cake. Sometimes we had a basket social. It was always fun to see who bought our baskets.
(Van Johnson)

I remember practicing for our Christmas program from Thanksgiving on. On the night of the performance, the sight of the lighted schoolhouse caused flutters in my stomach. It was always a thrill getting a box of three pencils with my name on them from the teacher.
(Alice L. Soffa)

Christmas programs were big events. I always had a piano or an organ. In one of my last schools, I taught piano and accordian at noon. I had an eight-piece accordian band, which made programs easy. At the end of one school year, I was given a TV table and lamp at the picnic as thanks for the music lessons.
(Emily Sedlacek)

Christmas programs were always necessary, and we had to get all the children to participate. We had no musical instruments the first years, so the singing was not always kept in tune! Later, we got a phonograph, which helped a lot.
(Signe Haraldson)

Christmas programs were a necessity. They were fun to have, with the makeshift curtains (sheets strung on a wire). My sister (also a teacher) and I bought a record player for the music. I had my program first. The record player was stolen before her program, so I had to sing behind the curtain to help her pupils out!
(Eldora Nannestad)

School holidays were listed on the contract, as was the need to have Christmas programs. There were corn picking and seeding vacations, so we really managed only eight months of school.

For the Christmas program, a stage was set up with blocks, and planks were laid across them. Some schools had old curtains. If not, sheets were used. They sagged, wires broke, and down came the curtains! A placard with instructions was fastened with rope, so all the pupils had to do was walk on, follow the directions, and walk off. Children drew names and gifts were exchanged. Teachers gave a gift to each child and received one in return. Apples, which were furnished by the school board, were passed out to the audience. Teachers filled the children's sacks with goodies.
(Arlie M. Klimes)

We enjoyed getting ready for programs for our parents. There were songs, recitations, and dialogues. We would practice and practice. Sometimes my brother, two sisters, and I could go through the whole program at home because we had learned everyone's part. Sometimes some of us were asked to put on a dialogue at a Farm Bureau meeting.

We always had a Christmas program for our parents. We had a big Christmas tree, on which we put real candles. We lit the candles on the night of our program when the schoolroom was packed with people. As I remember those Christmas trees, I still shake my head and wonder how we dared to do such a thing. We were so lucky.
(Selma Anderson Hughes)

Christmas programs were big events for the whole neighborhood. The teacher would hang up sheets on wire for a curtain. We were all so excited. Of course there was no electricity, so lamps and lanterns had to be brought from the homes for this occasion. I especially remember one time when I was an angel and my wings kept falling off. I almost missed my cue for my part in the program!

We also had pie socials sometimes, where the men would bid on the ladies' pies. Entertainment was cheap in those days, and more

things were done on the local level — such as card parties and even dances in the farmhomes.
(Mary D. Thompson)

In December we worked hard getting a Christmas program together that we could present to the parents. I always enjoyed that when I was a child attending the country school. The school board erected a stage in the front of the building.

After the program, there was a box lunch auction. The women of the district decorated a shoe box which contained lunch for two people. The men were good bidders and wanted to buy their spouse's box. If anyone knew which box was the teacher's, the bidding would usually go high, since the bachelors always wanted to get the teacher's box.
(Agnes Brenden)

Everyone always had a part in the Christmas program. My dad was Santa Claus, and my mother made him a suit. Kids' parents brought quantities of food for lunch after the program. My dad made coffee in a copper-bottomed wash boiler! Later, one of the mothers fiddled and my dad called square dance routines.
(Ruth Aleda Johansen)

School holidays were memorable, as in the fall around Halloween or Thanksgiving, we would put on a program for the neighborhood, with singing, plays, pageants, recitations, etc. Following the program, the ladies' baskets, which had been decorated and filled with lunch, would be auctioned off to the highest bidder; then they ate the lunch together. This was great fun and exciting, especially if there were unmarried ladies in the group. Sometimes the bidding would really be competitive for these baskets. The money from these auctions would then be used to buy Christmas gifts for the school children at Christmas time. The teacher bought these gifts, sometimes with the help of the parents. Some of the money was used to buy Christmas candy and peanuts, and also a box of apples. The candy and peanuts were then put in individual sacks and each child received one. The apples were passed out to everyone.

The Christmas program was quite an event. The real "Christmas Story" was always given as a pageant, along with much singing, other plays, and recitations. Someone always came in dressed as Santa Claus and distributed the gifts.
(Margaret Thompson Cimenski)

64

Any little programs given by the children were looked forward to by the whole community. Box socials were a way to make a little extra money, which was usually used for books, playground equipment, and other supplies. A program was given, and then the boxes were auctioned off. Each lady or girl packed a box with lunch for two, each one trying to outdo the others. Usually the boxes contained sandwiches, fried chicken, cake, cookies, and fruit. Then she decorated the box, trying to keep her design a secret, and hoping a certain person would get it. The men and boys bought the boxes and then ate with the owner.
(Dorothea Thompson)

A big event in rural schools used to be the basket socials. People came from miles around. Ladies decorated baskets and packed a lunch for two in them. The baskets were then auctioned off to the highest bidder. Usually they went for a couple dollars or less. Once in a while, someone found out whose basket was up for sale and, just for meanness, would run the price up, so the boyfriend might pay up to $10 or more. The money was usually used to buy library books.

People would come in bobsleds, with ten or more people in them. They'd tip the sled over into snowdrifts on the way, just for fun. They played "Four in the Board," "Gustav Skaal" (Norwegian), and many other games before the baskets were sold.
(Helen C. Williams)

As a means of getting some extra equipment for the school, we would have some way of raising money. One year, instead of the ordinary basket social, the ladies and girls brought unusually decorated hats. It was great fun seeing the men and boys bidding on their favorite hats. The rule of the evening was that each owner must wear his hat to get to eat the very delicious lunch the ladies and girls had brought.

At this event the children usually gave a short program. This particular year, the men agreed to entertain the group. Their skit happened to be their impression of the local ladies' bunco club. It was hilarious to see them all dressed as ladies and hear their conversation, which centered on recipes, housework, bits of gossip, and their operations. The evening was a great success and the children thoroughly enjoyed it. With the money earned, the children decided on some new balls and bats, a soccer ball, and games that could be played indoors in cold weather or on rainy days.
(Magdalene Waite)

Something that was done in those days in country school was to have a "Home Talent Play." People from the community were the actors and I, as teacher, was usually the director. Often we put the play on in other communities once it was whipped into shape. That was really fun. You learned a whole different side to people that you didn't know they had.
(Helen C. Williams)

For special fun there were sleigh rides and picnics for the "young people," all of which the teacher was obligated to attend. One time in the fall, all the neighborhood young people went to the woods about two and one-half miles away to gather walnuts and to have a wiener roast. Picnics and wild flower gathering were also sources of amusement.
(Reba Clark Meixell)

A big event in the rural school I attended was "Play Day," a county-wide gathering of school children. The first part of the day was given over to music and "declamation" contests. For weeks before the big event, we'd practice. I always was chosen to speak a "piece." This meant memorizing a story or poem and delivering it with impressive gestures and voice inflections. How nervous I would be! There would always be at least three trips to the bathroom in the hour before it was my time to be "on." Afternoons were given over to track and field contests. Because I was not much of an athlete, my afternoons were free to roam through the stores uptown, admiring the trinkets in the dime stores and eating ice cream cones.
(Pat Hanson)

The last day of school always was the picnic for the entire family. This was usually held in a farmer's pasture, not too far from school. After we'd eaten all the food which had been brought, the softball game was an important event. Others then wandered along the creek.
(Margaret Jenkins)

School picnics at the end of the school year were of special importance. It was about this time of the year that our mothers would let us roll down our socks after a long, cold winter of wearing long underwear and long socks. We felt FREE! I can remember watching other schools in the park that had a big ten-gallon container of vanilla ice cream as a special treat, but we didn't have any. I guess

our school board thought it would cost too much money. How we longed for one of those ice cream cones! I'm sure in the later years we maybe had some, but I especially remember the picnics when we didn't have any.
(Mary D. Thompson)

A big spring event in our rural school was the all-school picnic. At nine o'clock in the morning on the last day of school, several carloads of students (our entire school) would go to a nearby state park. It was a glorious day — not too organized! Several tables would be put together and that would become our headquarters. We could run and play. By noon, parents had arrived with food, and a potluck dinner would be held. Dessert would be ice cream — a real treat for kids who lived in a town or on farms that had no electricity — and so no refrigeration. The ice cream had been ordered from the Bridgeman-Russell Company in Grand Forks. It would be brought to our little town by truck, carefully packed in dry ice. It was always my dad's job to wait for the ice cream and then bring it out to the picnic. One year the truck failed to show — what a disappointment! An hour after eating, we would be permitted to go swimming in the river.

Another annual event in the spring was "Clean-up Day." We'd all bring our rakes from home and spend the afternoon raking the schoolyard, cleaning away the winter debris. What treasures were to be found!
(Pat Hanson)

In the spring of the year, we had "Clean-up Day." After raking and starting the bonfires, I furnished all the ingredients for a wiener roast. What fun!

Then on May 1, I hung a "May Basket," filled with goodies, on each desk. The pupils were allowed to eat out of it all day long. One little girl came to me at recess time to see if she could remove her gum. She said, "My jaws are just so tired." Needless to say, I never had any problems with the pupils eating candy or chewing gum in all the rest of the days.
(Frances Crook Olson)

I remember the school picnic at the end of the term, with all those wonderful games of baseball, tug-of-war, gunny sack races, wheelbarrow races (one unlucky kid got to be the wheelbarrow), relay races,

and — prizes! And, of course, food — lots and lots of home cooking. Ladies would pile it high on the tables. I remember taking some corn. It looked so beautiful in the dish, all gold and shiny, but yuk, it was so salty! But we had a good time. It was time to take our shoes off for the summer.
(Jerrie Steinwall Ahrens)

The picnics at the end of the school year were generally held in the woods next to the schoolyard. There would be potato salad, sandwiches, beans, cake, cookies, and lemonade; and the inevitable ants, flies, and mosquitoes (they didn't know of any sprays in those days). And so it was that we said "good-bye" to our teacher and friends until the fall, when in September the term started again.
(Lauretta Cords)

All social life — Christmas programs, social picnics, school plays, community clubs — revolved around the schoolhouse as the one meeting place available. When the country school went, much of the rural social life disintegrated. Its common center, the school, was no more.
(Milton S. Johnson)

FROM SKUNKS
TO SNOWSTORMS

FROM SKUNKS TO SNOWSTORMS

Nature believes in making use of any space available. In 1928, the space under the school seemed a good home for a family of skunks. All went fairly well, with just a slight disagreeable odor at times, until some woodchucks moved in, and ownership of the space was challenged with a fight. We all cleared out of the school in a hurry and rushed home, only to be ordered to leave our clothes and everything else that had been in the school outside. Help had to be called in to gas the animals and deodorize the place, an ordeal which was not perfectly satisfactory.
(Ruth V. Esping)

One dark morning while I was putting lessons on the blackboard at the front of the room, I heard footsteps pacing back and forth in the basement. I was alone and thought perhaps I was imagining things, but the pacing continued. With no telephone or car, I had no way to get help, so I stayed in the room, wondering who or what would open the door and walk in. When the door finally did open, luckily it was a school board member with his children. I told them about the mystery in the basement, and the dad went down to investigate. When he returned, he told us that there was a large skunk in the storeroom trying to get out. He went to get the other two school board members, and when they returned, they used a poisonous spray to kill the animal. They brought it up by the tail and displayed it to us in the schoolroom. Then they went to town to claim the $6 bounty. The skunk had done no damage in the basement, but it always remained a mystery how it had gotten in there.
(Kathleen Rietforts)

I came to the Maker School about 1929, facing a terrific discipline problem. There were five or six "big boys" who were really ruling the roost. The room was so full that the ringleader had to sit on a folding chair behind the last desk in the row. With all those grades, my class time was limited, so I had told the pupils not to ask any questions while I was teaching a class; I'd answer all questions between classes. Almost the first day this fellow raised his hand, and when I didn't come at once from class, he shoved his chair clear back to the wall and sat there defying me. I knew I must

do something drastic or be driven out as the teacher before me. So I walked back to him, tipped him back in his chair to the floor, and got my knee on his chest. Then I said, "Now will you do what I want you to, *when* I want you to?" In a very frightened voice he answered, "Yes." Then I told him to get up, get his dinner bucket, and get out of there. I didn't want to look at him any more that day. He left, but he didn't go home. He stayed in a nearby gravel pit until school was out. He never told anybody at home either, but I did. I heard reverberations of, "I guess that new teacher *means* what she says." I never had any more discipline problems all the years I taught there.
(Helen C. Williams)

Teaching in the early 1900s and during the war and Depression years, as my sister did, brought about some interesting and exciting happenings. My sister told of entering her school one morning and finding it warm. A hobo had slept there and kept the fire going. Gypsies were a common sight, sometimes scary, as most of the children had been told that they stole little ones.
(Dorothea Thompson)

I shall not forget an experience from which I learned a valuable lesson. It happened on a windy, late fall day when I discovered, upon leaving for the day, that I was locked in the schoolhouse. Since there was no telephone or lights in the building, I knew my only way out would have to be through a window. Luckily, they weren't double windows, so at least I could open one. The drop to the ground was too far without something to step on. The only loose objects were six orange-crate chairs for little folks, so I capitalized on using them. The first four fell over as they were dropped, but the fifth one stayed upright. Three times I was about out when I'd hear a car coming, so I'd crawl back in, lest I would be seen. Finally, it quieted down on the road and I made a safe landing, picked up the chairs, and found out why I was locked in. The metal bar had fallen over the padlock staple when the door was slammed shut. From then on I supervised every dismissal of the pupils.
(Hannah Lambert)

In the spring of the year, the creek that was between our farm and the schoolhouse always went out of its banks and made a new path (not under the bridge). When it appeared to be a bit hazardous,

my brother went that far with me in the morning and drove the car across, so that we made it safely. But one afternoon the water got higher and higher and was flowing much more swiftly. He called the neighbors to catch me and tell me to go another way (several miles farther), but because of a snowstorm that afternoon, the neighbors didn't see me come. I approached the watery roadway with caution, but decided to try it anyway. The whole front end of the Model A fell into the washout on the road, and I had to crawl out in ice water up to my hips! Luckily, there were neighbors just a few yards away, and an old German lady found me dry clothes. Then we called my folks, and my dad and brother came after me. But the car had to stay there overnight, and the next day it was completely frozen in. It didn't hurt the motor, but it was not an easy task to get it out and running again. It is a miracle my brother let me keep on driving his car after that episode!
(Mary D. Thompson)

One day I heard a loud bellowing noise, and for some reason I thought the boys were teasing a bull across the road. When I went out to stop them, I discovered that it was the bull himself pawing the ground and trying to get at the children. I called the children in, and in a few minutes the bull tore down three fence posts and brought his harem onto the playground. It was after five o'clock before it was safe to send the children home, as by then the cows went to the barn. In those days no parents rushed to see where their children were. They just assumed they would be home sometime.
(Dorothea Thompson)

One morning in May, the children came to school as usual. There seemed to be an air of expectancy as mischievous eyes watched me during the opening morning exercises. Then out of the desks came noisy sacks. Down the aisles rolled all kinds of canned fruits, vegetables, and glass jars of jelly and pickles. For once, I couldn't say anything, as I didn't understand what was going on. Then one little girl gave me a pretty card with all the children's names on it. She explained that they were having a food shower for me as a going-away surprise. I appreciated the food and the thought that went into planning it, and the surprise became another nice memory of teaching in days gone by.
(Kathleen Rietforts)

One day, before I was old enough to go to school, a teacher who stayed at our place offered to take me along to school. It was a very cold, snappy winter's day, so someone took us to school in a bob-sled pulled by a team of horses. When we got to school, the teacher had to start a fire in the big old pot-bellied stove that stood in the back of the room. As soon as she had the fire going good, the children started to arrive and crowded around the stove to get warm. The teacher, thinking my feet might be cold, sat me in a chair next to the stove and put my feet up against its side. She was getting ready for school to start, when someone yelled, "Lauretta's feet are burning!" Well, it didn't take her long to find out that the stove was red hot, and the soles of my shoes were beginning to smoke. She grabbed me away in a hurry and removed my shoes. Although my feet were beginning to feel hot, luckily I wasn't burned.
(Lauretta Cords)

Things had been going along smoothly for some time, when our teacher made the shocking announcement that from now on only English should be spoken on the playground. Uff da! What a headache! Did we have to use our company language even on the playground? Our household language was Norwegian, and that we enjoyed. It wasn't as if there were pupils who couldn't understand Norwegian. Every one of the forty pupils spoke it well. It wasn't that the teacher couldn't understand it either, because she did. We stormed about on the playground, declaring how downright unfair this new rule was to each and every one. The teacher had said that she thought American children should speak English while at school. We were patriotic, but this was carrying patriotism too far! When my mother heard the sad tale, she reacted calmly. "If you can talk Norwegian going to and from school, I am sure you will keep in trim," she said. Other parents must have taken it coolly as well. The threatened rebellion never took place.
(Ingeborg Bolstad)

We had a rule that no one was to leave the school grounds with-out permission. One day at noon, several of the older pupils took off without permission. They were even tardy for the opening of the one o'clock session. I thought that called for punishment, so I said that each of the offenders had to remain after school for one-half hour, especially since they wouldn't say where they had been. Classes proceeded, but with considerable tension. At about three-thirty,

several cars drove into the yard — out piled the mothers, laden with goodies for a picnic. The children had gone to a couple of homes to tell the mothers that it was my birthday and asked if they would bring the makings for a surprise party. Those mothers alerted the other mothers, and the result was a full-fledged party. No, the offenders did not have to stay an extra half hour!
(Mabel Winter)

It was December 1941, and all was in readiness for the afternoon performance of our Christmas program. The school was small, and parents and friends would have to come in the front door, across the stage, and go between the sheets which were used as curtains, before taking their place at desks in the back of the room. It was about one-thirty, with the program to start at two-thirty. The boys had been excused for a short time, and the girls were putting the finishing touches on the stage furnishings. The water fountain, which stood on a stand in the corner behind a sheet, had just been filled with water. When it was time for the boys to come back into the school, one lively ten-year-old came tearing in and crossed the room to get a drink. He couldn't stop in time and hit the fountain, overturning it, with about five gallons of icy water flooding the floor and soaking the hanging sheets. The boy was not hurt and the fountain did not break, but the frustrated teacher started to cry. What a mess! I sent some children to the neighbor's place for mops and more sheets. My landlady came to my rescue and brought extra sheets for curtains. She helped hang them, and after mopping up the water, we were pretty much ready for the program at two-thirty. The water fountain was not filled again until *after* the program. Santa Claus arrived on time with presents and candy, and the teacher regained her composure. Now I can smile when I meet that boy, grown to over six feet, who almost ruined the Christmas program.
(Kathleen Rietforts)

When I was in the sixth or seventh grade, we had terrible dust storms (the dust bowl days of the early 30s) that made our classroom so dark we could not see to do any work. Of course we had no lamps, etc., so we had to go home. I also remember that our Model T would choke up and die from all the dust in the engine.
(Mary D. Thompson)

It was in the Maker School that one of the practice teachers brought us scarlet fever. I got it, so was quarantined, as was customary to do then for contagious diseases. The local doctor gave me the word when I could go back to school. Someone saw the skin peeling off between my fingers, and one mother said that spread the disease. I had to get the doctor out to meet with those mothers and explain to them what they really *didn't* know about scarlet fever before they believed what I had told them.

Another time I had the doctor out to prove that some kids had impetigo. Most of the kids and I got that catchy stuff. I remember coming home when school was out in the spring and being banished to the attic with a complete cure or treatment to get rid of whatever I had before I could sleep in the beds or mingle with the rest of the family. Those were the days!
(Helen C. Williams)

Sadly to say, the death of a young child or baby was not uncommon in the days I attended school, and the family's grief was shared by the whole community. Funeral homes were not used at that time, so the visitation was always held at the family home. The teacher always spoke to the pupils about the tragedy, and then she and all the pupils would march, double file, from the school to the home of the bereaved, walk silently past the casket, and then back to school. This usually took about an hour, but it left a lifelong impression on everyone.
(Ida Posteher Fabyanske)

In one school, I opened the door one morning to find that the room was black dark. In a split second I knew what had happened. The oil burner had plugged up in some way and smoked until it burned out. There was no phone, so I had to get to a neighbor's house and let them know what had happened. There was no school that day or the next. The ladies in the district came to help clean up. No spot was left untouched by the soot. Even the books were smoke damaged.
(Signe Haraldson)

The schoolroom was heated by an old round stove that stood in the center of the room. It stood high on legs, and almost caused a disaster one time. One of the boys, who was being dragged by the teacher to the front of the room where he was to stand in the corner as punishment, hooked his foot behind a stove leg, pulling it down. Fortunately, there was no fire in the stove, but you should have seen the mess!
(Ruth V. Esping)

I had a first grader whose mother came for her after school was out each day. The first graders were let out at three-thirty to play in the yard until the older pupils got out. (I had six or seven classes of older ones in that half hour.) One day the first grader's mother came to the door to tell me her daughter wasn't waiting for her as usual, and we became alarmed. There were high cornfields on three sides of that schoolhouse, and I was afraid she'd gotten lost. So I sent my two big eighth-grade boys out to find her. They came back and reported that they had looked everywhere — even in the toilet holes! They couldn't find her anywhere. So I sent scouts out to track her route home, thinking maybe she had decided to walk home. They finally found her, hiding in a culvert with a boy, as a joke on her mother. Her mother had driven right over the culvert on her way to the school, and they had laughed and laughed.
(Elma Summers)

I remember one day sitting across the aisle from an older kid, say three or four years older than I. He had drawn a picture of a girl with no clothes on, and he passed it across the aisle for me to see. As I was passing it back to him, the teacher looked up and assumed that I had drawn the picture. Of course she didn't bother to ask. She told me to pass to the corner of the room. As I got up, the boy who had drawn the picture whispered to me, "Run for it." So that's what I did — straight to the outhouse! I got in and bolted the door with a 2 x 4 so the teacher couldn't get in. I waited until the teacher went back inside and then hightailed it for home. I told my parents about the episode, but was told I'd have to go back to school the next day to "face the music." When I came back, the teacher took my hand and slapped it with a ruler. I had a sore on that hand from a previous injury, and that now broke open. As it started to bleed, the teacher got a little worried about the action she had taken.
(David Wendell Hughes)

Opening day at school was quite chilly. The stove was the usual huge black hulk. I opened the door and saw that it was filled with scraps and waste paper. "Just enough to take off the chill," I thought. I threw in a match, and immediately a nice blaze erupted. But horrors! I realized, too late, that there were no stovepipes!! I almost panicked. I ran outdoors and was relieved to see one of the school board members driving in with his children. He told me to stay out;

he would take charge. Somehow he managed to put out the fire without it doing too much damage. He said that when a group had cleaned the schoolhouse, they decided also to clean the pipes, never thinking that the stove would be used on the first day of school. Luckily, I was not "fired."
(Mabel Winter)

How can I ever forget the morning in May when a thundershower came up and a bolt of lightning struck the schoolhouse. I think I never shall hear such a deafening sound again. First, we were just numb and couldn't move. When we got over being stunned, we got up and ran out of the schoolhouse — through a muddy field to a neighbor's place across the road. The family there was watching us, and they claimed there were splinters from the strike falling to the ground all around us as we ran; luckily, none hit us. The splinters came as a result of the lightning striking the roof of the schoolhouse and also the bell tower. The entry was moved inches away from the schoolhouse itself. The children's tin lunch boxes that sat on the floor in the entry were melted away — doughnuts, sandwiches, etc., burned and charred black. Needless to say, school was dismissed for the rest of the day.
(Lauretta Cords)

One of my first experiences after starting school in the fall of 1911 is maybe worth relating. There was no well on the school grounds, and water had to be carried from a neighbor's place. At one of the afternoon recesses, Sixten Swenson and I volunteered to fetch a pail of water from Magnuson's home. They had a large storage tank in the haymow of their barn; from there it flowed by gravity to the house, and was tapped from a faucet in the kitchen. This is where we got the water. When we returned to the school grounds, one of the older boys met us and spit in the pail of water. When we got inside with the water, we told what had happened. At once the teacher, Nancy Magnuson, stepped out on the porch and called this big boy to come forward. Then she asked Sixten and I what had happened. Sixten would not say anything (he was smarter than I — had started school the fall before in 1910). I told the teacher the facts and she made the boy empty the water pail, get it cleaned and go for another pail of water. For several weeks I hardly dared step outside of the school for fear of this big boy who was going to get even

with me for telling. I might add that I learned early that it doesn't pay to tattle on your friends.
(Holger O. Warner)

I think the first time I can remember going to school was as a guest of my older sister. It was not unusual to bring a younger brother or sister to school for a day. You shared the wood desk all day — all those wonderful books, a tablet of lined paper, and the smell of the wooden cedar pencils. It was always a very special treat to borrow the teacher's pencil. It seemed to be yellow, unchewed, had an eraser intact, and was long and well-sharpened. It felt clean, too. Being all of five years old, I noticed that the other students would get up and recite for the teacher. I heard a rooster crow off in the distance, so I stood up and did a very nice "cock-a-doodle-doo" for everyone, to their amusement and my sister's embarrassment. She never forgave me or took me along again!

Another time, I remember I had to stay after in first grade and write "get" on the blackboard (I had spelled it "git"). I had to write it a million times, it seemed, while my sister and brothers stood waiting, with their silent glare. I never had to stay after again!
(Jerrie Steinwall Ahrens)

I had a boy pupil who had grown to about six feet at grade school age. One day he got into a fight on the playground. When I saw the boys were fighting, I dashed out and got between them and sent them both in to their seats. When I later met up with a farmer who had been working in the field near the school, he laughed and told me how funny it was to see a little woman control those big boys!
(Edith O. Chaffer)

I had a little girl in the first grade who wouldn't read aloud; she would only whisper. She was a good reader and talked aloud in other classes. It went on like that for a month or more, when one day I asked her, "Virginia, will you read aloud for me if we send the pupils out to play?" Her answer was, "Yes." She started to read and was so pleased with herself. I stopped her and asked, "Shall we have Geraldine (her sister) come in to hear you read?" Again, her answer was, "Yes." It wasn't long before we had all the pupils back in the school listening to Virginia read aloud. What a happy little girl she now was!
(Marjorie Sperry)

One time in the school where I had twelve first graders, I had introduced the process of addition to them and most had gotten it right away. However, one little fellow just couldn't understand. I drew pictures, used objects, and things were getting pretty tight and heavy, since I was becoming very frustrated. The classroom was very quiet, and all the pupils were wondering what I was about to do to the poor little fellow. Finally I said, "Raymond, what is 1 + 1?" He replied with a pitiful look in his eye, "n-n-n-numbers." Needless to say, that broke the tension. I laughed, gave him a hug, and said, "Yes, Raymond, they are numbers." Everyone in the room laughed in relief. That was such a mistake; I should have realized that he just wasn't ready for addition.
(Margaret Thompson Cimenski)

The clothes we wore were simple. My brothers wore sweaters and knee pants — never, never jeans or overalls; that was for work in the fields. Poor as we were, that was a strict rule. My sister and I always wore dresses. We might have had two each, one for school and one for Sundays. The bloomers most always matched the dress, and there was a pocket on the front of the bloomers to carry a pretty hankie. Our stockings were heavy lisle, many times mended by spring, and in cold weather, the long underwear — yes, with the trap door! You were lucky if you had short sleeves on the underwear. Otherwise, you spent a lot of time tucking it up under your dress sleeve, pretending it didn't exist. I don't know why we were so concerned, because everyone wore it.

Shoes were practical brown oxfords, hand-me-downs, and worn until there were lovely holes in the leather soles. Then you could add a piece of cardboard for an inner lining, and when Daddy had time, he'd get his shoe-fixing tools out and repair the shoes himself. We had rubber gaiters and wool snow pants, coats, hats, and mittens. Snow stuck to everything, and once you went into a warm room, the snow on your clothes melted, the clothes got wet, and it was a while before you went out again. I remember my hands and wrists were always chapped to bleeding in the wintertime.
(Jerrie Steinwall Ahrens)

In the spring when the ground warmed up a little, nearly all of the boys and some of the girls went to school barefooted, and of course did not wear shoes during the summer vacation. So you can imagine the agony in the fall when the weather got cold and we had

to try to crowd our widened feet into the shoes we had set aside in the spring.
(Holger O. Warner)

The clothes worn on a cold winter's day consisted of one-piece long johns — better known as a "union suit" — cotton or wool socks, long shawls and heavy sweaters, petticoats, and skirts for the girls. We wore buckle boots over our shoes. The mothers usually made most of our clothes. I remember how much fun it was to go in to town to buy new long johns!
(Lucina E. Valento)

I remember wearing aprons over my dress to protect it — and wearing full, black, sateen bloomers. Also, I remember wearing long-legged underwear and trying to pull the long, ribbed stockings over them so they weren't bunchy. I wore bibbed blue overalls in the winter to further protect my legs. New ones faded and stained my stockings blue.
(Alice L. Soffa)

The following episode taught me a valuable lesson. A snowstorm had drifted the snow in the schoolyard in such a fashion that the schoolhouse appeared to be in a saucer. Since I was an inexperienced car driver, I didn't realize that the brakes were frozen until I tried to stop near the building. Since the only passable place to drive was around the building, I circled it three times without stopping, and then steered toward a snowbank. I didn't know I could have shut off the ignition! Anyway, I didn't stop until I hit the fence in front of the boys' toilet! One of my pupils asked, "Why didn't you stop where you always do, Miss Lambert?" Imagine my embarrassment when the wrecker men came to take the car to the garage from that location, and again when I had to report the damage to the school board clerk!
(Hannah Lambert)

I remember the Armistice Day snowstorm of 1940. It was in my teaching contract that school was to be in session on Armistice Day. I was at my boarding place, one-fourth mile from the country school, since my father took me there on Sunday afternoon. By seven-thirty on Monday morning, a school board member called and said that there would be no school that day. I didn't get to my country school until Wednesday afternoon, walking through snowdrifts up to my hips, since the gravel road had not been plowed out. There were snowdrifts in the schoolyard up to the steps and porch, and some snow had blown into the hall. I had to dig a path to the woodshed to get wood and coal, and then carry it into the schoolroom to build a fire in the large jacketed heating stove. After getting a fire built, I tramped through snowdrifts to try to check the outdoor toilets. There was snow packed solid above my head in the two toilets, as a result of the strong whipping winds of two and one-half days and nights.

I had school on Thursday, with one pupil present. By Friday I had gotten one toilet shoveled out so it could be used. I had seven pupils on Friday. The girls and boys took turns using the one toilet. On Friday at two o'clock, water started dripping from the ceiling onto the large dictionary toward the back of the room. Snow had blown into the attic and was starting to melt, after having heat in the schoolroom for two and one-half days. Drip! Drip! Drip! Yes, the dictionary was promptly moved!

(Orline Golden Foelschow)

A SPECIAL TOGETHERNESS

A SPECIAL TOGETHERNESS

A feeling of nostalgia often accompanies memories of the years spent teaching in a rural school. There was a togetherness or companionship there which was not found in other schoolrooms. If an older child got through with his lessons, he would, and did, help a younger sister, brother, or friend with his spelling, arithmetic, or reading.
(Dorothy Powell)

I still maintain that youngsters who attended a rural school had a special kind of education. We were like one big family. Everyone knew everyone else's hurts and problems, and showed their sympathy in many ways. They learned how to study on their own because most of their work was done by themselves. They "absorbed" much education, too, from listening to other classes that were reciting. We had some excellent students.
(Helen C. Williams)

The one thing that makes the country school special to me is the closeness that was felt between all of the students. There was also a certain closeness with the teachers. I had one teacher for grades one through four and then another for grades five through eight. Having the same teacher for so long gave me an opportunity to get to know each of them very well.
(Van Johnson)

When I was a child, people didn't go to town very often, and the country school was the center of community life. Neighborhood children would meet on the way to school and walk the long distance together. This provided for friendship and closeness. The Christmas program and box socials at Valentine's time brought the community together and were great fun. The Mothers' Club programs and lunches were also special times. Each one was happy when their mother attended.

I enjoyed everything about school and took it very seriously. Good grades and perfect attendance awards were important to me. And how I loved my first grade teacher! Recently, after so many years, we have resumed contact through an article I read about her in a Minneapolis newspaper.

There is much to be said about the goodness of that simple way of life. Surely, we were a healthy bunch — simple food and lots of exercise and fresh air!
(Mae Hanson Hughes Kjos)

I would like to say that rural schools were special. They provided a life-like situation. Children learned to share and to understand schoolmates of different ages. Honesty, self-discipline, patience, and respect were learned by close contact. It was necessary to work independently if one was to succeed. Neither money nor machines guarantee any better education. It's people who count. All in all, the rural school life is a time to remember. There is nothing else that can take its place. The rural school added much to our heritage. I am glad that I was able to participate. My earnest hope is that I gave a few, at least, a lift to a fulfilling life.
(Arlie M. Klimes)

I will always feel that the days spent in a rural school had something which could never be found in a city school. There was a closeness, togetherness, and friendship which brought everyone on an even basis. My four years of teaching are some of the happiest of my life, and my pupils will always remain very dear to me.
(Ada Ronnei Pederson)

To anyone not familiar with the excitement and trauma of being a pupil in District 11, our one-room school must have appeared prosaic. But to us who struggled over our "times tables" and went sliding on the "rubber ice" until someone broke through it, this was a place of laughter and tears, of challenges and surprises — the center of our lives. We who are products of District 11 treasure happy memories of the days we spent there. The friendships have been lasting, and some of the lessons have not been forgotten.
(Ingeborg Bolstad)

Country school was very special because all the people in our district knew each other and were involved in the programs, picnics, and box socials. There was a special togetherness — people caring about people.
(Elsie Fredericksen Williams)

I have many, many pleasant memories of my days of teaching, but perhaps the greatest reward came forty years after I quit teaching — on my eightieth birthday. Several of my friends and former pupils had a colossal idea. They went to the court house and got the names of all my former pupils and wrote to them, inviting them to come to an open house party or to write to me. What a thrill when the mailbox started filling with cards from all over the United States. I received about 150 beautiful cards and letters, and the church overflowed with former pupils and friends. That party climaxed an era of a life made full by country teaching and living.
(Mabel Winter)

As a farewell gift to me at the end of my four years of teaching, I was given a quilt. It was put together by the mothers, using the shirts and dresses of the children, and pieced together in blocks. What a precious reminder of the togetherness we shared.
(Ruby Vickers)

ACKNOWLEDGMENTS

I am deeply grateful to the following individuals for sending me their "Country School Memories." By taking the time to write down some of their recollections of country school life, that part of our heritage can now be preserved.

Ahrens, Jerrie Steinwall
— pupil, 1934-35, Dist. 1, Dakota Co., MN
Anderson, Clara
— teacher, 1927-45, Aitkin, Pope, and Swift Co., MN
Ball, Marva Rumelhart
— pupil, 1942-50, Budde School, Jerauld Co., Wessington Springs, SD
Barsness, Mabel
— pupil, 1907-17, Dist. 45, Pope Co., MN
Barsness, Olive
— teacher, 1918-26, Dist. 94, 52, and 88; Loury, Farwell, Kloten, ND
Bieberdorf, Ella
— pupil, 1913-20, Dist. 137, Hartford, SD
Block, Clarence
Bolstad, Ingeborg
— pupil, 1913-19, Dist. 11, Pope Co., MN
— teacher, 1924-28, Pope Co., MN
Brenden, Agnes
— pupil, 1909-18, Blue Mounds Township, Dist. 42, MN
— teacher, 1923-48, Pope and Kandiyohi Co., MN
Burtness, Hannah
— teacher, Waseca Co., MN, 3 years; Freeborn Co., MN, 25 years
Campbell, Viola Burnett
— teacher, 1935-39, Nicollet and Judson, MN
Chaffer, Edith O.
— pupil, 1912-20, Ten Mile School, E. Peoria, IL
— teacher, 1925-36, various rural schools near E. Peoria, Mackinaw, and Morton, IL
Cimenski, Margaret Thompson
— pupil, 1920-28, Dist. 3, Crow Wing Co., Brainerd, MN

— teacher, 1934-55, various rural schools in Crow Wing
Co., MN

Cords, Lauretta
— pupil, 1904-12, Grams School, Blue Earth Co., MN

Cummings, Frances E.
— pupil, 1921-29, Wolverine and Imlay City, MI

Cummings, Wallie D.
— pupil, 1910-18, Huckins School, Croswell, MI

Delage, Deloris
— pupil, 1940-47, Poplar River School, Brooks, MN

Demuth, Ann

Esping, Ruth V.
— pupil, 1909-17, Dist. 55
— teacher, 1924- (11 years), Dist. 55, 24, and 35, MN

Fabyanske, Ida Posteher
— pupil, 1920-27, McCarron's Lake School, Dist. 29, MN

Foelschow, Orline Golden
— pupil, 1925-31, Dist. 74, Swift Co., Milan, MN
— teacher, 1939-41, Dist. 64, Swift Co., Benson, MN;
1945-46, Dist. 74, Swift Co., Milan, MN

Fredericksen, N. Wyelene
— pupil, 1920-28, Maker School, Lincoln Township, Blue
Earth Co., MN

Hagedorn, Clara G.
— teacher, 1935-37, Willow Lawn School, Clay Co., IA

Hanson, Pat
— pupil, 1935-40, Honeyford, ND
— teacher, 1949-50, Walcott, ND

Haraldson, Signe
— pupil, 1912-18, Rock and Pipestone Co., MN
— teacher, taught 31 years in all

Hardin, Mae F.
— pupil, 1924-30, Royal School #1, Starkweather, ND

Hauge, Sophie C. Vold
— pupil, 1914-22, Dist. 87, Pope Co., Glenwood, MN
— teacher, 1928-29, Dist. 9, Pope Co., Glenwood, MN;
1929-30, Dist. 24, Pope Co., Sedan, MN; 1932-36,
Dist. 37, Pope Co., Starbuck, MN

Hedlund, Margaret Seeger
— pupil, 1925-33, Minnesota and North Dakota
— teacher, 1938-41, Dist. 73, Pope Co., MN

Hughes, David Wendell
— pupil, 1908-16, Dist. 11, Cambria, MN
Hughes, Selma Anderson
— pupil, 1918-26, Dist. 122, Blue Earth Co., MN
— teacher, 1932-38, Dist. 78 and 11, Blue Earth Co., MN
Jeddeloh, Carol Johnston
Jenkins, Alice M.
— pupil, 1927-32, Horeb School, Cambria, MN
Jenkins, Margaret
— pupil, 1927-33, Dist. 11, Cambria, MN
Johansen, Ruth Aleda
— teacher, 1920-23, Four Mile Creek School and Long
Lake School in rural Northern Wisconsin
Johnson, Blanche Lindholm
— teacher, 1917-23, McPherson Co., KS; 1930-31, Saline
Co., KS
Johnson, Milton S.
— pupil, 1918-26, Dist. 36, Lincoln Co., SD
Johnson, Van
— pupil, 1942-50, Dist. 139, Browerville, MN
Jones, Roland H.
— pupil, 1905-16, Llanfairfechan, North Wales
Juhl, Elizabeth
— pupil, 1901-09, near Fenton, IA
Kjos, Mae Hanson Hughes
— pupil, Lincoln Township, Blue Earth Co., MN
Klimes, Arlie M.
— teacher, 1927-71, Nobles, Rock, and Pipestone Co., MN
Lambert, Hannah
— teacher, 40+ years in Waseca and Steele Co., and
Madelia, North Mankato, and Faribault, MN
McKinley, Ethelyn
— pupil, 1911-16, Waseca Co., Waseca, MN
McKinley, Forrest
— pupil, 1907-16, Dist. 162, Stearns Co., Paynesville, MN
Meixell, Reba Clark
— teacher, 1926-31, Dist. 119, South Lincoln, and Dist. 92,
Good Thunder, MN
Nannestad, Eldora
— pupil, 1911-17, Sherburne Co., MN
— teacher, 1924-53, Douglas, Sherburne, Pipestone, and
Rock Co., MN

Norton, Mary Ann

Oldenborg, Harley
— pupil, 1921-30, Lake Benton, Marshfield, Lincoln Co., MN

Olson, Frances Crook
— pupil, 1917-18, Pleasant View, Blue Earth Co., MN
— teacher, 1931-45, four schools in Blue Earth Co., MN

Ose, Sally L.
— pupil
— teacher, taught 29 years in various rural schools

Parquet, Hazel Hubbart
— pupil, 1929-35, Manley School, Beaver Township, Miner Co., SD
— teacher, 1944-48, Manley School, Beaver Township, Miner Co., SD

Pederson, Ada Ronnei
— pupil, 1913-21, Dist. 45, Pope Co., MN
— teacher, 1927-31, Dist. 90, Pope Co., MN

Powell, Dorothy
— teacher, 12 years in Steele and Waseca Co., MN

Quissell, Mrs. Julian
— teacher, 1939-41, Quissell Country School, Moody Co., SD

Rietforts, Kathleen
— teacher, Kilkenny Co., Nebraska; Waseca and Steele Co., MN

Sanvik, Selma O.
— pupil, 1917-25, Dist. 44, Pope Co., MN
— teacher, 1930-41, Pope and Stevens Co., MN

Schlichter, Norma Hughes
— pupil, 1947-52, Maker School, Blue Earth Co., MN

Sedlacek, Emily
— pupil, 1920-26, Dist. 29, Moody Co., Ward, SD
— teacher, 1931-56, Dist. 19, 69, 64, 62, 36, 9, 12, 46, 73

Siefkes, Lucille
— pupil, 1926-29, Dist. 162, Andover, SD

Soffa, Alice L.
— pupil, 1924-31, Clear Grit
— teacher, 1936-45, Larson, Watson Creek, Brokken, Zion, Maple Lane, Clear Grit

Sperry, Marjorie
— pupil, 1910-11, in rural school
— teacher, 1927-30, in rural school
Studt, Lorena
Summers, Elma
— teacher, 1941-50, Butternut, Maker School, Helleckson School, Watonwan School, MN
Thompson, Dorothea
— pupil, 1918-24, Hardwick, MN
— teacher, 1931-69, Rock, Pipestone, and Nobles Co., MN; and Lyon Co., IA
Thompson, Mary D.
— pupil, 1928-36, Hanson 25-1 and Hanson 25-2 and Ferney, SD
— teacher, 1941-43, Hanson 25-1 (south of Groton, SD)
Valento, Lucina E.
— pupil, 1923-29, Richmond, MN
Vickers, Ruby
— pupil, 1916-23, Huffton, SD
— teacher, 1927-31, Barnes School, Claremont, SD

Waite, Magdalene
— pupil, 1914-20, Trosky, MN
— teacher, 1926-59, Dist. 13, Hatfield, MN; Dist. 51, Trosky, MN; Dist. 17 and 24, Pipestone Co., MN
Warner, Holger O.
— pupil, 1911-19, Dist. 33, Fish Lake Township, Chisago Co., MN
Williams, Elsie S. Fredericksen
— pupil, 1923-31, Maker School, Dist. 89, MN
Williams, Helen C.
— teacher, 1925-72, Yellow Medicine Co., Judson, and Blue Earth Co., MN
Wilson, Diann Lundeby
— pupil, 1952-59, Mission #2 School, Devils Lake, ND
Winter, Mabel
— pupil, 1910-17, Dist. 52, Traverse Co., Wheaton, MN
— teacher, 1922-41, various rural schools in Traverse Co., MN

This book evolved from a project I started in an American Folklore class at Lakewood Community College several years ago. I would like to thank John Schell, my folklore instructor, for his inspiration.

I would like to thank the following individuals and organizations for providing me with sources for this book and helping me in various other ways.

INDIVIDUALS: Marian Anderson, Ken Brauns, Allan F. Degnan, Dawn Blair Gullickson, Mary Hilke, Janet Huber, Vicki A. Johnson, Sherry Jones, Peggy Korsmo-Kennon, Robert Kuehn, Darlene Lenard, Minnie Osterholt, Shirley Selzer, Diane Skelnik, Terri Snider, Gail Westby, and Bertha Zniewski.

A special thank you to Nick Cords for his valuable advice, support, and encouragement.

I would also like to thank my husband, Tom, and sons, Scott and Andy, for their patience and understanding while I worked on this book.

HISTORICAL SOCIETIES: Cass County, Dakota County, Douglas County, Fillmore County, Koochiching County, Mille Lac Lake, Paynesville County, Pipestone County, Pope County, and Waseca County.

The Minnesota Historical Society was a valuable resource for researching the history of one-room schools in Minnesota.

ABOUT THE ILLUSTRATOR

Nancy Delage Huber graduated from the University of Minnesota—Morris, with majors in studio art and biology. She has been drawing since she was a small child, and now specializes in pen and ink illustration.

Nancy and her husband currently live in the Twin Cities area, where she works as a graphic designer.

ABOUT THE AUTHOR

In 1951, I attended first grade in a country school in southern Minnesota. It was called the Maker School and is located in Lincoln Township, Blue Earth County. At the end of that school year, the school district was consolidated, and I attended grades two through twelve in Lake Crystal, Minnesota.

Although I only attended a country school for one year, I have many pleasant memories revolving around that little building. Through the years, it has been used for Farm Bureau meetings, 4-H Club meetings, elections, box socials, potlucks, bridal showers, etc. When I was in the seventh grade, I even hosted a class party there for all my "city friends." The schoolhouse, which is located about one-half mile from the farm where I grew up, is still standing and is now called the Lincoln Township Hall.

I currently live in White Bear Lake, Minnesota, with my husband and two teen-age sons. I enjoy writing about everyday people and events. I specialize in researching and recording stories and events of the past — preserving our heritage. By integrating the fields of journalism, history, folklore, and design, I facilitate others in telling their stories. This is the second book I have published. My first book, *Forget-Me-Not*, is a collection of verses written in autograph albums from the 1880s to the present.

Bonnie Hughes Falk

My first day of school
1951

The above photographs were taken about 1948–1950 at the Maker School, located in Lincoln Township, Blue Earth County, Minnesota. In the middle photo, I'm the little one on the left, with my sister Norma standing behind me. (It must have been visiting day!)

"*Country School Memories* fascinated me, and I read it almost from cover to cover without putting it down.

The one-room school was a significant phase in our American culture, and Bonnie Hughes Falk has rendered us all a service by assembling and publishing these anecdotes of country school life."

— Dr. H. Conrad Hoyer

"My children are enjoying their copies of *Country School Memories*, and my grandchildren are learning (and laughing!) about the way things were when grandma was young."

— Margaret Seeger Hedlund

"In a unique and entertaining format, Bonnie Hughes Falk has brought us nostalgic recollections of a way of life that today exist only in our childhood memories.

Bonnie is to be commended for her outstanding effort in recording and preserving an important part of our heritage!"

— Allan F. Degnan

will to power, a sense of moral adventuring beyond good and evil, with the goal of evolving the superman, a term that we still use today, in German the *Übermensch*. In Germany, such ideas captured a generation that felt dissatisfied with the crisis state of German politics as well as culture, and who took aboard these ideas. In particular, a back-to-nature movement of hikers, called *Wandervogel,* in Germany represented in remarkable ways an anticipation of the hippy generation of the 1960s, as they turned away from a present day that they saw as commercialized and not idealistic, and longed for a world somehow remade by idealism and generational revolt. However misguidedly, when war came in 1914, many of them would feel that their hour had arrived.

To many it seemed that Europe was moving towards war. It wasn't clear when it would happen or precisely how, but tension certainly had been growing. According to the eminent military historian John Keegan, turn-of-the-century Europe was "pregnant with war." In particular, military planning had increased the likelihood of the destructive potential of this war. In its victory over France in 1870–1871, the Prussian and then later the German army had seemingly demonstrated the key to military success on the battlefield: universal conscription, the nation at arms—drafts, in other words, for everyone—large reserves, so that there would be manpower to throw into huge battles and—and this was crucial planning with scientific precision—in order to achieve speedy mobilization.

The Germans seemed to have arrived at a recipe for victory, and soon other Great Powers were imitating them. Military planning among all the Great Powers grew ever more detailed, dominated by that key symbol of industrialization, the railroad. Soon railroad timetables planning down to the minute for when what troop trains would be crossing which bridges at what precise moment had become an art or a science. Mobilization increasingly implied war, as once these plans had been started they had to continue unfolding less they dissolve into chaos. If speed was crucial, this simply underlined the importance of being there to strike with maximum force the first blow.

Germany's case was unique in one aspect in particular; for Germany mobilization meant war. The German army's secret plan, the Schlieffen Plan, sought to deal with a particular German problem, the geopolitical problem that Germany faced a war probably on both fronts—both in the east against Russia and in the west against France. This plan had been crafted by the German chief of general staff from 1891–1905, General Alfred von Schlieffen. Its aim, as a project, was to find a way of knocking France out of the war within 42 days by a sweeping movement of armies through neutral Belgium and Holland, violating their neutrality, plunging through northern France, to encircle French armies and Paris. And then, after winning against France, German armies could turn to face the slower Russian enemy.

We need to observe about the Schlieffen plan that its disregard of political and diplomatic realities—not least the invasion of neutral counties—made it a clear example of militarism abstracted from the realities of politics. The French Plan, Plan XVII, projected a glorious frontal attack into Germany to regain the lost provinces of Alsace and Lorraine. Russia, for its part, also had plans for an attack on Germany. All of this was given further impetus by a so-called "cult of the offensive." In a counterpoint to military planning and technocratic organization, military planners also emphasized the spirit of attack, the cult of the offensive. Generals and officers argued that fiercely dedicated soldiers could overrun even far larger forces as long they had the requisite ferocity and morale. And thus, military training often emphasized direct attacks and bayonet charges. In the French case, the crucial quality of spirit was even given a glorious name, "*élan vital*." It implied an all-out extreme attack, which was necessary to compensate for a hard reality: France's smaller population versus its German enemy. Once the largest nation in Europe, France by 1914 could field only 60% of German potential manpower; and thus it was clear that the argument for greater morale took on a special resonance. A young officer, Charles de Gaulle, later the leader of a recovered France, proclaimed in 1913, the year before the war broke out, "Everywhere, always, one should have a single idea: to advance." This cult of the offensive, this militaristic thinking, these trends in the culture, represented an explosive mixture, which would be ignited in a 1914 July crisis that we'll examine in our next lecture.

Lecture Four
Causes of the War and the July Crisis, 1914

Scope:

Fierce debate has surrounded the causes of the war ever since it took place. In this lecture, we consider first the prehistory of growing tensions in European foreign affairs. Next we analyze the immediate events that led to war, from the assassination of the Archduke Franz Ferdinand of Austria-Hungary at Sarajevo in June 1914 to the diplomatic chain reactions that followed in the July Crisis. We weigh the dominant positions in debates on the origins of the war, including the crucial Fischer Debate on Germany's role and intentions in the unleashing of the conflict. Who or what ultimately was responsible for the outbreak of the war?

Outline

I. Analysis of Causes

    A. Because tipping over into war in 1914 is a classic case of escalation, it is urgent to understand how it happened.

    B. The inquiry has led to one of the most voluminous debates in historical scholarship, with many hundreds of books on the topic.

    C. Debates concern questions of whether long-term or short-term factors predominated, the role of individuals versus structural factors, intention versus miscalculation, and clear culpability versus collective responsibility.

II. Prehistory

    A. Events unfolding in 1914 built on earlier diplomatic history.

    B. German unification in 1871 changed the balance of power.

        1. Bismarck's often secret diplomacy sought to reinforce stability and make Germany indispensable to European order.

        2. The conservative Three Emperors' League that Bismarck crafted in 1873 to join Germany, Austria-Hungary, and Russia failed.

3. Bismarck then set up the Dual Alliance with Austria-Hungary in 1879. Joined by Italy in 1882, this became the Triple Alliance.

4. At the same time, Bismarck also signed a secret Reinsurance Treaty with Russia in 1887.

5. When Bismarck departed in 1890, this special tie with Russia was dropped.

6. In 1894, contrary to German expectations, Russia and France entered into a military alliance.

7. In terms of the balance of power, at this point a German-British alliance would have made most sense.

8. Britain grew worried by its isolation and sought allies, among them Japan in 1902.

9. However, Wilhelm II announced a new course called *Weltpolitik* (world policy) in 1897 and began construction of a great fleet.

10. Britain approached its traditional rival, France, and settled colonial frictions in the 1904 *Entente Cordiale*, from which further cooperation would develop.

11. German diplomats provoked colonial crises over Morocco in 1905 and 1911, which cemented French and British cooperation and increased suspicion of Germany.

12. In 1907, Britain and Russia settled their conflicts.

13. From 1907, increasingly rigid alliances bestrode the European continent: the Triple Alliance (Germany, Austria-Hungary, and Italy) and the Triple Entente (France, Russia, and Britain).

III. Balkan Crises

A. It is sometimes said that World War I started as the Third Balkan War.

B. As Ottoman control receded before the power of nationalist independence movements in Serbia, Bulgaria, and Romania, the region became a power vacuum in which both Austria-Hungary and Russia got involved.

C. Austria-Hungary considered it imperative to impede Serbian ambitions, lest the empire's own South Slavs be drawn to Pan-Slavism.

D. In the 1885 Bulgarian Crisis, Germany supported Austria-Hungary, leading to worsening German-Russian relations and breakdown of the Three Emperors' League.

E. The Balkan Wars then followed, with increased tension.

    1. In 1908, Austria annexed Bosnia-Hercegovina, which it had administered since 1878. Serbia, coveting the area, was infuriated, but when Germany supported Austro-Hungary, Serbia and its patron Russia were humiliated and backed down, but resolved not to do so again.

    2. In 1912, a Balkan League of Serbia, Bulgaria, Montenegro, and Greece expelled the Ottoman Empire from most of the Balkans and then fell out over the spoils in the Second Balkan War of 1913, with the former allies fighting with Bulgaria.

    3. Serbia's size doubled, but it still lacked access to the Adriatic and wanted union with Serbs in Bosnia.

    4. These unresolved conflicts provided an explosive mixture.

IV. July Crisis

    A. Sarajevo

        1. World War I began due to a terrorist act.

        2. Obviously, however, other factors came into play, as earlier assassinations had not led to world wars.

        3. On June 28, 1914, the Habsburg heir, Archduke Franz Ferdinand and his wife, Sophie, were assassinated by Gavrillo Princip, an 18-year-old student affiliated with a Serbian underground group, the Black Hand, whose motto was "Union or Death."

        4. Although not organized by Serbia's government, the Black Hand was supported by the head of Serbian military intelligence, Col. Dragutin Dimitrijevic, a.k.a. "Apis," a mysterious figure.

        5. The Archduke's visit to Sarajevo on the day commemorating the Serbian nationalist anniversary of the 1389 defeat of Kosovo was extremely ill-timed.

    B. Ultimatums

1. The Austro-Hungarian government saw the assassination as an opportunity to stage a showdown with Serbia.

2. When Austria-Hungary inquired whether Germany would support a responsive action, the German leadership gave a "blank check" of support on July 5, 1914, although the risk of general war was present.

3. On July 23, Austria-Hungary presented a deliberately unacceptable ultimatum to Serbia, to be accepted in 48 hours.

4. On July 25, Serbia accepted most conditions.

5. On July 28, Austria-Hungary declared war on Serbia.

6. To support Russia's Serbian ally, Tsar Nicholas ordered full mobilization on July 30.

7. On July 31, Germany sent Russia an ultimatum to stop its mobilization within 12 hours or face war.

8. Events show the importance of military planning: When Kaiser Wilhelm II suggested not going to war in the west as well, his panicked generals, having no other plans, had no response.

C. War Declared

1. On August 1, Germany declared war on Russia.

2. On August 2, Germany delivered an ultimatum to Belgium to allow German troops to pass through its territory.

3. Britain, which had repeatedly proposed mediation or peace conferences, now communicated to Germany that, if Belgian neutrality were violated, Britain would go to war.

4. On August 3, Germany declared war on France and on August 4 invaded Belgium, putting the Schlieffen Plan into action.

5. On August 4, Britain entered the war, officially for "Little Belgium," whose neutrality it had guaranteed in 1839 (which Bethmann-Hollweg called "a scrap of paper"), but also for its importance to the balance of power.

6. Italy stayed out of the war, tending to "sacred egoism."

7. By August 4, 1914, this war had become a general one, which Europe had not seen in a century.

8. The Central Powers (Germany and Austria-Hungary) faced off against the Allies (France, Great Britain, and Russia).

V. Debate on Causes

   A. Debate began with the war itself.

      1. Governments published "colored books" claiming justification.

      2. Scholarly debates have undergone enormous shifts.

   B. One key formulation was the War Guilt Clause, part of the Versailles Treaty.

      1. The Versailles Treaty at the end of the war claimed in Article 231 that Germany and its allies were solely responsible for launching the war.

      2. Reflecting wartime sentiment, the clause also justified reparations.

   C. In the 1920s and 1930s, the notion of a collective responsibility became prominent.

      1. In the interwar years, as international tensions relaxed, opinions shifted toward the notion of shared responsibility.

      2. British wartime leader David Lloyd George suggested that all European states "slithered over the edge" into war.

   D. In the 1960s, the Fischer Debate renewed the question of the causes of the war.

      1. Renewed debate exploded in 1961 when German historian Fritz Fischer's *Grab for World Power* (published in English as *Germany's Aims in the First World War*) argued that Germany launched the war to become a superpower and developed war aims that anticipated the Nazis.

      2. In the furious confrontations that followed, the debate itself changed. Fischer's critics came to argue that Germany miscalculated its gamble, rather than that the country intended world war.

3. In a later book, Fischer claimed Germany had planned war from 1912.

E. Other explanations have also been advanced by historians through the years.

    1. Other interpretations stressed different causal factors.

    2. Did alliances themselves cause the war? "Secret diplomacy" was denounced after the war as a crucial factor.

    3. Did arms races and military planning cause the war by forcing a timetable? Henry Kissinger argues that alliances and mobilization plans created a "Doomsday Machine."

    4. Was war an accident, as British historian A. J. P. Taylor argued, turning politicians into "prisoners of their own weapons?"

    5. Was imperialism the cause? Although colonial competition certainly poisoned the atmosphere, earlier clashes were negotiated.

    6. Was capitalism the cause, as Marxists argued? On the contrary, German industry's dominance grew in peacetime.

    7. Though this is not a scholarly theory, were the Balkans to blame (as some hinted during the Balkan wars of the 1990s)? Rather, outside involvement of the Great Powers was the crucial variable.

F. Where does the current interpretation of the causes of the war stand today?

    1. Most scholars today see Germany as bearing the main responsibility for the war, as it was willing to risk general war, though not aiming for it.

    2. Even as Germany is seen as mainly responsible, some degree of responsibility is shared by other actors in this tragedy.

    3. Although Fischer moved the debate forward on war aims, his arguments on intentions are not accepted.

    4. The debate continues today.

VI. Fatalism

   A. A shared sense of fatalism and misunderstanding as to the true nature of modern war among Europe's political leaders helped *make* the war inevitable, if it had not already been so.

   B. The compulsion to think the unthinkable was expressed in the German saying, "Better a terrible end than endless terror." Contemporaries were about to discover that one could have both.

Essential Reading:

Annika Mombauer, *The Origins of the First World War: Controversies and Consensus*.

Supplementary Reading:

Henry Kissinger, *Diplomacy*, pp. 168–217.

A. J. P. Taylor, *The First World War: An Illustrated History*, pp. 13–20.

Questions to Consider:

1. If Wilhelm II had not been Kaiser, would war still have broken out?

2. Was there too much or not enough secret diplomacy before 1914?

Lecture Four—Transcript
Causes of the War and the July Crisis, 1914

In this lecture, we'll be considering the causes of the war and the July Crisis of 1914 as Europe plunged into the conflict. Fierce debate has surrounded the question of the causes of the war since the very event took place. In this lecture, we'll consider first the prehistory of growing tensions that led to the war; next we'll analyze the immediate events such as the assassination of Archduke Franz Ferdinand at Sarajevo in June of 1914 that touched off a diplomatic chain reaction that produced the conflict itself; we'll weigh the dominant positions in the furious debates that have raged on the origins of the war; and we'll seek to understand better some of the issues at stake, who or what ultimately was responsible for the outbreak of the war.

Now, clearly in terms of the largest issues, an analysis of the causes of the First World War is existentially important. The very fact of how the Great Powers tipped over into a general war in 1914 is considered a classic case of escalation in diplomatic and military history, and thus, it's very urgent to understand how it happened. Indeed, this is one of the most voluminous debates in all of historical scholarship, and many hundreds of books have been written on the topic; the debates center on many issues, which are key questions of historiography. The debates concern questions of whether long-term or short-term factors were more important, whether the role of individuals should be stressed or rather structural factors took on great importance, whether the policy makers who produced this disaster did so by intention with malice of forethought, or whether miscalculation, instead, guided their steps. Questions, also, ultimately of whether culpability can be clearly assigned to one or another party or side, as opposed to a collective responsibility for this manmade disaster.

We need, first of all, to understand some of the prehistory of these events, because 1914 and the crisis of that year, in fact built on earlier diplomatic history. German Unification in 1871, Bismarck's German Revolution of unifying Germany nation-state, had changed the balance of power. After this German Revolution of German Unification, Bismarck often sought through secret diplomacy to reinforce stability, to reassure Germany's neighbors, and to make Germany itself indispensable to European order. A key example of this was Bismarck's attempt to argue to the conservative powers of the continent—Germany, Austria-Hungary, and Russia—that they had shared interests and, in 1873, he crafted the Three Emperors League as an attempt to solidify that solidarity. But, ultimately it failed, in part because of conflicts between Austria-Hungary and Russia. Bismarck then scaled back his ambitions and set up the so-called Dual Alliance where Austria-Hungary joined Germany in an alliance relationship in 1879. When Italy joined as a third power in 1882, this became the so-called Triple Alliance. But at the same time, pursuing his canny diplomatic manipulations, Bismarck also kept open lines of communication with the conservative power of Russia by singing the secret Reinsurance Treaty of 1887, which promised that neither power would aid another power attacking either Germany or Russia. When Bismarck left office in 1890, essentially dismissed by the new fiery Kaiser Wilhelm II, this special German tie with Russia was dropped.

In 1894, contrary to German expectations, Russia and France, in what amounted to a diplomatic bombshell, announced that they had entered into a military alliance. This took German diplomats by surprise; their expectations were that the political systems of both of these countries were so different that they wouldn't be able to be reliable alliance partners. Russia, after all, was an autocratic empire; France, by contrast, was a republic. But as it turns out, their shared strategic interest overrode any domestic ideological differences. In terms of the concept of the balance of power that we've discussed in earlier lectures, at this point, with the emergence of a French and Russian alliance, the most natural outcome would have been a balancing off of this alliance by a revitalized German-British relationship or friendship or alliance, which would have balanced off against this constellation of powers. It says much about the disastrous state of German diplomacy that this didn't take place. By contrast, Britain felt that though the time was right for an alliance—finding new partners—Germany was not a partner that came into question. Britain had grown worried about its own isolation at the start of the 20th century and had found allies, among them Japan in 1902. But ultimately, it was worried about German intentions.

When Wilhelm II, the Kaiser of Germany, announced a new aggressive foreign policy called *Weltpolitik*—or world policy—in 1897, which aimed to make Germany a world power and began construction of a great fleet, the British were worried. In a warped sense, Wilhelm II had intended this building of super navy in some sense to make Germany more desirable to the British as an alliance partner, because it would gain the respect of this maritime power. This was, again, a disastrous idea because Britain instead grew worried about rivalry on the seas. Britain then reacted by approaching its traditional enemy, France, and they settled their mutual colonial frictions in an agreement—not an alliance, not a formal alliance—from 1904 called the *Entente Cordiale*, the "Friendly Relationship." Now, while this was not a formal alliance, further cooperation could develop on the basis of this agreement. German diplomats worried about what they saw as an encirclement of enemy powers all around Germany and thus, they sought to provoke colonial crises that would fragment the alliances that they saw coalescing against them. The colonial crisis over Morocco in 1905 and again in 1911, in fact did just the opposite; they cemented French and British cooperation and increased general suspicions of Germany and its ambitions.

Completing this web of relationships and of friendships of powers that worried about Germany was in 1907 the understanding which Britain and Russia undertook in order to settle their colonial conflicts. So by 1907, a very key diplomatic moment had been arrived at throughout the European scene, increasingly rigid alliances covered the European continent. On the one hand, the Triple Alliance; Imperial Germany, Austria-Hungary, and Italy—though questions always remained about whether Italy could be trusted to ultimately participate actively in the alliance. The Triple Alliance was balanced by the opposing powers of the Triple Entente; France and Russia bound together in an alliance, and Britain bound to them through understandings or ententes.

Very clearly, the temperature was rising in terms of potential conflict in Europe, and nowhere more so than in the Balkan regions. The Balkans, as we'd already pointed out, was an area where, with the receding of the Ottoman Empire, a power vacuum had emerged, which presented a tremendously volatile political situation internationally. Such a keen diplomatic thinker and observer as the "Iron Chancellor" of Germany, Otto Von Bismarck, in one of the phrases that he just tossed off that later seemed to have almost a prophetic quality to it, Bismarck had worried that all of his careful undertakings to preserve European peace would be done by, as he put it, "Some damn fool thing in the Balkans." That was precisely what ended up happening in 1914. But in fact, a whole series of Balkan crises had preceded this ultimate Balkan crisis and they hadn't produced general war. It is sometimes said by historians that World War I really represented the Third Balkan War, one in a series that ultimately escalated into a worldwide conflict. How had that happened? As Ottoman control had receded in the course of the later 19th century, before the power of the uprising of nationalist independence movements in Balkan countries like Serbia, Bulgaria, and Romania, which became independent and clamored for more territory, this region became a power vacuum.

It was one in particular in which both multinational empires, Austria-Hungary as well as Russia, got involved feeling that their interests were implicated. In a very special sense, Austrian policy-makers felt that the Balkans represented a special threat. We'll recall that Austria-Hungary, as a multinational multiethnic construct with 12 major nationalities, felt especially threatened by the powers of nationalism. If nationalism truly came to the fore, the result would be that the empire itself might very well explode. The anxieties focused on the Balkans of Austro-Hungarian leaders; they considered it imperative to impede the ambitions of Serbia in particular, because Serbian ambitions involved the creation of South Slavic with Serbs in a leadership position, feeling that they had an essentially nationalist calling to achieve this Slavic unity. The anxiety of Austro-Hungarian policy-makers was precisely that their own South Slavic peoples, Croatians, Slovenes, Serbian minorities living under the Hapsburg rule, might feel the attractions of this Pan-Slavic ideology and be drawn to its message. If that were to happen, the other nationalities of Austria-Hungary might very well peel off as well, and the empire itself would be destroyed.

Events clearly had taken a bad turn already in the so-called Bulgarian Crisis of 1885, when Austria-Hungary and Russia had argued over who should have the most influence in the Bulgarian state. Germany, forced to choose between its alliance partners, had tried to steer a more neutral course, but was seen as supporting Austria-Hungary more. This led to Russian anger, hurting German-Russian relations, and breakdown of the Bismarck's conservative Three Emperors' League.

There followed, then, an increase in tension with a new 20th century, the Balkan Wars. In 1908, a crisis situation had developed in the Balkans when Austria annexed Bosnia-Herzegovina, an area that has been much in the news at the end of the 20th century and the start of the 21st. Austria-Hungary had administered this area since 1878, though it formally had remained under rule; but now to, in part, demonstrate the vitality of the Austro-Hungarian Empire, had formally annexed the area. Serbia, which had also coveted that area—there were Serbians living there—was infuriated and prepared for conflict. When Germany supported Austria-Hungary, Serbia and its great patron to the east—Russia—felt that they were not ready for war, were humiliated, and backed down, but both sides resolved that they would not compromise again. Wars then flared up in the Balkan area in 1912. A Balkan League—including Serbia, Bulgaria, Montenegro, and Greece—fought against the Ottoman Turks and expelled them from most of the Balkans and Europe, but then fell out themselves as allies over the spoils of their victory in the Second Balkan War of 1913, with most of the former allies ganging up to fight against Bulgaria. The outcome of the Second Balkan War was a remarkable one. Serbia had gained new confidence, its size had doubled, its confidence had grown in sense of nationalist mission, but it still lacked access to the Adriatic, and the fact that Serbs in Bosnia had come under the rule of Austria-Hungary still rankled. These unresolved conflicts provided an explosive mixture, which ultimately would help to produce the July Crisis.

The July Crisis of 1914 began with a terrorist act; so, in a very real sense, World War I began due to terrorism. Now, obviously other factors came into play, earlier assassinations or acts of terrorism had not led to world wars, this one was different. On June 28, 1914, the heir to the Habsburg throne, Archduke Franz Ferdinand and his wife Sophie, were visiting the provincial capital of Bosnia-Herzegovina, Sarajevo. At 11:15 in the morning, they were both assassinated. The assassination itself proceeded with essentially, a comedy of errors, though a dark comedy, as the gang of assassins failed in repeated attempts to destroy the procession of the royal couple. When, however, the car that was to take the Archduke and his wife away from the scene took a wrong turn by chance, one final assassin saw his opportunity; he was very surprised to see the car unexpectedly loom up before him. He stepped up to it and fired into the car itself and assassinated the couple. The young assassin was an 18-year-old student, Gavrillo Princip, who was affiliated with a Serbian underground group called the Black Hand. Its motto was "Union or Death," meaning union in a great South Slavic Serbian state or death, which he now had meted out. He was immediately arrested and investigations followed as to how this could have happened. The assassination itself, contrary to the suspicions of the Austro-Hungarian government, had not been organized by Serbia's government itself, but it had been supported by shadowy mysterious figures within that government; in particular, the head of Serbian military intelligence, Colonel Dragutin Dimitrijevic, also known as "Apis."

The Sarajevo visit had coincided with a moment of nationalist fervor. It had, as it happened, fallen on an anniversary, the Serbian nationalist anniversary of the defeat of the battle of Kosovo of Serbian forces by the Ottoman Turks in 1389, and had been seen as a special provocation by the nationalists who had brought off the assassination. Outrage internationally spread at this cruel act. Gavrillo Princip, who was taken to prison, was soon tried and spared the death penalty because of his youth; he eventually died of tuberculosis in prison in 1918 before the war ended. Now the Austro-Hungarian government proceeded to respond to what was seen as a provocation, a challenge to the very existence of Austria-Hungary as a Great Power. The Austro-Hungarian government used this tragedy as an opportunity to stage a long-awaited showdown with Serbia to finally settle the score.

When Austria-Hungary inquired whether Germany would support vigorous action by the Hapsburg Empire, the German leadership agreed. It gave what later historians have called a "blank check" of support on July 5, 1914, even though it understood that the risk of general war was certainly present and might break out. On July 23, thus, a crucial diplomatic event took place. Austria-Hungary presented an ultimatum to Serbia, one that had been very carefully crafted to be unacceptable to the Serbian government. It was to be accepted by them, the ultimatum announced, within 48 hours. On July 25, Serbia went the extra mile by accepting all but a few of those conditions, excepting those which interfered with or didn't correspond to its national sovereignty; in particular, the demand for an Austro-Hungarian commission of investigation to investigate what they felt was probably the complicity of the Serbian government. Nonetheless, in response to what it considered an unsatisfactory answer on July 28, Austria-Hungary declared war on Serbia.

Now events began to unfold with tremendous rapidity. To support its Serbian ally, the Russians now came into play. Tsar Nicholas ordered full mobilization of Russia's armies on July 30. The next day, on July 31, Germany came to the support of its Austro-Hungarian ally. Germany sent to Russia an ultimatum that it had to stop its mobilization within 12 hours or face war. At this point, events show the importance of the detailed military planning and the rigid timetables, which had been developed by generals' staffs in the years previous. Kaiser Wilhelm II, at this point, suggested, contrary to earlier plans, that perhaps one should not go to war in the west as well. His panicked generals almost experienced, by some accounts, a nervous breakdown at this and tearfully explained to the Kaiser that there were no other plans. The war now proceeded and war was declared.

On August 1, Germany declared war on Russia. On August 2, in line with its earlier plans for a knock victory in the west before moving east, Germany declared an ultimatum to Belgium that it must allow German troops to pass through its neutral territory on their way to attack France; Belgium refused. Great Britain, which had repeatedly throughout these hours proposed mediation or peace conferences, now communicated to Germany that if Belgian neutrality were violated, Britain would go to war. On August 3, Germany declared war on France and on August 4, invaded neutral Belgium, putting the long ago crafted ideas of the Schlieffen Plan into action. On August 4, Britain also entered the war; it did so officially for its commitment to respect the neutrality of little Belgium, which had been guaranteed by the Great Powers in 1839. The German Prime Minister, or Chancellor, von Bethmann-Hollweg, told a horrified British ambassador that this neutrality was merely a scrap of paper. Nonetheless, Britain respected its obligations, and also realistically, in terms of power politics, was concerned about the balance of power. It could not allow France to be crushed and for the channel to be dominated by German power. As many had suspected would happen, Italy did not honor its treaty obligations and instead stayed out of the war, tending to what it called its "sacred egoism" in defense of its own interest. Thus, by August 4, 1914, this had become a general war such as Europe had not seen in the course of a century. At this point, the Central Powers—Imperial Germany and Austria-Hungary—the Central Powers faced off against the Allied Powers—France, Great Britain, and Russia. The war now had become a general war.

The debate continues to this very day about the causes of this conflict. Debate had begun with the war's start itself. Governments published so-called "colored books" claiming that their side was just, that they were reacting to aggression by the other side. Scholarly debates that have proceeded with ferocity in the years afterwards have seen enormous shifts since the war itself. One key formulation of an explanation of the causes of the war was provided by the Versailles Treaty. The Versailles Treaty, at the end of the war imposed upon a defeated Germany, included Article 231; the so-called "War Guilt Clause" in which Germany was forced to accept sole responsibility along with its allies for launching the war. This clause was also intended to justify the payment of reparations by the defeated side as well. It provided a very clear answer; Germany accepted the responsibility for the war. However, in the next years, in the 1920s and 1930s, different interpretations instead because prominent, including the notion of collective responsibility. In the inter-war years, as international tensions relaxed, as some of the passion of the war died down, opinions shifted instead towards the notion, not of sole German responsibility, but instead of shared responsibility by many irresponsible European politicians for this tragedy. Even British wartime leader, David Lloyd George—about whom we'll be talking much more about his energetic leadership in the war—afterwards suggested that perhaps all European states had somehow inadvertently, as he put it, "slithered over the edge" into war.

In the 1960s, however, debate grew once again; this is the famous Fischer Debate. Renewed debate exploded in 1961, in particular when German historian Fritz Fischer published a book, which in German was entitled *Grab For World Power*. It had the weaker title in its English translations of, *Germany's Aims in the First World War*. Fischer's book argued that Germany had launched the war to become a superpower and developed war aims, which, in many cases, anticipated those of the Nazis in the Second World War. Furious confrontations followed, but in the process of the debate itself, positions changed. Even Fischer's harshest critics came to argue that while Germany had played a very important role in starting the war, it had miscalculated rather than intending world war. Fischer's positions became more extreme with time in a later book that Germany had planned the war years previously from 1912.

Other explanations also were advanced by historians in the furious debates about the causes of the war. Did alliances themselves cause the war? Indeed, after the First World War itself, secret diplomacy was sometimes denounced as a crucial factor. A diplomat like Bismarck had tended to believe by contrast that alliances and webs of networks and relationships made war less likely. Did arms' races and military planning in all of its detail and inflexibility cause the war by forcing war by timetable? The diplomat and diplomatic historian Henry Kissinger has argued that alliances and mobilization plans created what amounted to a "Doomsday Machine" that moved Europe towards war. Was the war then an accident, as the provocative British historian A.J.P. Taylor argued? He proposed that politicians had been turned into the "prisoners of their own weapons." Was this really the case? Was, perhaps, imperialism the cause? Was it the scramble for colonies, the frictions that had grown over imperial competitions?

While colonial competition certainly poisoned the atmosphere between the Great Powers, Germany and Austria-Hungary had been less prominent in such colonial competition and earlier colonial clashes had indeed been negotiated peacefully. Was, perhaps, capitalism the cause, as Marxists and Marxists historians argued? On the contrary, the war would take an incredibly economic toll, as we'll see in later lectures, and Germany's own industrial dominance had grown in peacetime only to be frustrated in Europe as a whole by the ravages of the war. Finally, there's a kind of explanation that gets advanced, which is not really a scholarly theory, but I think nonetheless needs to be put on the table. Some people feel that there's something about the Balkans themselves, the Balkanize—that word has even entered in the English language—the fragmented or Balkanized nationalist passions of the region, that somehow made it a powder keg that blew up. This sort of not quite scholarly explanation was hinted at also during the 1990s, as Balkan wars raged there, in part as an excuse for not intervening. There was something about the Balkans, some suggested, that made those people kill one another and hate one another. I think that this explanation needs to be looked at quite critically because, in fact, it wasn't only the Balkans themselves under the nationalist passions that reigned there, but indeed the outside involvement of the Great Powers was the crucial variable in bringing the explosive situation to its flash point.

Where do interpretations in the causes of the war stand today? Most scholars today do see Germany as bearing the main responsibility for the war. Germany was willing to risk general war, though perhaps not aiming for it. Even as Germany is seen as mainly responsible, some degree of responsibility is seen by many historians as shared by other actors in this tragedy, at least in the sense of not having tried hard enough to prevent a general war. Historians are currently focusing renewed attention on the role of Austria-Hungary as the beginning, the flash point of this conflict; as Austria-Hungary, in part as they saw it, to defend their own survival initiated the process itself to cause a regional war. Not desiring general war, as erupted, but a localized conflict that they felt would insure the continued survival of the Austro-Hungarian Empire. In terms of the Fischer Debate, many of Fischer's arguments about war aims and the extensive nature of German war aims have been accepted, but some of his more far going claims about German intentions or premeditation have not been accepted. I think it's safe to say that the debate continues today and will continue into the future as well.

We might usefully add into our considerations of the causes of the war one more psychological element shared by many European politicians at this time, which is hard to quantify, hard to capture exactly, but which nonetheless must have played a role. A shared sense of fatalism played an important role in the unfolding of these events, in addition to misunderstanding of the true nature of modern war. Europe's political leaders, in some sense, by believing that a war was inevitable helped to make that war inevitable, if it had not already been so. The conviction that Europe was moving inevitably towards a great clash, a great general war, had something in the nature of a self-fulfilling prophecy.

I'd like to give one particular example of this that was tremendously evocative. The compulsion on the part of some politicians, some intellectuals, to think the unthinkable and to view the war, the coming war, as inevitable and perhaps even, in some sense, desirable, at least to clear the air and to finally break the great tension, was expressed by a famous German saying that was much current at the time and that saying went in translation: "Better a terrible end than endless terror." Better a terrible end than endless terror—the argument was in essence that if the conflict was inevitable, better that it should come now and finally break the tension that had been building over previous years. Later this saying, "Better a terrible end than endless terror," would take on a dreadful significance because contemporaries were about to discover that it wasn't an either-or proposition; in fact, in terms of the First World War, one could very well have both. We'll examine next the intensity of illusions and misapprehensions and failed plans with which this terrible war would begin in our next lecture.

Lecture Five
The August Madness

Scope:

Turning to the intriguing realm of mass psychology, we seek to plumb the so-called "August Madness," the hysterical celebration of the outbreak of war that took place in European capitals. Crowds paraded in the streets and squares with songs and flags, while young men rushed to volunteer. Historians are now questioning how widespread this emotional outburst really was. We will analyze new research and assess the variety of reactions to the start of the war, including the avowal of domestic truces in an exalted mood of national unity (soon to break down), paranoid waves of spy manias, and tempered anxieties about what was to come.

Outline

I. The Myth of the August Madness

    A. By "myth," historians mean not outright falsifications but rather powerful shared conceptions that command belief in a society.

    B. The events of late July and August 1914 were mythologized and invoked repeatedly throughout the war and after.

    C. In August 1914, with the declarations of war, scenes of jubilant excitement played out in Paris, London, St. Petersburg, Vienna, and especially in Berlin on Unter den Linden Boulevard.

        1. Crowds cheered, waved national flags, and sang national anthems and patriotic songs.

        2. Contemporaries celebrated a feeling of social unity, with internal differences swept away.

        3. In sociological terms, society (*Gesellschaft*) was supposed to have turned into a true community (*Gemeinschaft*).

        4. Many nationalist hopes of achieving true inner unity were vested in cementing these emotions.

5. Beyond this, the breaking of the feverish anxiety of waiting produced hysterical relief.

6. For some, war could be a redemption from ordinary life or social crises.

7. Expectations of heroism and glory played a role.

8. Some were simply caught up in the mood of excitement.

D. The memory of these events was politically instrumentalized in many different ways afterward as the "Spirit of 1914."

II. Recent Research

A. Recent study has strongly qualified these collective memories.

B. Historians have pointed out that the enthusiasm was strongest among the middle class and elites, students, and in urban centers.

1. In rural areas and frontier regions, there were more sober reactions and worried anticipation.

2. Men were more strongly affected than women.

3. There was also public opposition to the war, so this reaction was not monolithic.

4. Ethnic minorities in the empires lacked this enthusiasm.

5. Jaroslav Hasek's comic classic, *Good Soldier Svejk*, lampooned the August Madness.

C. Historian Jeffrey Verhey notes that less than one percent of Berlin participated in the fabled first mass gatherings.

D. Clearly, one needs to speak of a range of reactions to the outbreak of the war.

E. Nonetheless, after qualifications, this outburst, and especially how it was later used, need further investigation.

III. Spontaneous Mobilization

A. Many intellectuals and artists have left testimonies as to how they were caught up in the initial enthusiasm.

1. These people included the psychologist Sigmund Freud, the German historian Friedrich Meinecke, and the British poet Rupert Brooke.

    2. The Austrian writer Stefan Zweig, though passionately antiwar, recalled these first hours of war as rapturous.

  B. All the warring powers claimed to be acting in self-defense.

IV. Social Reactions

  A. Inner Truces

    1. In all the combatant countries, "domestic truces" were ceremoniously declared, pledging to put aside internal conflicts in this time of emergency. They were not to last.

    2. In France, a *Union Sacrée* ("sacred union") was declared.

    3. In Russia, imperial unity was invoked.

    4. In Germany, the inner truce was called the *Burgfrieden*, recalling the unanimity of a besieged castle.

    5. Kaiser Wilhelm II famously announced that he no longer saw people of different parties or religions, but "only Germans."

    6. In the *Reichstag* parliament, the German Social Democratic Party voted for the war by authorizing credits, revealing its own nationalism.

    7. In the exalted mood, German Jews participated fully in this mood of nationalism, though they continued to face social discrimination and anti-Semitism.

    8. Germany would need this inner truce, as the British naval blockade would begin to bite and grind down the economy, with painful sacrifices required.

  B. Inner Paranoia

    1. Wartime societies also evidenced strong paranoia about the crisis and feared disruptive forces within. This was a worrying portent of the singling out of minorities.

    2. Absurd epidemics of spy chases and a mania for denunciations (called "*Spionitis*" in Germany) set in.

    3. Enthusiasts demanded a cleansing of languages from enemy influence.

    4. In Russia, German-sounding St. Petersburg was renamed Petrograd.

5. The British royal family (with the German name of the House of Saxe-Coburg-Gotha) assumed the name of Windsor.

6. Signs on shops became targets.

C. Spontaneous Propaganda

1. It is a truism of research in propaganda that it is most effective when building on things that people already believe.

2. In this case, self-propaganda took place, as an enormous and spontaneous wave of testimonials to the justice of one's own cause arose, at first without governmental urging.

3. The universal claim of going to war in righteous self-defense was an effective rallying cry.

4. In the first months of the war, more than a million war poems were published in German newspapers.

5. Governments would later learn to harness this enthusiastic impulse in systematic ways.

6. The self-mobilizing impulse proved crucial over the next years in sustaining morale and determination.

7. The churches played an ambivalent role in this enthusiasm.

V. The Failure of International Socialism

A. Contrary to expectations, the international socialist movement, which had earlier pledged internationalist unity, broke down with the outbreak of war.

1. At the 1907 Stuttgart conference, the Socialist International promised to stop a capitalist war, perhaps with a general strike.

2. In practice, socialists discovered that their patriotism trumped their earlier ideological avowals.

B. Surprised by the outbreak of war, the Russian Bolshevik revolutionary Vladimir Ilyich Ulyanov, known as Lenin, was living in exile in the Austro-Hungarian Empire, where he was disgusted with this socialist failure.

1. Ironically, he was at first arrested as a suspected Russian spy.

    2. Lenin was able to leave for neutral Switzerland.

    3. Lenin saw the war as the final crisis of capitalism and unsentimentally advocated that the war among the Great Powers be converted into a worldwide civil war of classes.

VI. Mobilizations

    A. The Great Powers mobilized and volunteering stations were crowded.

    B. Throughout Europe, 20 million men were mobilized.

Essential Reading:

Modris Eksteins, *Rites of Spring: The Great War and the Birth of the Modern Age*, pp. 55–94.

Supplementary Reading:

Peter Fritzsche, *Germans into Nazis*, pp. 1–82.

Jeffrey Verhey, *The Spirit of 1914: Militarism, Myth and Mobilization in Germany*.

Stefan Zweig, *The World of Yesterday: An Autobiography*, pp. 214–237.

Questions to Consider:

1. What forces worked most effectively against enthusiasm for war?

2. Under what circumstances would Lenin's message become more appealing?

Lecture Five—Transcript
The August Madness

In this lecture, we'll be turning away from the sort of high politics and diplomatic maneuverings that we've discussed in our earlier lecture on the outbreak of the war, and turn instead to the intriguing realm of mass psychology. We'll be examining the mysteries of a truly strange event to our present day sensibilities, the mysteries of the so-called "August Madness," that hysterical celebration in August of 1914 of the news of the outbreak of war in European capitals. As crowds paraded in the streets and the squares with songs and flags, young men rushed to the volunteering stations to sign up for a role in the conflict. Today, historians have started to question how widespread this emotional outburst really was and what it all meant. In this lecture, we will analyze some of this new research and assess the real variety of reactions to the start of the war, including the avowal of domestic truces which were supposed to summon up a sense of national unity—which, as it turned out, would soon break down—as well as other psychological reactions to the news of war, such as paranoid waves of spy manias, seeing conspiracies everywhere, and the growth of anxieties about what was to come.

Historians speak of the myth of the August Madness. It would be profitable here to stop and think about how we use the word "myth." We don't mean merely the event itself of the August Madness, those celebrations themselves per se, but also how it was mythologized, dramatized, and played up and used in propaganda for years afterwards. When historians talk about myth, they generally do not mean outright falsification or lies—though it certainly can be that as well—but rather by myth, they mean powerful, shared conceptions that command belief in a society and can motivate people in one direction or another. In this lecture, we'll be talking about real events that happened, the events of late July and August of 1914, which where then depicted in certain ways, or mythologized in certain ways. These events were repeatedly invoked again and again throughout the war, when it became necessary to get energized again in the fighting countries in support of the conflict. These mythologized experiences also played a very important role after the war in trying to understand what it all had meant. These scenes, in and of themselves, were compelling. Crowds gathered in the last days of July, as the diplomatic maneuverings and diplomatic news filtered in. They gathered around newspaper offices and telegraph posts in order to share in the sense of these world-changing, historical events in the making.

In August of 1914, as the declarations of war rolled in, tremendous and compelling—and to our sensibilities, strange—scenes played themselves out. While we might today more soberly consider war a disaster, an event not to be met with anything but grim foreboding, at this time, in August of 1914, the scenes were very different. Jubilant excitement played out in the capitals of Europe and in the boulevards of Paris, as crowds gathered, cheered, and marched, as they did in the squares of London, Vienna, and St. Petersburg. In Berlin in particular, along the main boulevard through the center of the capital, along the famous street Unter den Linden Boulevard, crowds marched up and down on sides, singing and moving between the royal castle at the center of the city and the parliament off to the side in a patriotic celebration. In all of these European capitals, crowds cheered, waved national flags, sang patriotic songs, and national anthems. Nationalists who participated in these events were celebrating a feeling of social unity. Whatever might have divided them earlier, or whatever internal differences might have wracked the politics and the social divisions of a country, were now in an instant swept away as part of a larger cause and a larger mobilization. German sociologists had earlier tried to understand how society was to be conceived of and how social organization was to be understood, and some of the terms that German sociologists had come up with, were now deployed to analyze these exalted feelings. In sociological terms, society or what the German sociologists called *Gesellschaft* had been something artificial founded on a social contract and utility.

Now supposedly, this society of *Gesellschaft* had turned into something finer, something more authentic, and more real; a true community or *Gemeinschaft*, based not on who and what is of use to you and vice and versa, but rather on true solidarity and a true feeling of unity. Many nationalist hopes of achieving a true inner unity of the nation, earlier frustrated by social, regional, or religious divisions, now were invested in using the opportunity invoked by this emotion of the August Madness events to cement their nationalist cohesion. Beyond this, contemporaries also pointed out that this hysterical reaction was not only a positive emotion and a feeling of unity; it was also something more elemental. The sense of hysterical relief, which at last followed upon the breaking of the growing, feverish anxiety, had been building for days, weeks, months, and maybe even for years. At the same time, for some individuals, war felt like redemption from the boredom or the quotidian nature of ordinary life and of a society that was not living up to expectations. A famous British war poet Rupert Brooke—who later was killed in the war—summed up these thoughts in famous poems treating the war as a moment "where God had intervened in order to bring a young generation to a moment of a high calling." Such expectations of heroism, of breaking through ordinary life to horizons of glory and drama, certainly played a role for many. At the same time—and here we speak obviously of mass psychology and its mysteries—some individuals might simply be caught up in the mood of excitement, without thinking through what it was that they were hurtling towards collectively. The mythologization of these events certainly played a very important role in years to come. The memory of these events reproduced in newsreels, photographs, and in contemporary testimony, became political instruments with many different political orientations in different countries. A common touchstone called the "Spirit of 1914," an exalted emotion, which greeted the war, united all the countries.

One of the main themes of our course that we will be pursuing is the notion of the First World War as a series of shocks of the new: a series of shocks of one novelty succeeding upon another. This would be a good moment to mention that the sort of mass emotion and mass mobilization that the crowds represented in the August Madness, really added a new and dynamic element that many traditional politicians that were quite concerned about and not quite sure what to do with. The sort of mass enthusiasm which later would become so very important in sustaining total war, was here presented as a new and dynamic element for the first time. Now, historians have, in more recent research, started to look more closely at the evidence that we have of the August Madness and its true dimensions. Recent historical research has strongly qualified over large generalizations about the August Madness itself. One might say that historians here are performing a role they often play of being spoilsports of deconstructing myths and legends, but in this case, it is important to point out that the enthusiasm, contrary to what the mythological images would later be; the enthusiasm, while strong, was not universal. It gripped certain elements of society more than the others.

How did this more recent research suggest these events and enthusiasm broke down? Historians have been careful to point out that enthusiasm was strongest in particular segments of society; strongest among the middle class, among the elites that identified themselves with the government, especially strong among university students, and especially strong in urban centers as compared to the rest of the country, where obviously one could gather such massive crowds to participate in an event like the August Madness. By contrast, historians point out, in rural areas or in frontier regions, which would be the first to be hit probably in a territorial conflict, there were certainly more sober reactions and much more in the nature of a quieter and a more silent and worried anticipation might bring.

One might also add that some of the scurrying about and frenzied energy of the August Madness was not merely preparing for war itself with enthusiasm, but was also an expression of other anxieties. While some crowds celebrated the outbreak of the war with national songs, other crowds rushed to the banks to withdraw their savings, and yet other crowds rushed to the stores to stock up on staple goods before the inevitable rise in prices in a time of war. Another qualification is that from the evidence gathered, it appears that men, especially young men, and especially those young men that were university students, were more strongly affected by this enthusiasm than women. Let us also carefully note the considerable public opposition to the outbreak of war, so contrary to the exalted myth of the "Spirit of 1914," that was gripping entire societies and unifying them. In fact, the reaction was not monolithic in all the countries. In many cases, socialists were prominent among those who spoke up against what they denounced as a war of capitalist exploitation, in which the workers inevitably would be among those hardest hit.

At the same time, as crowds were gathering for nationalist celebrations such as in Berlin for example, socialists were mustering their followers in Berlin as well to march for peace. In fact, and this is often forgotten in the exalted mythology of the August Madness, in the center of Berlin on that same beautiful boulevard Unter den Linden, as nationalist crowds sang national anthems, they were joined by socialist crowds of protesters who sang socialist songs.

Observers at the time spoke indeed of a war of the songs that took place on this boulevard in Berlin, as contending crowds were matched one against the other.

Another qualification that needs to be registered is that ethnic minorities in the multinational empires, especially of Austria-Hungary and of Russia, lacked this sort of enthusiasm. They felt alienated from the mobilization in many cases for war for the imperial cause. In a book that is one of the great comic classics of world literature—unfortunately not as widely known in English as it should be—Jaroslav Hasek's *The Good Soldier Svejk*, the figure of the good soldier Svejk is by his very passivity and following of orders is a constant reproach to the attempt to mobilize the masses. A Czech soldier in the comic classic, Svejk lampoons the August Madness taking place around him, by having himself wheeled around in a wheelchair, while shouting, "Long live the emperor," and "Long live the Austro-Hungarian Empire," thus making a farce of the entire venture.

Among the historians who have shown yeoman work in bringing us a closer view of what the August Madness meant, is a historian called Jeffrey Verhey, who in really a masterful work of detective investigation, has reconstructed the events in Berlin, and provides us with one very important fact that puts in perspective how we need to be cautious in our generalizations about the August Madness. He notes that perhaps less than 1% of Berlin participated in the fabled first mass gatherings of the August Madness. Clearly, one needs to speak of a range of reactions in answer to the outbreak of the war. Instead, we are left with this: after all of those qualifications, this remarkable mass outburst—and especially how it was used later—was real and need further investigation.

We might further talk about the larger phenomenon of which the August Madness just represented the tip of the iceberg, such as the spontaneous mobilization of Europeans for war. Many intellectuals and artists of many different countries have left testimonies to how they too were caught up in the initial enthusiasm. There are especially compelling in cases where people later turned against the war, but are honest enough to talk about the emotions they felt at the start. These figures included the psychologist Sigmund Freud in the Austro-Hungarian Empire, the German historian Friedrich Meinecke, and the British poet Rupert Brooke, whom I mentioned some moments ago. The Austrian writer Stefan Zweig, though passionately against war, still recalls these first hours of war as rapturous, something special and out of the ordinary. A key aspect, perhaps *the* key aspect in this spontaneous mobilization of populations for the cause of war, was that all the warring powers claimed that they were going to war and acting in self-defense. This deserves to be underlined. One of the main themes of our course is the different meanings that were assigned to the war. Here quite simply was a universal meaning in 1914 assigned to what it was all about: the World War was about self-defense.

Let's look a more closely at some of the social reactions which typified the response to the start of the war. A key notion of the August Madness was that it symbolized the greater reality of societies experiencing a perfected unity. This is a concept often summed up in the notion of an inner truce. In all the combatant countries, where domestic truces or inner truces were ceremoniously declared, all parties were supposed to pledge to put aside their internal conflicts, their ideological quarrels, at a time of emergency when all had to rally to the national or imperial cause. These domestic truces were very important at the start of the war, but they were not to last. In France, which had a famously fragmented political force, the republic declared a *Union Sacrée*, a sacred union where all Frenchmen would rally to the defense of their fatherland to expunge the humiliation of defeat against Germany back in the 1870s, and to regain the lost provinces of Alsace Lorraine. In Russia as well, imperial unity was invoked, and even some disaffected minorities felt themselves nonetheless able to participate in this domestic truce, in the hope of gaining greater autonomy and greater cultural rights after a victorious conclusion of the war. In Germany, this inner truce was called the *Burgfrieden*, the term, which has almost sort of a medieval resonance that quite deliberately tried to conjure up of the unanimity or the piece of a besieged castle. *Burgfrieden* quite literally means the piece within a castle, with a clear implication that one is facing enemies on the outside.

Kaiser Wilhelm II was overwhelmed by the August Madness, a real remarkable testimony to the novelty of the August Madness and the self-mobilization of the crowds. German politicians had been worried about how the news of war might be met, and some of them advised the Kaiser to actually make himself scarce in the first hours of the declaration of war, in case sentiment turned against it. On the contrary, vast crowds came to the royal palace and demanded to see their emperor. Kaiser Wilhelm II famously stepped out in front these crowds and announced that he no longer saw Germans as separated groups belonging to different parties or different religions, but rather, he saw only Germans, all united in their national identity, all needing to treat one another from now on as brothers and as fellow fighters in the common cause. Swept up in the emotions of this event, another truly remarkable circumstance played out in the Reichstag parliament, where it was necessary to vote for war credits to fund the war.

The German Social Democratic Party, caught up in this enthusiasm, voted for the war, authorized credits, and revealed its own German nationalism in this moment, coming as a real surprise to German political leaders. There had actually been plans for fanning out and arresting the leaders of the Social Democrats if they protested actively against the war, so their participation in this nationalist mobilization came as something of a surprise as well. Also caught up in the exalted mood of those days and weeks were groups within German society, which had not fully been allowed to participate in German nationalism. German Jews, as a minority representing about 1% of the population, participated in a very patriotic sense in this mood of nationalism, even though they still continued to face social discrimination and anti-Semitism. As it would turn out, Germany would be very much in need of this inner truce in the years to come as the British naval blockade would begin to bite and grind down Germany's economy and painful sacrifices would become requirements in the months and years that lay ahead.

Another reaction psychologically to the outbreak of the war was not a sense of inner truce and inner unanimity, but rather one of inner paranoia, a fevered and frenzied examination of one's society for elements that were considered subversive or burrowing into the unity that had been established. Wartime societies showed a strong paranoia in these hours of crisis and feared disruptive forces within. I just want to hint at what we will discuss in some of our upcoming lectures. This first instance of paranoia and anxiety about traitorous elements within was the first worrying omen or portent of the singling out of minorities in later years, who would be blamed for the defeat and for reverses on the battlefield.

In these first days and weeks and months of the war, one could see in all of the combatant countries, really absurd epidemics of spy chases, and a mania for denunciations which set in. In Germany, there was even a word for this. It was called *Spionitis*, meaning suffering from spy paranoia. There were absurd cases even of German officers being suspected of being spies and arrested by local police. There was also an attempt, less dramatically, to not only find putative spies within one's midst, but also to eliminate what were seen as disruptive cultural influences from the outside. Chauvinist enthusiasts in many countries demanded a cleansing of the national language from enemy influence. In Germany in particular, French words were to be eliminated from the language, even if that meant the need to produce clunky, German equivalents. This trend was seen in other countries as well. In Russia for instance, the German-sounding name of the imperial capital St. Petersburg, was renamed Petrograd, or Peter Town or Peter City. Britain was not immune either. The British royal family had to change its name for its originally very German name of the House of Saxe-Coburg-Gotha and now assuming instead, the much more British-sounding name of the family of Windsor. Signs on shops became targets throughout Europe, especially if they bore foreign names of enemy nationality, with a spontaneous mass mobilization against these symbols of outside influence.

We come here to a crucial theme, that of the spontaneous self-mobilization and enthusiasm for the war. It really is a truism of research and propaganda—it is self-evident in fact, but still a valuable insight to keep in mind—that propaganda, even when it is directed from above, is most effective when it builds on things that people already believe. In this case, we might speak of the August Madness as a self-propaganda of entire populations, an enormous and spontaneous wave of testimonials which ordinary people give at first without governmental urging as to the justice of their own nation's cause and their support for it. We'll come back to this key insight that the universal claim of going to war in righteous self-defense would be an effective rallying cry in the start of the war. This spontaneous outpouring of support for one's own national cause actually surprised the different governments that had entered the war. The magnitude of this was truly remarkable—just to mention one fact which never ceases to both amaze and appall me—that in the first months of the war, more than a million war poems are counted as having been published by German newspapers. More than a million war poems, not ordered by the government but spontaneously flowing from the pens of ordinary citizens, many of them of just truly astonishingly horrible quality but testifying nonetheless, to the enthusiasm and self-mobilization of a society. The governments, at first surprised by this course of events, would later learn how to harness this enthusiastic impulse with much more manipulative and scientific ways in systematic fashions. The self-mobilizing impulse would prove crucial over the next years in sustaining the morale and determination of societies suffering under the strain and stress of total war.

In the context of this self-mobilization, the churches and organized religion played an ambivalent role in this enthusiasm. One could understand the quandaries that the churches were facing. The quandary of the Catholic Church for instance was obvious as an international institution with French Catholics, and German Catholics, and Polish Catholics fighting in the different armies. How could the Catholic Church speak clearly of the necessity of peace and of neutrality? In the Protestant churches, the problem was a little different. The Protestant churches were much more nationally identified with the particular countries in which they were based. Still, how could they give their endorsement to the force of arms as representatives of a religion proclaiming peace and humanity? In this case as well, the notion of a war of defense would provide the rhetorical opportunity for the churches to share in the mobilization and the enthusiasm.

I want to talk before concluding about the record of the mobilization that we have been discussing by mentioning a key case that came as a great surprise but nonetheless, was of tremendous historical significance for the course of the war later, as well as for twentieth century history. That was the unexpected—and in many cases, surprising—failure of international socialism to react to the war in a fashion similar to what it had threatened it would. Contrary to the expectations of many political observers, and contrary in fact to its own promises about what it would do, the international socialist movement, in the European countries in particular, which had earlier pledged to shut down capitalist wars, and not to participate in this sort of conflict but instead to emphasize internationalist unity, had found itself unable to react in a unified way and all of its promises broke down with the outbreak of war. This ran completely contrary to earlier vows.

In the 1907 Stuttgart Conference, the Socialist International group, a gathering of all of the different socialist parties of the world, had resolved in a solemn way to stop this kind of a capitalist war. Capitalist war would be stopped by concerted and unified action by socialists everywhere. How this was to be done was left a little bit vague, but one suggestion, which certainly worried conservative authorities, was that this might be done through the means of a general strike, i.e. to say all workers simply laying down their tools and stopping their machines and not participating, and simply abstaining from the preparations for war. Now in practice, these sorts of earlier pronouncements simply went by the board. In the initial enthusiasm for war in August of 1914, many socialists, but not all, discovered that their patriotism and their identification with their own nations, in fact, trumped many of the earlier ideological avowals. One might think of it in this way: French socialists discovered that they were French; German socialists discovered that though they still prized their socialist ideas, they were Germans as well. The national identity in some sense had been more rooted far more deeply than many had been aware of earlier.

Not all socialists felt this way, and we want to focus on one particularly important and fateful example of a socialist who reacted differently. Surprised by the outbreak of the war, a Russian revolutionary belonging to a faction of radical socialists called the Bolsheviks—and we'll talk more about in later lectures—by the name of Vladimir Ilyich Ulyanov, but better known by his revolutionary pseudonym of Vladimir Lenin, who was living in exile in the Austro-Hungarian Empire, was simply disgusted by what he saw as the total failure of the socialists to live up to their own ideas. Ironically, in the first opening stages of the war, he was actually arrested by the authorities of Austro-Hungarian Empire as a suspected spy for the Russians. Nothing could have been further from the truth. He actually wanted to overthrow the empire. Lenin was able to leave for neutral Switzerland and there he crafted a program for revolutionary action. He saw the war as nothing less than the final crisis of capitalism and very unsentimentally preached a revolutionary message that the war should be turned into a worldwide civil war of the working classes against the capitalists. Nonetheless, at this point, in spite of Lenin's lone voice in the wilderness, Europe was mobilizing. The Great Powers mobilized and volunteering stations were crowded, jammed with young men who were sure that they would be home by Christmas and whose great fear was that they might miss out on the drama of the war itself. Twenty million men were mobilized throughout Europe and they hurdled forward into the great battles that we'll consider in our next lecture.

Lecture Six
The Failed Gambles—War Plans Break Down

Scope:

The opening stages of the war were marked on all sides by surprises, shocks, and the failure of established war plans. This lecture follows the logic of the plans of the Great Powers, especially the German Schlieffen Plan (a bold blueprint for victory on two fronts, but with disastrous political implications) and the proud French Plan XVII, which aimed to seize the initiative against Germany and win nationalist redemption for lost French territories. Next, we observe the collapse of these military plans in practice, replaced by a desperate defense of France (the Miracle of the Marne River), German atrocities in Belgium and northern France, an improvised "Race to the Sea," and an unexpected German victory in Eastern Europe at the titanic Battle of Tannenberg.

Outline

I. The Plans in Abstract and Surprises

    A. The opening stages of the war were marked by tremendous violence and surprises that left commanders baffled.

        1. Six million men were rushed into the initial collisions of the war.

        2. This Battle of the Frontiers, which lasted from August 14 to September 6, 1914, saw the failure of prepared plans. Some historians consider it the biggest battle in history.

        3. German forces were directed by Helmuth von Moltke (the younger). General Joseph Joffre commanded French forces, and the British Expeditionary Force was under Sir John French.

    B. Let us look first at the Schlieffen Plan.

        1. The plan was developed long before the war, by 1905, by General Alfred von Schlieffen (1833–1913), chief of staff 1891–1905.

2. It was a sweeping, bold plan for victory in a two-front war, which called for first destroying France and then turning on Russia. It called for the violation of Belgian and Dutch neutrality to achieve surprise in the attack on France, arcing around Paris to achieve victory in six weeks.

3. Moltke altered the plan's emphasis on a huge concentration of force on the right flank. Declining to invade Holland, he drew off troops to the Eastern Front and diverted other forces to Lorraine.

4. Debate continues today concerning the practicability of the plan, as troops outdistanced their own supplies and artillery and were expected to march 20–30 miles a day.

C. Now we turn to the French Plan XVII.

1. The French plan, endorsed by Joffre, called for an attack to regain the lost territories of Alsace-Lorraine, avenging the humiliating defeat of 1871.

2. Stressing the cult of the offensive, the plan underestimated German reserves and actually played into the Schlieffen Plan's expectations.

D. In practice, both plans broke down.

1. Launched August 14th, the French plan broke against German defenses, and the French suffered enormous losses of the best officers and men.

2. The Schlieffen Plan at first seemed to be succeeding, but then broke down in the Miracle of the Marne.

II. In Action

A. The Miracle of the Marne

1. On August 4, 1914, German troops invaded Belgium, then France, and by early September were at the Marne River, some 20 miles from Paris.

2. German advance was hampered by Belgian resistance, destruction of railroads, and fear of snipers (leading to atrocities).

3. On August 7, a younger officer named Erich Ludendorff captured the main Liège citadel, as heavy guns demolished other forts.

4. As German armies approached, the French government fled to Bordeaux.

5. Contrary to German expectations, the British Expeditionary Force mobilized quickly and was thrown into battle. After reaching Mons, British and French forces moved back in a fast retreat.

6. A gap opened up between the advancing German armies, the First Army under General von Kluck (which altered its planned direction) and the Second Army under General von Bülow.

7. French and British forces counterattacked on the Marne from September 6–10. The fabled effort included troops brought in taxicabs from Paris.

8. Following an order by Colonel Hentsch, German forces fell back to the Aisne River and dug in.

9. Though these were shallow trenches, German forces could hold off attackers and the war of the trenches began.

B. Outcomes

1. The Schlieffen Plan had failed. Germany would now face war on many fronts.

2. As a result of this failure, Minister of War General Erich von Falkenhayn replaced Moltke as Chief of German General Staff on September 14.

III. "Race to the Sea"

A. The next stage of the war, October–November 1914, was called the "race to the sea," but was actually a series of attempts to turn the flank of the enemy until the front reached the English Channel and the North Sea (Antwerp fell on October 11).

B. At the First Battle of Ypres ("Wipers" to British soldiers), October 18–November 22, British forces repelled German attacks. At the Yser River, Belgians opened sluices, flooding the battlefield.

C. Failed French winter offensives in the Champagne region followed.

IV. Atrocities

    A. The German advance through Belgium and northern France was marked by atrocities that were disastrous for German standing in international opinion.

    B. German forces panicked at the prospect of civilian resistance and suspected snipers.

    C. Confused incidents led to atrocities.

        1. Recent research shows that during their invasion of Belgium and France, German troops killed more than 6,000 civilians as suspected guerrilla fighters or in taking reprisals. This total included men, women, and children.

        2. The Belgian university city of Louvain, including its library, was burned on August 25–28, 1914, and hundreds of civilians killed.

        3. Reims Cathedral was shelled September 19, 1914.

        4. The Allies effectively argued that these incidents showed Germans to be "barbarians" and "Huns."

V. Surprise Victories in the East

    A. Ironically, as war plans in the West were overturned, unexpected victories resulted on the Eastern Front, after initial disasters.

    B. Seeking to aid their French ally, Russian armies moved against East Prussia, as well as against Austria, earlier than German planners had expected. East Prussia had been left lightly guarded, as part of a calculated risk.

        1. As the Russian armies occupied German territory, German commanders panicked and prepared for a mass retreat.

        2. Two new generals were sent to East Prussia as replacements: the elderly General Paul von Hindenburg and his chief of staff Erich Ludendorff.

        3. Together with Lieutenant Colonel Max Hoffmann, these generals scored a vast victory against the Russians at the Battle of Tannenberg, August 26–30, 1914.

    C. Hindenburg and Ludendorff were hailed as saviors and became German war heroes (later essentially war dictators).

D. This German victory could not hide the failure of the initial plans for the war. At great cost, Russia had made a vast contribution to the French war effort by drawing away troops from the Schlieffen Plan.

VI. Verdict

    A. With the failure of war plans, the war took on unfamiliar forms and patterns.

    B. Historians debate whether Germany had already lost the war in a strategic sense, facing a long war on many fronts. In economic terms, the Central Powers were seriously outmatched by the Allies in this industrial war, and the British naval blockade threatened to choke the Central Powers.

    C. Tactical victories might not alter the strategic equation.

    D. The unfamiliarity of this form of war would have devastating results in practice.

Essential Reading:

John Keegan, *The First World War*, pp. 48–137.

Supplementary Reading:

John Horne and Alan Kramer, *German Atrocities 1914: A History of Denial*.

Jack Snyder, *The Ideology of the Offensive: Military Decision Making and the Disasters of 1914*.

Questions to Consider:

1. How would the war have unfolded if the Schlieffen Plan had been more successful?

2. Why was there no negotiated peace at the end of 1914, when all military plans had failed?

Lecture Six—Transcript
The Failed Gambles—War Plans Break Down

In this lecture, we will be examining how the extensive war plans of the fighting powers broke down in practice. One of the major themes that we are weaving through our course is that of a succession of shocks of the new. In some sense, in this lecture we are covering a tremendously important shock and that was the failure of the gambles and the war plans with which the war had begun. One might say that the opening stages of the war were marked on all sides by surprises, shocks, and the collapse of established war plans. This lecture follows the logic of the plans of the Great Powers, especially the key plan, the German Schlieffen Plan, a bold blueprint for victory on two fronts, but with disastrous political implications diplomatically, because of the violation of neutrality of Belgium; as well as the proud French Plan XVII, which aimed to seize the initiative against Germany and win a redemption of the lost French territories Alsace and Lorraine, both of which had been taken from France after the Franco-Prussian war in the 1870s. Next, we will observe how these plans collapsed in practice and how they were replaced by a desperately improvised defense of France—the Miracle of the Marne River. We will examine the atrocities that accompanied the German invasion of Belgium and Northern France. We will examine the improvised Race to the Sea, and the unexpected German victory in Eastern Europe at the titanic battle of Tannenberg, all surprises.

First, let us consider the plans in abstract. The opening stages of the war were marked by tremendous violence; a tremendous clash of many mobilized armies, which produced surprises and unexpected reverses that left commanders baffled, and scrapped earlier war plans. Six million men rushed into the initial collisions of the war, trying to enact the plans that had been produced in the abstract, and this was called the Battle of the Frontiers. The Battle of the Frontiers raged from August 14–September 6, of 1914 and it represented ultimately the failure of prepared plans. Some historians consider this the biggest battle in history involving as many soldiers as it did. German forces were directed by Helmuth von Moltke, the younger. French forces were commanded by General Joseph Joffre. The British Expeditionary Force was under Sir John French. We need to consider first of all the German Schlieffen Plan as it was developed in the abstract and as it was put into action. The plan was developed long before the war itself as part of this extensive military planning precision of preparations that we have already discussed in an earlier lecture.

The man who had crafted it was the German General Chief of Staff, General Alfred von Schlieffen. General Alfred von Schlieffen was Chief of Staff from 1891–1905, and excelled precisely at careful preparation and thinking in abstract terms about the military challenge which Germany's geopolitical position represented. Simply put, Germany's geopolitical challenge was the possibility of war on two fronts simultaneously. At the center of Europe, it might find itself forced to fight against both France in the west and Russian in the east. Schlieffen's plan was a sweeping, bold conception of how to win victory in a two-front war. Essentially, speed would be of the essence. First, by very quickly destroying France, and then turning on the Russian great power, a country that would be expected to be slower to mobilize and more ponderous in its preparations for war. The Schlieffen Plan was very much a product of the militarism that we have described in an earlier lecture in that it tended to disregard the political implications of what was regarded by Schlieffen essentially as a technical solution to a military problem. It called for the violation of Belgian and Dutch neutrality, by invading through both of those countries to achieve surprise in a vast attack on France. A huge German force would come swinging through Northern France after invading Belgium and Holland, arcing around Paris in order to achieve decisive victory by a timetable of about six weeks. It was hoped that Paris itself would be surrounded, French armies and French leadership would be surrounded, and that this would represent a military masterpiece, a battle of annihilation.

The Schlieffen Plan's emphasis thus, was on a huge concentration of force on the right wing, whereby German movement, which would come plunging through Belgium and Holland and through Northern France. After von Schlieffen died, this plan was further worked on and altered as military plans were by von Moltke, his successor. Von Moltke changed certain aspects of the plan. He did not solve the political problem of violating neutrality, but lessened it by declining to invade Holland. Then he also took troops away from vast movement that was projected for the invasion of Northern France and instead, drew off some of those troops to the Eastern Front and others for the defense of the territory of Lorraine to the south. Debate continues today concerning a key question, whether the plan was even in fact possible and whether it could have been brought off in its original form or in the altered form that Moltke later devised.

Military historians point out that the German troops were having tremendous demands made of them in practice. As they marched the predetermined stretch of territory per day, they would outdistance their own slower moving supplies and artillery, and the demands included marching 20–30 miles a day and fighting through encountered resistance, which some military historians see as completely unrealistic to begin with. You will note that I had mentioned earlier that Schlieffen, the original architect of this plan, had actually died before the First World War, in 1913. Nonetheless, his plan with some alterations was the one chosen to be put into action. It is sometimes said that in a sense, a dead man had his finger on the trigger, as the Schlieffen plan was enacted.

We need to speak at the same time of a plan that would be tickling down at precisely the same time as the Schlieffen plan was put into action; the opposite plan, the French Plan XVII. The French plan endorsed by the commander Joffre, called for an all-out attack into Germany to regain the lost territories of Alsace-Lorraine, avenging the humiliating defeat of 1871, and redeeming this French honor. Stressing the "cult of the offensive," the French Plan XVII actually tended to underestimated German reserves that could be deployed in the defense of these territories, and in a very real sense, actually played into the expectations of the Schlieffen Plan. An attack of the south would ensure what the German planners hoped for: that their sweeping movement would capture even more French troops. In practice, however, as we will see shortly, both plans broke down in disaster. The French plan which was launched on August 14th, broke against German defenses in Lorraine, and suffered enormous losses of some of their very best officers and men, as they sought to put into action the cult of the offensive with the disastrous consequences. The fate of the Schlieffen Plan was proceeding a little bit more positively at first and it seemed to be succeeding, but then broke down in what afterwards was called the "Miracle of the Marne" by French patriots, a truly remarkable moment of salvation and national mobilization to expel the German invader.

On August 4th, German troops invaded Belgium. As they moved through Belgium, they encountered more resistance than they had expected and then plunged into France. By early September they had reached Marne River, some 20 miles from Paris. It is said that German advance troops could see the Eiffel Tower off in the distance. The German advance however, had been slowed with the Schlieffen plan running behind schedule at crucial moments. The German advance had been hampered by fiercer Belgian resistance than had been taken into account, as well the destruction of railroads and other strategic assets by the Belgians or the French, and also slowed by German anxieties about the fear of snipers. This was not entirely without some reason in a sense that the anxiety about snipers or guerilla warfare looked back to an earlier encounter, the Franco-Prussian war of 1870 to 1871. That war had devolved into a guerilla conflict at times in its later stages, which indeed, had seen snipers picking off German soldiers. This anxiety would not only slow the German advance making them more careful, but would also lead to atrocities that we will be discussing later in this lecture against the civilian population.

Nonetheless, there were remarkable and celebrated successes that gave a sense of optimism about the enacting of the Schlieffen Plan. On August 7th, the main citadel of Liege, a key strategic point that was supposed to hold up the German advance, was captured. It was captured by a younger officer who pulled up in his car and demanded its surrender, which he then promptly received. That younger officer was named Erich Ludendorff and he later would play a very important role in the German war effort that we will be discussing in our later lectures. Heavy German guns were brought up to demolish other forts and soon this resistance was quelled. This represented, it seemed to some, the triumph of military technology over old style fortifications, a success it seemed, for the cult of the offensive. As German armies approached Paris, the French government packed up and fled to Bordeaux. Nonetheless, Paris was to be defended and indeed the bridges of Paris were mined in preparation for blowing them up in case the German troops actually reached the capital. At the same time, another factor came into play, which had not expected to come into play quite as soon. Contrary to German expectations, the British Expeditionary Force as it was called, the BEF, mobilized quickly and was thrown into battle in Northern France. The British forces moved forward and reached Mons.

However, upon discovery that they were overextended and in peril of being simply overwhelmed by the German advance, both British and French forces moved back in a fast retreat, seeking a place to make a concerted stand. In the process of the German advance, as the Schlieffen plan continued to move through the stages of its prospective sections, it was discovered that a gap had opened up between the advancing German armies, between the First Army under General von Kluck and the Second Army under General von Bülow. This came to be a concern, and the result was that the German armies moved closer together. The German armies, in an alteration of the plan, thus did not come around Paris to encircle it, but instead began their inward turn that had been projected for the Schlieffen plan, further east. The result strategically was that the German armies had left their flanks exposed to Paris itself, not expecting that Paris would be the site of considerable resistance or military peril.

This was the opportunity, which the allies had been waiting for. French and British forces counterattacked on the Marne from September 6–10, 1914. They were aided in this by a heroic and legendary effort, which was celebrated ever afterwards as hundreds of taxicabs, 600 of them to be precise, brought troops that had been stationed in Paris, from Paris itself all the way out to the battlefield, shuttling these men back and forth to get them to the places where they needed to be. Clearly the taxicabs and their forces were not the sole decisive element here, but it certainly gave a sense of the heroism that was involved in this mobilization to expel the invader. Following an order from Colonel Hentsch, German forces fell back to the Aisne River and began to dig in. This was a crucial moment, as it was admission that the Schlieffen Plan had not ultimately succeeded, and it was also the beginning of trench warfare. Though these were shallow trenches ditches, essentially dug into the ground only several feet, they had very important implications for the conduct of war. The German forces here could establish themselves and hold off the attackers, the allied side, and the war of the trenches now meant that the shovel had become a crucial weapon in this conflict.

We need now to consider some of the outcomes that this first failure of the military plans had represented; in addition, of course, to the massive losses that they implied. The Schlieffen Plan had failed. Germany now would face the very geopolitical nightmare plan that the Schlieffen Plan had been intended to deal with—the reality of the challenge of fighting war on many fronts. As a result of this failure, on September 14, 1914, Moltke was replaced by the Minister of War, General Erich von Falkenhayn, as Chief of German General Staff. Falkenhayn would now face the challenge of improvising a solution for a war that had begun in ways that were not anticipated.

From October through November of 1914, this next stage was called the "Race to the Sea." It conjures up images of the Germans, as well as the French and the British, plunging northwards now in order to reach the British Channel to secure strategic position. However, this name "Race to the Sea" which has stuck nonetheless, is actually something of a misnomer because it wasn't so much a race to the sea, as a succession of attempts to turn the flank of the other side, until ultimately without a decision, the front simply reached the English Channel and the North Sea.

Antwerp, an important port, had fallen on October 11. As part of this race to the sea, the first battle of Ypres—which British soldiers gleefully mispronouncing the name of the place, calling it "Wipers" for the rest of the war—took place on October 18 through November 22. British forces repelled German attacks and dug in as well. At the Yser River, Belgians used natural forces in order to hold off the Germans, simply opening up sluices to the canals and flooding the battlefield, producing a nearly impenetrable barrier. Failed French winter offensives in the Champagne region followed, but ultimately were not able to break through the growing stasis of trench warfare.

We need to take a step backwards to examine a phenomenon that was playing itself out at the same time as the German invasion of Belgium and Northern France, one that would have enormous significance in terms of political terms, in terms of international public opinion and the like. This was the vexed and debated question of German atrocities in this invasion of 1914. The German advance through Belgium and Northern France as we now know, because of careful historical research, was in fact, marked by atrocities which were disastrous for German standing in international world opinion. German forces as they moved forward into unknown territory, were on occasion, panicked by the prospect of feared civilian resistance and suspected snipers. There was something else at work as well. The German military often saw tactics that we today would call "terror," as a useful way of quelling even potential civilian resistance, which its own philosophy of war saw as fundamentally illegitimate and illegal. According to German military professionals, war should be left to professionals rather than a mobilized nation at arms with civilian resistance.

Nonetheless, confusion and chaos, what was often called the "fog of war," also played a role as confused incidents could lead to atrocities. Examples of this could be as follows: German troops moving into a enemy village or a city might actually encounter friendly fire as fellow troops mistook them for enemy forces and the result could be very well be that this would then be mistaken for sniper fire. The Germans on occasion would find that shots were coming from somewhere and it was not clear from where and the cry would go up from the German troops, shouting in German, "*Man hat geschossen*," a very interesting passive construction, meaning that 'one has shot at us.' What was clear from the statement was that it was not entirely clear to the soldiers themselves who was doing the shooting, but increasingly it was suspected that civilian resistors, people not in uniform, fighting in guerilla fashion, were the ones doing the shooting. The chase could further be increased and made lethal by the presence of alcohol on the battlefield, as troops moved forward. Human nature being what it was, alcohol would be looted and the result would be the drunken troops might be even more prone to such misunderstandings or miscalculations.

Recent research which painstakingly has tried to exactly reconstruct what actually happened, has found that in these first stages of the invasion of Belgium and France, German troops in fact, killed over six thousand civilians in Belgium as well as Northern France, taking them to be suspected guerrilla fighters or in the form of reprisals against resistance. This number of civilian victims included men, women, and children. Another very famous and indeed notorious instance of these atrocities took place in the Belgian university city of Louvain, often considered to the Oxford of Belgium. In this university city of Louvain, shots broke out and German troops responded with reprisals. The famous library of Louvain, as well as much of the city, was burned from August 25–28, 1914, and hundreds of civilians were killed in the process. In other instance of damage to cultural property and cultural monuments that would later be trumpeted as an example of German barbarism, the cathedral at Reims was shelled on September 19, 1914.

It was instances like this that were deployed to tremendous propaganda effect by the Allies in the initial stages of the war as they argued that the Germans had shown themselves to be barbarians or Huns, as they often called, the Germans, the enemies of civilization as shown by their disregard for culture, for monuments, as well as for civilian life. Rumors proliferated about German barbarism and German atrocities, a really remarkable case of this are the many rumors that spread that German troops, systematically, as a way of showing German beastliness or frightfulness, had actually been cutting off the hands of Belgian children, as a way of discouraging resistance. As it turned out upon closer investigation there does not seem to be cases of this that actually recorded, but nonetheless the rumor was believed. Another rumor that circulated was that priests or other civilians had been used as clappers inside church bells as another instance of atrocities against civilians. Oddly enough, as recent historical research shows, this dialectic of true instances of atrocities being followed by the proliferation of what seemed to believable rumors about the enemy's atrocities ultimately produced a strange effect that came into play later in the 20th century. Later in the war, as disbelief grew in such rumors, the true atrocities also were considered more skeptically and to a great extent were considered later not to have taken place. In fact, as recent historical research has shown, they certainly had. In a sort of bitter irony in the Second World War, when rumors started to filter out about the Nazi's genocidal policies of the Holocaust, these stories were on occasion, disbelieved or not taken aboard precisely because they were seen as propaganda of a sort that had been denounced in the First World War in a tragic misunderstanding.

While the plans for victory in the west had collapsed for the Germans, they did encounter surprise victories in the east. Ironically, in a turn of events that had not been anticipated, victories were won on the Eastern Front after initial disasters by the German armies. Germany's eastern territories had been imperiled at the start of the war because Russian moved more quickly than had been expected in order to invade Germany to aid their French ally to draw off German forces by invading East Prussia as well as against Austria. As part of the Schlieffen Plan, eastern parts of Prussia had been left lightly guarded, in a calculated risk in order to shift as many troops as possible over to the Western Front. This calculation looked like it was about to turn into a disaster because Russian armies occupied

German territory. This was the only truly large-scale invasion of German territory during the First World War and would represent a very traumatic experience.

German military commanders in East Prussia panicked and prepared for a massive retreat. In order to stiffen the resolve of these forces, two new generals were sent to East Prussia as replacements. One of them was an elderly General by the name of Paul von Hindenburg, the descendent of many generations of East Prussian nobility, and attached to him as his chief of staff, was the young hotshot officer Erich Ludendorff, who had helped in the capture of the citadel of Liege. Together with Lieutenant Colonel Max Hoffmann, these generals crafted a vast victory against the Russians at the Battle of Tannenberg, August 26–30, 1914 even as the Schlieffen Plan was playing itself on the Western Front. Hindenburg and Ludendorff were hailed as nothing less than the saviors of East Prussia and of Germany. They had beaten back larger Russian forces and had become German war heroes. Later in the war, as we will see in the following lecture, they essentially would become the war dictators of Germany, building on the enormous popularity as they had won as a result of this victory, the Battle of Tannenberg. Nonetheless, there were some harsh truths that needed to be confronted, despite the tremendous victory of the Battle of Tannenberg, the remarkable decisive results that had been won there, and even the masses of Russian prisoners of war and of artillery that were captured as a result of this war. All these victories could not hide certain very harsh and realistic truths. German victory on the Eastern Front, welcome as it was and unplanned as it was, could not hide the failure of the initial plans for the war and the west. Russia as it turns out, at great cost to its own, had made a vast contribution to the French war effort, by drawing away troops from the Schlieffen Plan in a sacrifice that was quite deliberate.

We need to consider a verdict then of what the failure of these war plans ultimately implied. With the failure of the war plans, the war would take on increasingly unfamiliar forms and patterns. One might say that improvisation would now rule the day. In a larger sense however, historians are still debating the significance of these failed plans and in particular the Schlieffen Plan's failed gamble for achieving an answer to the geopolitical challenge of fighting a war on two fronts. Some historians actually believe that in a very real sense by the fall of 1914, Germany and its ally Austria-Hungary had already lost the First World War in a strategic sense. They would know face a long war on many fronts, and increasingly, in a total war or a battle of attrition of resources, they were outmatched. In economic terms, the Central Powers, that is to say Germany and Austria-Hungary, were seriously outmatched by the Allies, by Great Britain, France, and the Russian Empire in what would now be a drawn out industrial war.

At the same time, to make matters worse, the British naval blockade that we will be discussing in more detail later, threatened to choke the Central Powers in their embattled economic position. Clearly, even the welcome victory on the Eastern Front was a tactical victory that might not alter the overall strategic equation. Ultimately, the unfamiliarity of the forms of war that would now evolve after the failed plans would have devastating results in practice. The learning curve was one that would be counted in vast causalities. We have encountered in the course of this lecture the key question of how expectations with which the Great Powers that entered the war were ultimately frustrated and were not put into effect. The result that would follow would be the need to improvise or reinvent in a series of shocks of the new, the art of war itself. What this improvisation, this costly improvisation would look like on the Western Front in particular, we will be examining in our next lecture.

Lecture Seven
The Western Front Experience

Scope:

The Western Front was soon frozen into immobile front lines hundreds of miles long, static trench warfare, and a horrific slaughter resulting from attempts to break this deadlock. We outline the reasons for a crucial phenomenon, which contemporaries only slowly came to understand and at great price: the superiority of the defensive position in this war due to the state of military technology. Despite the ways in which the American Civil War and Russo-Japanese War (1904–05) had hinted at this development, commanders in World War I showed appalling incomprehension of the reality unfolding before them and at first blindly ordered frontal attacks against machine guns and barbed wire. To their minds, a breakthrough would at last allow sweeping offensives and glorious cavalry charges: these never came. We survey the horrific record of these initial attacks and the psychology behind them, including the 1914 Battle of Langemarck.

Outline

I. Deadlock Established

    A. It was (or should have been) clear that by the winter of 1914–1915, deadlock had descended on the Western Front, stretching some 500 miles, from the Channel to the Swiss border.

    B. The Western Front experience that unfolded, though little understood at first, left a decisive imprint on modern consciousness.

    C. Though the form of this war was unfamiliar, aspects of the American Civil War (1861–1865) and the Russo-Japanese War (1904–1905) anticipated this modern industrial conflict.

    D. Attempts to break the deadlock led to debate about where decisive victory could be won. Both among the Allies and the Central Powers, "Westerners" and "Easterners" championed very different solutions.

II. The World of the Trenches

A. The trench landscape was marked by increasingly elaborate earthworks and fortifications, but the simple product of barbed wire played an important role.

B. Between the opposing lines of trenches lay a territory called No Man's Land.

    1. It was usually about 275 yards across, but in some places the trenches lay much closer together.

    2. Smaller trenches were dug into this territory for observation, scouting, or launching attacks.

C. Trench lines represented a crucial feature of this war.

    1. The front line was dug in zigzag pattern.

    2. Wooden boards covered the bottom of the trench, and a "fire step" was used for observing and shooting.

    3. Lines were punctuated by machine gun nests, mortar batteries, and concrete pill boxes.

    4. Behind the front line were many other lines: support lines, reserve lines, and retreat lines.

    5. The complexity of these lines required maps or guides.

    6. Bunkers were built to house up to a dozen men.

    7. Further behind these lines were the heavy artillery positions.

    8. Soldiers in the front lines were exposed to the weather, as the trenches were often wet and sometimes flooded. Mud made it difficult to move across the landscape.

    9. Rats and vermin proliferated.

    10. Existence in the trenches was marked by vast boredom, punctuated by acute terror and horror.

C. Gunfire traversed the landscape.

    1. Machine guns, developed in the 1880s, had a range of more than 1,000 yards and fired 600 rounds per minute.

    2. One machine gun crew could hold off masses of enemies.

    3. New recoilless artillery was an important advance.

D. On April 22, 1915, German forces used poison gas at Ypres. The yellowish-green clouds inaugurated general gas warfare, as the Allies soon responded in kind.

E. Soldiers felt their own status was changing.

    1. Soldiers themselves became increasingly anonymous, as individual heroism seemed obsolete in industrial war.

    2. This trend was illustrated in changes in uniform and in the language of the soldiers themselves.

III. Primacy of the Defensive

A. The key fact of this new warfare was the strength of the defensive, for technical reasons.

B. This fact was discovered only slowly and understood in practice. In practice, this new reality totally contradicted the reigning military doctrine of the cult of the offensive.

C. Mass attacks often turned into massacres, as the defenders enjoyed tremendous advantages.

D. A typical attack makes this clear.

    1. A massive artillery barrage would be unleashed, intended to cut barbed wire and "soften up" enemy forces, leaving them in shock.

    2. In practice, the barrage would signal the attacker's intentions, losing the element of surprise.

    3. After the barrage, attacking troops would go "over the top" with fixed bayonets and advance through No Man's Land and into enemy trenches.

    4. As the barrage had torn up the ground, it was difficult to advance and easy to lose one's way. Friendly fire was also a danger.

    5. In practice, barrages often did not do their intended work: wire remained uncut, and defenders would emerge from deep bunkers to mow down the attackers. At the Somme, German machine gunners could be back in position in less than three minutes.

    6. Even if a breakthrough was achieved, reserves were lacking or could not move fast enough to exploit the gap.

7. By contrast, defenders could use railways to bring up troops as reinforcements, while the attackers advanced slowly on foot.

8. Historian A. J. P. Taylor remarked on the contrasts of fast arrival at the front and slow progress afterward: fundamentally, "defense was mechanized, attack was not."

E. The general's response, however, was to increase the mass of the attack, preceded by ever larger and heavier barrages.

IV. Frontal Attacks

A. For two years, generals tended to show appalling incomprehension of this new reality.

1. Many held to the persistent dream of cavalry breaking through.

2. "Offensive spirit" continued to be a mantra. The British had a special instructor who traveled around preaching the virtues of the bayonet charge.

B. As a result, frontal attacks at the start of the war took a devastating toll.

C. Let us now examine the Legend of Langemarck, the site of one such frontal attack.

1. Langemarck in Flanders, near Ypres, became the site for the creation of a German nationalist myth centered on such a failed attack in November 1914. Poorly trained volunteers had been thrown against British lines, taking some 41,000 casualties.

2. On November 11, 1914, a Germany army dispatch wrote of young units attacking enemy lines, singing the national anthem.

3. The myth, elaborated in propaganda, claimed that German students and *Wandervogel* idealists had shown a sublime spirit of self-sacrifice in this attack.

4. A soldier named Adolf Hitler claimed later that he had witnessed the attack and seen a new spirit forged there. After the war, he would create a party around the idea of war forging a race.

5. The myth in many ways does not bear close examination.
6. The encounter actually took place at Bixchote, where student volunteers made up only 18 percent of the regiments.
7. Those not taken in by the myth spoke instead of a "*Kindermord*"—the slaughter of the innocents.
8. The actual magnitude of losses was not hidden.
9. It is estimated that only a third of the German Wandervogel, or youth movement participants, returned from the war. Similarly, officers experienced especially high casualty rates (six times the ordinary rate at the Somme).
10. The notion of a shared "front community" growing out of these terrible experiences was a potent idea.

D. Allied offensives in 1915 on the Western Front merit our attention as well.

1. The Allies felt a special urgency in retaking lost ground, in particular the French, and in helping to relieve the Russians.
2. The start of the war produced extremely costly engagements, with the French army taking a million casualties in the war's first five months. More French soldiers were killed in 1915 than even in the terrible Battle of Verdun in 1916.
3. A long series of attempted attacks yielded disappointing results: the Battle of Artois on December 17–29, 1914; French attacks in February and March of 1915 in Champagne; the French attack on Saint-Mihiel in April; the Second Battle of Artois from May 4–June 18, 1915; the Third Battle of Artois from September 25–October 14.
4. In 1915, the French suffered 300,000 casualties.
5. In the British attack at Neuve-Chapelle on March 10, 1915, and in the attack at Loos in late September, breaches were created in the German lines but could not be exploited before the front again stalemated.

6. In December 1915, General Douglas Haig replaced General John French as commander in chief of the British army in France until the end of the war.

V. A key question, given this stalemate and futility, is how soldiers were able to endure.

Essential Reading:

John Keegan, *The First World War*, pp. 175–203.

Supplementary Reading:

Olivier Razac, *Barbed Wire: A Political History*.

Denis Winter, *Death's Men: Soldiers of the Great War*.

Questions to Consider:

1. What single aspect of the Western Front came as the greatest surprise to contemporaries?

2. Why were the experiences of the American Civil War and Russo-Japanese War not prominently integrated into the popular imagination of war?

Lecture Seven—Transcript
The Western Front Experience

In this lecture we'll be beginning our examination of the Western Front. In essence, in this lecture we'll be exploring what it was that followed after the failure of the plans for the start of the war in the west. The Western Front, contrary to all earlier expectations, was soon frozen into immobile front lines hundreds of miles long that saw static trench warfare rather than glorious charges and war of movement, and degenerated into a horrific slaughter resulting from attempts to break this deadlock. We'll outline the reasons for a crucial phenomenon which contemporaries only slowly came to understand—and did so at a great price—this key dynamic: the superiority of the defensive position in this war due to questions of military technology, which we'll look at more closely in today's lecture. Despite the ways in which recent wars had hinted at this development, commanders in World War I, nonetheless showed on occasion, appalling incomprehension of the reality that was unfolding before them, and at first sought through ever larger frontal attacks, to overcome this challenge. In their mental world, the tantalizing prospect of a breakthrough that would finally allow sweeping offensives and glorious cavalry charges was a great prize, but this never came. We will survey the horrific record of these initial attacks, and the reality of trench warfare and the psychology behind them, including a particular and very telling instance such as the 1914 Battle of Langemarck and all that it implied about the war.

First, we need to understand how it was that the deadlock was established. It was, or at least should have been clear that by the winter of 1914–1915, deadlock in a very real sense had descended onto the Western Front. The Western Front now stretched for some 500 miles, all the way from the Swiss border, the Alps, through France to the English Channel in parallel lines. The British and the French held lines in the west, and the German lines to the east. The Western Front experience that unfolded there, though little understood at first, has left a decisive imprint on modern consciousness. It indeed is often almost synonymous with collective memory of the World War, at least in the west. Though the form of this war with its fortifications, its trenches, its dugouts was unfamiliar, there were probably instances that should have suggested that this might be a reality that came before. These included the

American Civil War from 1861–1865, or even the more recent Russo-Japanese War of 1904–1905, both of which had already anticipated some of these traits of modern industrial war and the importance of fortifications or the defensive. Attempts to break the deadlock that had descended upon the Western Front also produced vigorous debate on all sides about where decisive victory could be won given this deadlocked situation. Curiously enough, both among the Allies, that's to say France, Britain, and Russia, and on the part of their enemies the Central Powers, the Germans and Austro-Hungarians, there emerged differed schools of thought that had the same names, "Westerners" and "Easterners." In both cases, these camps championed very different solutions for where war might be won.

The world of the trenches soon took on a reality as a world apart. A surreal, unreal existence was to be found there. The trench landscape was marked by increasingly elaborate earthworks and fortifications, and indeed those first initial trenches that we talked about from 1914, shallow dugouts, were now replaced by ever more elaborate building. In the process of this fortification, the role of technology was a fascinating one. The simple product of barbed wire, a very ordinary form of technology that had helped in the cultivation of the American West, here played an important role in fortifications. Between the barbed wire barriers, between the trenches on either side, between these opposing fortifications lay a very special and strange territory called "No-Man's Land." No-Man's Land, as the named implied, signified land that was owned by no one, belonged to neither side, and thereby, represented the focus of attacks on either side. It was an area that was pockmarked with shell holes with the remains of trench fortifications, and ultimately with dead bodies as well. Usually this territory was about some 275 yards across, but in some places the trenches of the enemy sides could lie much closer to one another, in other cases much further apart. Nonetheless, smaller trenches were continually being dug into the No-Man's land in a sort of probing action, and their purposes were for observation, for communication, for scouting, or even for preparing attacks that would be launched against the opposite side.

The trench lines themselves represented a crucial feature of this 'us versus them' geography that was omnipresent on the Western Front. The front lines on either side increasingly were dug in zigzag patterns, which had the specific aim of not allowing free fields of fire by enemy troops that might surge into the opposed trenches. Instead, they would have to more laboriously conquer those fortifications. It also meant that explosions of shells, for instance, would be deadened in their impact rather than simply hurtling down channels that the trenches might represent. The trenches themselves also were, as they were increasingly elaborated and built up, provided with wooden boards that covered bottom of trench, and this was a necessity as photographs from the period can make abundantly clear precisely because in this wet soil, in areas with little drainage, water would gather at the bottom of the trenches and they would represent an unhealthy and very wet environment. The wooden boards covering this wetness would allow at least for a little bit of comfort and security. In addition, each trench would have a special "fire step," a board that allowed soldiers to stand up higher and to observe or to shoot at the enemy from the comparative safety of their trench. The trench lines were also punctuated with machine gun nests, mortar batteries, and as the lines grew, elaborate concrete pill boxes or bunkers as well. Behind the front line—that is to say, the very furthest fortifications—were many other lines that extended to the rear. These were support lines, so that in the case of an attack or even of the enemy breaking through the trenches, it would be possible for troops who had been waiting in readiness as reinforcements to be moved up.

Reserve lines as well as retreat lines if necessary so that soldiers could surge back to a second line of defenses in order to defend these newer positions of retreat. As one could well imagine, the complexity of these trench layouts was such that maps or guides and people who would serve to direct the movement of troops were necessary in order to even allow troops to navigate through this confusing geography. Indeed, many of these trenches could look very alike. Getting lost in them was a perennial reality, as well. Behind the lines, as increased fortification took place, bunkers were built up. The bunkers were intended to house up to a dozen men who thus could be shuttled as necessary to wherever they might be required in the front lines. It was attempted to reinforce the bunkers with concrete or with other fortifications, but the reality was that a direct hit from heavy artillery would of necessity endanger even men in such fortifications.

Yet further still behind these lines, in yet more placements, were heavy artillery positions. These heavy artillery positions were used to bombard the enemy's side and to target the artillery of the other side as well in what amounted to artillery duels taking place over No-Mans Land and over the opposed trenchers. It hardly needs saying that soldiers who were stationed in these front lines had an existence that was horrific to contemplate. Soldiers in the front lines were constantly exposed to the weather. The trenches, as we've already mentioned, were often wet, and at particular times of year could be flooded. Snow was certainly a reality in the winter. In the spring and fall, mud would make it very difficult to move across the landscape or even one's own trenches. Increasingly, soldiers who were positioned or stationed in the trenches took on the aspect of nearly primitive people in their state of filth, as well as disarray. Within the trenches, in this unhealthy environment, one marked by decay and putrefaction, rats and vermin proliferated and added to the horrors of this existence. The existence in the trenches as such was, according to soldiers who survived this experience, marked by vast stretches of boredom, at times punctuated by intense moments of terror and horror, an existence that they often summed up, as not being human at all.

Further, this environment obviously was tremendously dangerous as well, because gunfire, as well artillery, traversed the landscape. A crucial role here was played by an object, a machine, in fact, that really I think is synonymous as a terribly eloquent symbol of the industrial nature of this war, and that was the machine gun. The very name of machine gun signifies the ability to industrially produce mass death as a result of automated fire. Machine guns or guns that would spew fire at a steady rate with a pull of the trigger not requiring repeated aiming or repeated firing of the mechanism, had already been developed in the 19th century, in the 1880s, and these had a range of more than a 1,000 yards and they fired 600 rounds per minute, many times more than a trained marksmen could. One machine gun crew could hold off masses of enemies, many times larger simply by deploying this mechanized technology. In fact, the machine gun had often been celebrated as the ideal weapon for colonial warfare. It was seen as a vital demonstration of the technological superiority of Europeans over non-European peoples; and naively, it had been assumed in the past this weapon would not be deployed by "civilized peoples" against other "civilized peoples."

However, as soon as it was deployed to such destructive effect in the first stages of the First World War, it became clear that many more of these machine guns would need to be used, and they were ordered.

Another technology that was crucial was the new form of artillery that was "recoilless," which means that this was artillery which would not after every firing be jolted out of its position by the recoil of the gun as the missile was launched. Rather, it would absorb the shock of the explosion of the shell as it took its trajectory and would not need to be re-sited or re-calibrated in order to fire at the positions it originally had been aimed at. This increased rates of fire and allowed, later in the war, ever more precise artillery attacks to be planned as well as put into effect.

Another disastrous new technological advance that was put to murderous effect was poison gas. On April 22, 1915, German forces first used poison gas at Ypres. These yellowish green clouds of poisoned gas inaugurated a general gas warfare, as the Allied side, which at first had been the victims of this warfare, soon would respond in kind, with new and improved chemical weapons, as well. We will be speaking more in a later lecture about the horrors and nature of gas warfare.

The soldiers trapped in this environment felt that their status as individuals and as human beings was changing. Many of them record that they were becoming increasingly anonymous, and individual heroism seemed obsolete and ridiculous almost, in the context of an industrial war in which shells and artillery and machine guns mattered much more than an individual's personal heroism, bravery, or motivation. "A farewell to chivalry," is a phrase that was sometimes used to describe this final parting of the ways with the illusions with which the war had begun. This trend of acutely felt dehumanization of soldiers themselves and the divorce from earlier ideas of heroism and chivalry were probably best illustrated by the changes in uniform that were taking place out of necessity. Earlier, resplendent uniforms and bright colors with glittering badges and plumed hats had been the order of the day. Now by contrast, uniforms in dull earth tones and camouflage colors, as well as the ubiquitous steel helmets that made almost all soldiers look alike whether they were officers or enlisted now were the order of the day. In the language of the soldiers themselves, some of this dehumanization could be felt as well by the ordinary soldiers' dislike of big words such as "heroism" or of causes and duty. Instead, the language was replaced by words depicting a simpler struggle of survival and a feeling of obligations towards one's comrades in the trenches.

A key dynamic that was at work here that we need to understand in order to fully appreciate what it was that was taking place in these first attempts to deal with trench warfare was the primacy of the defensive. The key fact of this new warfare in military historical terms was the strength of the defensive side, those who were being attacked on the battlefield for technical reasons. This phenomenon, also known as the "primacy of the defensive," meant that soldiers in trenches trying to ward off an attack would be stronger than those attacking. This was only slowly discovered and understood in practice. One reason for the slowness in embracing this phenomenon was that the new reality totally contradicted the ruling military doctrine of the "cult of the offensive" whereby the more motivated and more spirited attackers would always overrun more cowardly defenders. As a result, mass attacks often turned into massacres, as the defenders it turned out, enjoyed tremendous advantages.

Let us try to follow through what a typical attack in all of its horror would have looked like at least in brief outline to make clear this phenomenon. First, a massive artillery barrage—that is to say, a volley of artillery fire, fired by a whole bank or group of artillery or cannon—would be fired in unison, all at once, with a particular goal. A massive artillery barrage would be unleashed, planned in advance, the intent of which was to cut barbed wire of the enemy's side, destroy the defenses and, as the phrase went, to "soften up" the enemy defenders, leaving them in shock, which would allow them to be easily overrun by the attacking side. In practice, this barrage very often did not cut the wire. If the defender's trenches were deep enough the shells would not destroy all of the defenses, and the barrage would have another devastating side effect instead, i.e. the barrage would actually signal to the defenders where the attacker was planning to attack. The element of surprise was lost in the long pounding, prolonged barrages, allowing the defender time to move up reserves of reinforcements to the support or reserve trenches. After the barrage had lifted, attacking troops would be ordered to proceed "over the top," or to leap up from the firing step out of their trenches to advance with fixed bayonets and with cheers through No-

Man's Land and into the enemy trenches, which now allegedly where ripe for the taking.

However, another side effect of the previous barrage that was supposed to make the attack easier now came into play. The barrage had pounded the ground of the defending side. It had torn up much of the No-Mans Land and made it difficult to advance and even easier to lose one's way than it might have been otherwise. It scarcely needs to be added that in the process, friendly fire from one's own artillery trying to support attacking troops, could also be a danger to the attackers. In practice, thus, barrages often had not accomplished what they were supposed to do. The wire remained uncut and soldiers would be caught on the wire. Once the barrage had lifted, the defenders would then know that this was the right time to emerge from their deep bunkers, to set up their machine guns and to mow down the lines of attackers as they advanced, now entirely visible and vulnerable against the defending trenches.

At the Battle of the Somme that we will be talking more about in a later lecture, German machine gunners could be back in position after a barrage had lifted from their bunkers and into readiness to fire in less than three minutes, more than enough time to encounter the attackers with deadly fire. Even if an attack should achieve breakthrough and a hole should be punched in the lines of the trenches of the defender, nevertheless, reserves had more than likely already been moved up by the defender and the attacker would not be in a prime position to exploit this opportunity. The reserves of the attacking side would encounter the same difficulty in moving forward quickly, and thus often could not move fast enough to exploit the gap that had been created—if it had been created. By contrast, the defending side could use the railways behind its own lines, out of the range of the attacker's artillery, to bring up ever more troops as reinforcements. Again by contrast, the attackers were advancing slowly on foot through No-Man's Land.

The noted British historian A.J.P. Taylor remarked in a very compelling way, with a wonderful coinage, on the contrasts that this form of battle represented. Troops could arrive very quickly at the front, but once they were to move forward and attack their progress slowed to a very, very, slow pace. Fundamentally, according to A.J.P. Taylor, the challenge was this, "Defense was mechanized and attack was not." Soldiers, once they had reached the front up to the

No-Man's Land, would move just as slowly as soldiers had ever done in earlier ages. On both sides, the generals' response, however, to this quandary, this challenge and insoluble problem, was to increase the mass of the attack and to increase the size of the force that was deployed, preceded by ever larger and heavier barrages. Bigger was to be better.

We need to survey then the record of these frontal attacks. For two years after the start of the First World War, many generals tended to show appalling incomprehension of this new reality. Some were wrestling with the problem, but many instead held to the persistent dream of decisive breakthrough, of soldiers moving forward at a rapid pace, of cavalry finally coming into their own. Many of these generals, in fact, had been trained as cavalry officers and had a soft spot or two for this particular arm of the military. The "offensive spirit" notion, the cult of the offensive, continued to be a mantra in these renewed frontal attacks. The British, in fact, even had a special instructor who traveled among the troops preaching the virtues of the bayonet charge. Another way in which soldiers were encouraged to really get into the cult of the offensive, also on the British side, was the tradition of kicking off attacks by quite literally kicking a football across No-Man's Land in order to mark the start of a sporting attack on the enemy.

The frontal attacks at the start of the war took a devastating toll on all sides. We want to examine these attacks in particular in a little more detail. A good example is the battle of Langemarck, which grew into a legend for the Germans. Langemarck, in Flanders, near Ypres, became the site for the creation of a German nationalist myth, which centered on a disaster, a failed attack in November 1914, where poorly trained volunteers had been thrown against British trenches and in the process took some 41,000 casualties. The myth grew up once a German army dispatch was produced. On November 11, 1914, an army news bulletin was published that reported a story of young German units attacking enemy lines, while singing the German national anthem, "Germany, Germany Above All." The myth, later elaborated in German wartime propaganda, claimed that German students, and especially *Wandervogel* hiking idealists, with Schiller and Gutte and Nietzsche in their backpacks, supposedly had shown their typical sublime spirit of self-sacrifice by attacking even when the odds were hopeless. A soldier, an ordinary soldier by the name of Adolf Hitler, claimed later that he had witnessed this attack and seen a new spirit forged there. Ominously in his memoir, he wrote that this was the beginning of something new. After the war he would create a party around the ideas of war forging a renewed race. Yet in many ways, the myth of Langemarck does not bear closer examination since so much of it was crafted or mythologized. The encounter was not actually fought at Langemarck, but instead fought at a place named Bixchote, which didn't sound quite as Germanic or legendary as Langemarck, so another name was chosen, and it is estimated that only 18% of the regiments that went forward in the purportedly self-sacrificing and vain way, were actually student volunteers, though in propaganda materials, they were all turned into young student idealists.

Not everyone was taken in by the myth. Those who were more skeptical spoke instead of a *Kindermord* of Langemarck, or the "slaughter of innocents" where young men had been sent to their death for nothing. The event certainly did show the actual magnitude of losses. It is estimated that only a third of German young student *Wandervogel* hiking enthusiasts returned from the war. Similarly, on all sides, officers experienced especially high casualty rates in leading the frontal attacks. It transpired at the start of the war that the flash of an officer's sword or saber as he rallied troops towards an attack or led them, made him an excellent target for snipers on the opposing side. At the Battle of the Somme, it is estimated that officers took six times the ordinary rate of causalities as enlisted men did. Nonetheless, the notion of a shared front community growing out of these terrible experiences was a potent idea.

We want to survey in a little more detail the 1915 allied offensives on the Western Front and their failure, since the Allies, as opposed to the Germans on the Western Front, felt a special urgency in recapturing lost ground, in particular, assisting the French whose own territory and own homeland was occupied, and also in helping relieve the Russians for whom the war was not going well in 1915. We will discuss the Russian experience in 1915 in a future lecture on the Eastern Front. The start of the war produced extremely costly engagements at the start on the Western Front, with the French army taking a million casualties in first five months of the war. This was followed by more losses in 1915 when more French soldiers were killed in attacks even more disastrous than in the terrible battle of Verdun in 1916.

A long series of attempted attacks yielded disastrous results such as the Battle of Artois on December 17–29, 1914; the renewed French attacks in February and March of 1915 in Champagne; the French attack on Saint-Mihiel in April; the Second Battle of Artois from May 4 through June 18, 1915; and lastly, the Third Battle of Artois from September 25–October 14, 1915. We see in essence here, the same territories being fought over again and again. In 1915, French suffered nearly a third-of-a-million casualties. In the British attack at Neuve-Chapelle on March 10, 1915 and the attack at Loos in late September of 1915, breaches were created in the German lines, but could not be exploited and once again froze in stalemate. As a result of these disappointments in December 1915, General Douglas Haig replaced General French as Commander in Chief of the army in France and remained in this position until the end of war. With so many unfamiliar, unexpected and nonetheless continuing methods of warfare being conducted at the cost of a great many lives, a key question to consider, given this stalemate and futility and senseless sacrifice, is how were the soldiers able to endure this sort of existence? How were the soldiers able to tolerate their own lives being placed at stake, while generals and leaders sought to improvise and deal with the new realities of trench warfare and the war on the Western Front? Ultimately, this was a question that the soldiers would answer with their own day-to-day existence and survival in the trenches, a topic that we will be considering in our next lecture.

Lecture Eight
Life and Death in the Trenches

Scope:

The trenches of the Western Front have been imprinted on collective memory as a crucial site of modernity. They were vivid symbols of how this industrial war stripped soldiers of human agency and mocked any concept of heroism. This lecture provides a detailed overview of the trench landscape from the perspective of ordinary soldiers: the increasingly elaborate fortifications, the omnipresence of death, and different national styles of trench construction. Distinctive codes of behavior evolved in the trenches, such as the informal truces of the "live and let live system," the Christmas fraternizations between the trenches in 1914, and elaborate superstitions growing out of the trench experience.

Outline

I. The Trenches

   A. The trenches of World War I mark a crucial site of modernity and are imprinted on the Western collective imagination.

      1. Traces of that experience remain in our language, in expressions like "over the top," "in the trenches," or "No Man's Land."

      2. Poems and prose by T. S. Eliot, Robert Graves, Eric Maria Remarque, and others recorded the impact and shock.

      3. Important examples include Wilfred Owen's "Anthem for Doomed Youth" and Siegfried Sassoon's "They."

   B. The trenches are a symbol for the loss of human agency and radically diminished individual heroism.

   C. Detailed descriptions of the trenches themselves from the perspective of ordinary soldiers can only approximate the lived reality.

II. Life in the Trenches

   A. Life in the trenches was enveloped in what Clausewitz called the "fog of war," obscuring a panoramic view of the battlefield.

   B. Soldiers could not have endured unbroken service in the trenches, so rotation systems were created.

      1. Typically, a soldier might spend one week of each month in the front lines, one week in the reserve trenches, and the rest of the time behind the lines and in the rear areas.

      2. The daily routine began with predawn preparations to repel an attack: the ritual of "stand to."

      3. Breakfast, inspections, sentry duty, and the repair of trenches and bunkers would follow.

      4. Nightfall also brought the possibility of an attack.

      5. The trenches produced their own maladies, like trench foot and trench fever.

   C. A disturbing feature of trench warfare was the omnipresence of death.

      1. Soldiers were often in close proximity to the remains of bodies, decay, and infestations of rats.

      2. Bodies resurfaced as shells churned up the soil.

   D. National styles of trench building emerged during the war.

      1. Trenches took on distinctively different styles.

      2. German propagandists celebrated the domesticity and elaborate care that German soldiers took of their trenches.

   E. Coping in this environment was an enormous psychological task.

      1. Letters and diaries written at the time have produced rich, historical sources.

      2. Grim humor was another way in which soldiers tried to deal with horrifying scenes.

      3. Trench newspapers tried to offer a voice to soldiers.

      4. Front theaters and cinemas tried to offer diversion.

F. Paul Fussell argues compellingly that this war's ironies changed the English language forever.

III. The "Live and Let Live" System

  A. Not all sectors were equally murderous. Some quiet sectors existed.

  B. Soldiers on opposing sides entered into informal truces.

    1. These truces could include such conventions as not attacking during breakfast or not aiming at latrines or men walking about the landscape.

    2. Soldiers might be careful to make noise on patrol to avoid enemy parties.

    3. Such arrangements, when suspected, infuriated commanders.

IV. Christmas Fraternization of 1914

  A. The most dramatic instances of informal truces were the scenes of fraternization on the Western Front during the first Christmas of the war, in 1914.

  B. German soldiers put up Christmas trees and Christmas hymns were sung on both sides.

    1. Meetings and games in No Man's Land were arranged.

    2. The truce did not obtain everywhere.

  C. Generals were furious at the news and effectively shut down any recurrence.

V. Superstitions

  A. Irrational mystical gestures were also attempts to cope, and the war evolved its own folklore.

  B. Such gestures and rituals were an attempt to reassert a measure of control in a situation of helplessness.

    1. Ordinary soldiers prized amulets.

    2. Taboos were developed that persisted long after the war.

  C. More elaborate legends also took on a life of their own.

    1. At the 1914 Battle of Mons, angels or medieval archers were said to have come to the rescue of British troops.

2. In the Somme, a statue precariously hanging from a church steeple was said to portend the end of the war when it fell.

3. Unfounded rumors, including those of a "Corpse Factory" and of a "crucified Canadian" expressed deeper existential truths about the terrors of the war.

VI. Trench Community

    A. The intensity of the front experience produced in many soldiers loyalty focused on comrades and one's immediate group.

    B. Propagandists and some soldiers asserted that front soldiers had been changed by their experiences and welded into a "trench community" in which class and regional differences supposedly melted away, producing a true community, property in common, and shared sacrifice.

        1. Hatred of officers and resentment of the home front could lead to a feeling of kinship with enemies in the opposed trenches.

        2. A gap of experience could lead to alienation from civilian life on the home front.

    C. A mythology of a new man and new community forged in the trenches had important political potential.

Essential Reading:

Paul Fussell, *The Great War and Modern Memory*.

Supplementary Reading:

John Ellis, *Eye-Deep in Hell: Trench Warfare in World War I.*

Stanley Weintraub, *Silent Night: The Story of the World War I Christmas Truce*.

Questions to Consider:

1. Was dark humor or superstition more important as a coping mechanism in the trenches?

2. What factors could lead to the breakdown of a "live-and-let-live" informal truce?

Lecture Eight—Transcript
Life and Death in the Trenches

In this lecture, we'll be examining aspects of life and death in the trenches of the Western Front. The trench landscape of the Western Front has clearly been imprinted on collective memory as a crucial site of modernity. They're for many people synonymous with the First World War as a whole, though obviously the war, as we'll be discussing, is far vaster and more diverse. But nonetheless, they seem to capture an essential truth about the war; they were vivid symbols of how this industrial war stripped soldiers of human agency, and human freedom, and instead mocked any concept of heroism or individuality. In this lecture, we'll seek to provide a detailed overview of the trench landscape from the perspective of ordinary soldiers. Clearly, it wouldn't even be possible to approach the horrors as they were lived in reality, but we'll try to understand certain aspects of this surreal situation—the increasingly elaborate fortifications, the omnipresence of death, different national styles of trench construction, the distinctive codes of behavior and ethos that evolved in the trenches—including between enemies—events such as the informal truces of the live-and-let-live system, or the remarkable scenes of the Christmas fraternizations between the opposing sides in 1914, an elaborate and vast world of superstition and myth that grew out of the trench experience.

I stated a moment ago that the trenches were a crucial site of modernity and are imprinted on Western collective imagination. I think that, clearly, the trench landscape has left its impact on Western art and literature both high and low, both elite and popular. One needs to think, just for instance, of the Peanuts cartoon series and Snoopy as a fighter ace crawling his way through the trenches, something that requires no explanation to a reader of the cartoon. Or, think of the appearance of the trenches in British comedy series like Monty Python. These are less serious examples, but at the same time our language itself has retained expressions that come from this unreal world of the trenches. Expressions, which some people use in the workplace, for instance, or in the context of popular sports without understanding precisely where these terms come from. These include words like "over the top," meaning the act of attacking out of the trenches, or even speak of being "in the trenches" during the workweek as a time when one is fully engaged, or speak of "No

Man's Land," a territory not held by any side. In literature and in the arts, the traces are significant in poems and prose by writers such as Robert Graves, Erich Maria Remarque who wrote the classic *All Quiet On The Western Front*, or T.S. Eliot who wrote *The Wasteland*, which presents the trench landscape with scurrying masses as a very symbol of modernity. All of these writers have recorded the impact and shock of the world of the trenches and what it represented.

Important examples, which one certainly could read at one's leisure, of poetry that does the same thing, that captures some elemental truth about the experience of the Western Front, include bitter poems by Wilfred Owen and Siegfried Sassoon. In a poem entitled "Anthem for Doomed Youth," Wilfred Owen wrote—and essentially the title says it all—of a time of parting, a time with the lights going out on an entire generation being sacrificed, and the implicit question is: For what? Siegfried Sassoon's poem entitled more tersely "They" speaks at first with the voice of a bishop, a bishop who is describing the young men in the trenches, the young men at war, and how they will most certainly be transformed in a spiritual sense, by the sublime experience of the test of war and its moral importance. The poem bitterly closes with the observation that yes, indeed, many young men will have changed as the result of the war, as they've lost legs, arms, and have been mutilated as a result. The trenches as a whole, thus, I would argue are a crucial site for modernity indeed, because they're a vivid symbol for the loss of human agency, radically diminished individual importance, and individual heroism against a backdrop of anonymous industrial forces, the destructive power of technology, and compulsions larger than those individuals' motivations. Detailed description of the trenches themselves, obviously that we'll speak about in a moment, can only begin to approximate the full impact of the lived reality, but it's nonetheless necessary to try to form a mental picture of them.

Life in the trenches was enveloped by, what the German philosopher Carl von Clausewitz has called, the "fog of war," meaning the uncertainties, the lack of perspective, the lack of clarity on where one is and what's going around one. Life in the trenches, by definition, is a subterranean form of existence obscured a clear or a panoramic view of the battlefield as a whole. Soldiers who existed in this unreal landscape could very clearly not have endured long unbroken service in the trenches, so instead, of necessity, rotation systems were created in which soldiers would be moved into trench duty and then after they had survived—if they had survived—were moved out once again. Typically, a soldier might spend one week of each month in the front lines, and then after the intense horror of that experience, one week further back in the reserve trenches, and the remainder of the time behind the lines or in the rear areas or, if one was especially lucky, on vacation at home.

The daily routine of the trenches had its own rhythm, its own rituals that needed to be observed. The daily routine began before dawn. Before dawn preparations would be made to repel an attack, which was likely at precisely this first glimmer of light. The name given to this ritual of preparing for an attack was "stand to." This was from an archaic term of military art, to stand to arms, meaning to prepare for an imminent assault. The "stand to" represented the moment when soldiers, often groggy from the night and from lack of sleep, would be roused to stand at the fire step of the trench and to see whether an attack might be coming. If it didn't, then the day took its ordinary round. This included breakfast, inspections, sentry duty, repairing trenches and bunkers—a seemingly never-ending taking—and then later another meal. Nightfall also would bring the possibility of an attack, and thus soldiers had to be on the ready once again.

What this should make clear, by the way, is the constant presence of insomnia, a chronic lack of sleep, which became a permanent feature of the trench existence. The trenches also produced their own maladies. This included diseases that had names essentially given to them as a result of the experience of the trenches, like "trench foot" or "trench fever." Trench foot was the name given to a form of frostbite that distinctively could be acquired by standing in the water-filled and water-logged bottom of the trenches, while trench fever represented an infection carried by the vermin and the lice that were a part of the ordinary life of soldiers, as well. One might mention, as well, the phenomenon of shell shock, that's to say the psychological impact of the constant horrors and the strain of combat and existence in the trenches, which we'll be discussing in more detail in a later lecture. Very clearly, a disturbing feature of this existence was the omnipresence of death. Soldiers were often in close proximity to death, to the remains of bodies, decay, and infestations of rats, as well as the reality of having lost close friends. In No Man's Land, the bodies, whether of enemies or of one's own, might very well be lying out in the open for all to see, but still too perilous to be reached and recovered for burial. Even in cases where bodies were buried, the bombardments, the barrages of artillery, could churn up the soil where those bodies had been either buried or had been lost in the mud and thus, bodies might reappear after a period of being buried, a horror revealed for all to see. The soldiers at the same time would throw themselves into the task of building these trenches, as it was an existential matter of importance. Oddly enough, contemporaries recorded that national styles of trench building emerged. This smacks very much of 19th century generalizations about national character, but it speaks a lot, also, to the self-understanding of soldiers as they celebrated their distinctively different styles of building these important fortifications. The British were, in some cases, proud of the fact that their trenches were less elaborate and less carefully tended than those, let's say, of the Germans.

By contrast, it was argued that the British were still hoping for that breakthrough, that decisive assault that would lead them into the heart of Germany and thus, there wasn't any point in getting too bogged down in domesticity. At the same time, even British forces weren't willing to give up entirely on domesticity and thus, the names that they gave for their trenches in this complicated landscape of avenues and of front lines, included names that were familiar. A trench might be named Piccadilly or the Strand or Hyde Park, a way of evoking home even in this unreal environment. The British also were well supplied; the cans of tinned beef that the British had became especially sought after by German raiding parties as a special delicacy. And, as we'll see in later lectures, as the war turned economically against the Central Powers, German raiding parties especially enjoyed success in which they'd be able to carry off much food and supplies from the better equipped British trenches. For their part, German propagandists celebrated what they took to be the virtues embodied in German trenches. These were ones that were carefully designed with eye to domesticity, civilization, elaborately cared for and with the comforts, in so far as this was possible, of home with mirrors on the wall, wash basins and everywhere, what was taken to be a national characteristic of cleanliness and order.

Trying to cope with this environment was obviously an enormously complex and challenging psychological task. Just consider the following question: For soldiers who were able to go home on leave, would the proximity of one's family or hometown or home lands, would that make it easier to cope or more difficult to cope with the trench landscape? The very proximity of home could be a bizarre counterpoint to the horrors on a daily basis, experience in the trenches. To give but one example that was ready to mind, for British soldiers, there one was in the trenches of northern France and yet one might very well be receiving with only short delay, one's hometown newspaper from Britain, perhaps from London. From London also came special care packages from proximity; an example would be that of Fortnum and Mason or Harrods, both famous department stores that specialized in care packages for the troops fighting at the front. Apparently, fruitcakes were especially suitable in this regard. Would this proximity make one long even more to be out of the trenches? Would the disjuncture, the radical difference between the normalcy of home existence and the new normalcy of the trenches, be too much to bear psychologically? This was a process, which had no clear answer, rather, the letters and the diaries written by soldiers who survived the experience of the trenches yield rich historical sources.

Historians point out that these were often the more literate and thoughtful soldiers who were recording their experience, very many instead would have to cope in a way that was far less eloquent but nonetheless, part of strategy for survival. Survival strategies could include grim, downright dark humor, which tried to deal with horrifying scenes. There's one in particular as an example that has remained with me still that I think sums this up perfectly. In the British lines, at the salient at Ypres, British soldiers would, upon going out to the trenches or returning from the trenches, would pass one spot in the fortifications of the trench landscape. As a result of bombardment or of the movement of earth, a common reality in the trench landscape, at first they were horrified to see an arm sticking out from the trench wall, the remains of a fellow fighter, perhaps a British man, perhaps not, sticking out from the wall exposed for all to see. One way of dealing with this horrific, mind-boggling sight was simply to respond to it with humor, which soldiers did. They gave the possessor of this arm the nickname "Jack" and would shake the hand as they moved out for good luck, saying "Hello, Jack," and then upon returning would shake the hand again. Once again, a ritual of superstition, which supposedly was to insure one's good fortune and survival and yet also represented grim humor trying to deal with the accumulated horror.

There were other ways in which soldiers also were urged to find a voice for themselves and express at least aspects of their condition. These included a strange artifact of the First World War, which is marvelously expressive and fascinating to read today—trench newspapers. These included publications that ordinary men, sometimes under the tutelage of their officers, were encouraged to produce as a way of perhaps humorously summing up and coping with life in the trenches. These exist on the side of the Central Powers, as well as the Allies. As did also front theaters, so-called front theaters or even front cinemas, where movies were shown, which tried to offer some diversion from the reality of warfare. These could obviously be primitive affairs; on occasion, one special challenge was producing plays or romantic comedies without the presence of women actors, but the soldiers improvised in this regard, as well. One German reviewer of military front theater even argued that it was a virtue to have these primitive conditions because this most closely resembled the conditions of Shakespeare's own time before technology and other aspect of modern stage craft had diluted an original and vital art form. Ultimately, the soldier's language as well, as we've mentioned before, changed and the literary historian Paul Fussell makes a compelling argument that ironies, the sense of helplessness within the war, changed the English language forever, so that soldiers no longer could be uttering—as he argues, we too cannot—could no longer utter words like duty, or honor, or glory without an ironic tinge.

Another element of coping—which was most definitely not allowed, most definitely a matter of improvisation, and of unofficial understanding—was the so-called live-and-let-live system. The live-and-let-live system was an informal truce that might be worked out, often with great difficulty and ambiguity, between enemy sides in trenches. Very clearly we've been talking about the horrific slaughter of frontal attacks and the dreadful record of the first years of the war, but it needs to be kept in mind that not all sectors, not all areas of the front, not all military theaters, were equally murderous. Some, in fact, were quieter sectors and these were much sought after as one might pass there in an existence which, while not without threat, was nonetheless, not quite as deadly as that of the more fought over sectors of the front line.

It was precisely in such quieter areas that in the name of simply living and letting live, informal truces evolved between enemies on opposing sides. These could range from the really quite ordinary to the tremendously elaborate and well thought out. Live-and-let-live systems could include conventions that were worked out spontaneously of not attacking at certain times, not attacking, let's say, during breakfast because everyone, after all, needed this first meal of the day; a convention, perhaps, of not attacking during religious holidays. A convention, perhaps, in quieter sectors where the was no need for a constant antagonism of even resisting the temptation of aiming at latrines or at isolated men walking about on the other side, so that snipers, in the name of keeping the peace, would refrain from shooting at such easy targets. The same could be true in No-Man's Land. Soldiers might be careful to make a lot of noise as they were on patrol in No-Man's Land at night, in order to give plenty of warning to an enemy scouting party that they were close by to avoid an unnecessary and ultimately futile mutual slaughter. At the same time, such arrangements, which could include pretending not to see one another in No-Man's Land as one repaired fortifications or repaired breaks in the barbed wire, very clearly would infuriate commanders if they learned of them. These were forbidden again and again.

The most crucial case of this sort of informal truce, and the most famous, the most riveting in human terms, was the Christmas Fraternization of 1914, the first Christmas of the First World War. The most dramatic instances of informal truces took place on the Western Front. It all started with a simple gesture. Mostly from the German lines, apparently soldiers put up Christmas trees. And, especially from the British lines, soldiers were shocked to see Christmas trees appearing with lights twinkling off in the distance and then starting to hear the sound of Christmas hymns being sung by the German side. After at first suspecting an attack or some subterfuge, this might be joined by a British response of singing or some other greeting or welcome. Soon meetings and games in No-Man's Land were arranged, food was traded, photographs were taken, signatures exchanged as mementos of this remarkable experience, and at least in this Christmas season, at least for this short space, a truce had descended and goodwill by contrast was visible. The truce, however, even during this Christmas of 1914, it needs to be noted, did not obtain everywhere. It turns out that the truces were far likelier to break out between the British and Germans than they were between the so-called hereditary enemies, the French and the Germans. It was also the case that some kinds of German troops, especially highly motivated and disciplined Prussian troops, were far less likely to engage in an informal truce. Nonetheless, generals on both sides were furious at the news of the Christmas truce; they tried to censor news of its existence and did effectively shut down any recurrence on a similar scale of such a phenomenon. It worried them as to what it might portend about the morale and the conviction of their own troops.

Finally, a fascinating area to discuss is the superstitions, the entire world of myth and of ritual, of irrational mystical gestures that grew up in this bizarre trench landscape. These irrational gestures were in a very touching way, we can understand, attempts to cope with the situation of helplessness. The war evolved its own folklore as an attempt to make sense of an otherwise mad world. This ritual clearly was an attempt, psychologically, to reassert some measure of control in a situation in which soldiers were without it. Ordinary soldiers might prize amulets—special lucky charms that were to them a protecting force. Some soldiers believed that through a kind of self-hypnosis they could make themselves invulnerable to bullets. Indeed, myths grew up about things that you should avoid doing so as not to be wounded or killed in the war, taboos, some of which persisted long after the war itself. It used to be a long-standing superstition— this has probably vanished now—that one should never light three cigarettes in a row with one match even if friends were sharing a smoke. The reason for that had everything to do with the reality of the trenches. From the opposite side, if a sniper was watching, the sniper would, with the first cigarette, see the match being lit; with the second being lit from the same match would take aim; and with the third would fire killing the third in the series, a ritual which had its grounding in the trench world.

More elaborate legends also took on a life of their own. In 1914, at Battle of Mons when British forces had retreated hastily before the German onslaught, a legend grew up that angels or medieval archers had stepped out of the clouds, a shining presence, and had come to the rescue of British troops against the pursuing Germans. The reason, as it turns out, why this myth grew up, it came from a short story that had fantasized about medieval archers of the British wars on The Continent coming to the aid of British soldiers in the Great War. The writer of this short story afterwards tried to sort of do a "time out" and to convince people that no, no this never actually happened, it was just a short story of his invention, but he was shouted down; it was unpatriotic, it seemed, to call it into question. At the Somme, a statue at a damaged church of the Virgin Mary took on a very special superstitious significance. This statue of the Virgin Mary held up a child—probably the Christ child—at the top of a church steeple, but it had been damaged in the course of the conflict itself and the statue was essentially poised to topple over. It was at an angle parallel to the ground. This was a bizarre sight for many soldiers on their way to the front. The legend grew up that when that statue finally fell, the war would end. This superstition unfortunately was not one that came to pass, the statue did fall and the war continued, nonetheless.

There were also other rumors that were marvelously expressive, but don't appear to have any basis in a concrete reality. One of those rumors was that of the so-called German Corpse Factory. The myth suggested that the Germans were running so low on supplies, including fats, that they were rendering human bodies in factories that were intended to recycle this human material. Though this myth didn't have truth to it—sometimes it was attributed to the British as well, that they had a similar installation—it certainly expressed some deeper intuition about how humans were raw materials for this war. Another rumor, which apparently was without basis in reality, was one that appeared again and again, was that of the "crucified Canadian." The Germans had allegedly crucified, in plain view, a Canadian prisoner of war above their trenches so that the opposed British side could view his torment in full detail. Very clearly, once again, even a myth without a basis in reality apparently expressed certain deeper existential truths about the terrors of the war and the way in which all soldiers were being crucified by this experience. The religious imagery that's behind much of this superstition is obvious as well.

One of the most powerful myths that grew up as a consequence of this experience was that of the trench community. The intensity of the experience of soldiers at the front did in fact produce, in many soldiers, a loyalty that focused not on the big words that were often scorned—concepts like loyalty and duty—but instead, a more intense personal obligation felt towards comrades and one's immediate group, one's fellow soldiers. This has been observed by psychologists, as well, as a very key element of the psychology of warfare. But the mythologizing of this notion of a trench community went beyond much of this. Propagandists on all sides, and some soldiers themselves, asserted that front soldiers who had existed in the trenches, who had fought in the trenches, had actually been changed in a moral or spiritual way by their experiences. The argument ran that they had been welded into a true trench community that something wonderful had happened out in the trenches. That what earlier had been fragmented, groupings of people from different parts of their nation-state or their empire, was now somehow coalescing into one.

With the melting away, supposedly, of class differences, differences of religion or confession, differences of region, producing a perfected national community, true community, which shared property in common, shared peril and shared sacrifice, this notion of a trench community was not without a potentially subversive edge, because it accented the cohesion of ordinary soldiers. It was argued that distinctions and hierarchies had been broken down in the common peril of the trenches. Hatred of officers—in particular, those men behind the lines who were directing this senseless slaughter—could grow up and be a cement for the trench community as it was mythologized. Resentment of the home front could also become a factor; people at home, it was argued, didn't understand what it was like. All of this could lead, finally, to a strange and unintended psychological consequence of feeling sometimes of kinship with enemies on the other side in the opposed trenches. It was sometimes argued, indeed, that enemy soldiers from the trenches on either side, as a result of this searing experience, had more in common with one another than they did with their officers, generals, or the home front. A gap of experience could lead to alienation from civilian life at home, as well as authority. A mythology of a new man and new community forged in the trenches would have important political potential. Let me leave you with one last myth that I think was marvelously expressive about this notion of a trench community. The myth grew up that in No-Man's Land, between the trenches, there existed another army, an army that was independent, an entire regiment, an entire grouping of deserters from both sides who refused to fight in the war, but instead survived in hidden lines, hidden bunkers in No-Man's Land. This myth, this dream of soldiers becoming once again in control of their destinies in however a limited way, speaks volumes of the helplessness of the reality of the world of the trenches.

Lecture Nine
The Great Battles of Attrition

Scope:

Once the new and distinctive dynamics of this industrial war had slowly been recognized, there followed in 1916–1917 a series of huge battles of attrition involving some 5 million men on a hitherto unprecedented scale on the Western Front, intended to grind down the enemy side but ultimately yielding little result beyond mass death and suffering. We examine the months-long battles of Verdun and Somme in 1916 and, in 1917, the French Champagne Offensive and the Third Battle of Ypres, also called Passchendaele. The lecture examines the guiding ideas behind the launching of these failed offensives and how the battles could take on a life of their own, escaping the initial premises of their planners, increasingly invested with dogged national pride and irrational psychological and symbolic importance.

Outline

I. Reasons and Commonalities

    A. Both the Allies and Germany planned decisive battles on the Western Front. These turned into disasters of attrition.

        1. "Attrition" means a grinding down or draining of the enemy's forces, rather than a decisive victory.

        2. These mass battles took on lives of their own, escaping rational control.

        3. They became symbols of national pride and assumed vast psychological significance.

    B. The battles revealed again the strength of the defensive, the generals' inability to understand how to employ new technology to break the stalemate, the growing callousness toward the expenditure of lives, and the unexpected endurance of ordinary soldiers.

II. Verdun

A. The titanic battle between the Germans and French at Verdun in 1916 illustrated the futility and destructive power of this new war (a lesson repeated at the Somme soon afterward).

   1. General Falkenhayn saw Britain as the decisive enemy, which could be beaten by knocking out its main ally, France.

   2. Falkenhayn's plans aimed to "bleed white" the French army, exhausting its reserves by drawing it into a "blood mill." The operation was named "*Gericht*" (Judgment).

   3. Historic Verdun, surrounded by 19 forts (Fort Douaumont dominating) was targeted because of its symbolic significance for the French. The location formed a salient jutting out into German-held territory (a bulge in the front line) and thus was more exposed and vulnerable to attack on three sides. As the point was to draw in French defenders, the salient did not even need to be taken, but this was not understood or forgotten by German commanders.

   4. On the first day, February 21, 1916, German guns fired a million shells: 20 tons of shells per acre.

   5. On February 25, German forces took Fort Douaumont.

B. As Falkenhayn had anticipated, the French could not sacrifice Verdun.

   1. General Philippe Pétain was brought in to lead the French defense. Unusual in having a defensive strategy, he was ideally suited for this task.

   2. Pétain set up a rotation system that moved troops through the battle. Three-quarters of the French army rotated through this meat grinder.

   3. Supply was ensured through the "Sacred Road," where 3,000 trucks rode out and returned daily under fire, one every 14 seconds. Pétain vowed: "They shall not pass."

   4. The battle fragmented into smaller encounters, like the one in March when Charles de Gaulle was captured.

   5. In May, Georges Robert Nivelle replaced Pétain in charge of Verdun.

6. The battle's highpoint was over after June 1916.

7. The Somme offensive, opening in July, also drew off resources from Verdun.

8. The battle drew to a close in November 1916, with French recapture of the forts from October 24 to December 18, 1916.

C. What were the outcomes of this battle?

1. In 10 months of inconclusive combat, 700,000 French and German casualties (nearly even) were sacrificed for a few miles. About 300,000 men were killed (one death every minute).

2. Arguably, this offensive was the only one of the war to take a marginally smaller toll than the defensive.

3. The toll for France was enormous, amounting to about 10 percent of all their war dead. (Throughout the war, one out of every two Frenchmen between the ages of 20 and 30 was killed.)

4. The French army's offensive capacities were shattered.

5. The experience led to changes in military leadership positions.

6. On August 29, 1916, General Hindenburg replaced Falkenhayn as German commander in chief, with Ludendorff as his quartermaster-general.

7. In December 1916, General Nivelle replaced Joffre as commander in chief of the French army. Pétain's reputation soared, and he was made Marshal of France.

D. The aftermath of the battle was remarkable.

1. An estimated 12 million unexploded shells still lie in the Verdun area. They are still being found, and hundreds of defussers have died over the decades.

2. One of the French defenders of Verdun, André Maginot, later became interwar Minister of War. The Maginot Line, which crumbled in World War II, was named after him.

3. Verdun became hallowed ground, with shrines like the famous "Bayonet Trench."

III. Somme

    A. The great offensive of the Somme had been long planned as a joint Allied operation.

        1. The defense of Verdun drew off French forces, leaving the British to take the lead.

        2. The territory chosen was unsuitable, as Germans held strategic heights.

    B. The first day opened with disaster.

        1. After an intense bombardment of five days, intended to cut the barbed wire, British troops were sent out on July 1, 1916, against the German lines.

        2. Expecting breakthrough and advance, soldiers carried about 70 pounds of equipment apiece, slowing their progress.

        3. On the first day, there were 60,000 British casualties, of which 20,000 were deaths. This loss was the greatest in one day of any army.

    C. Four months of battle ensued.

        1. Further assaults also failed.

        2. British tanks were used on September 15, 1916, but in insufficient numbers.

        3. Overall, by November, some seven miles were won at the cost of 400,000 British casualties. More than one million casualties were counted for the British, French, and Germans.

        4. Haig's reputation was battered by this "Great Foul-Up."

IV. Champagne

    A. In the spring of 1917, General Nivelle planned a great French-led offensive, combining force and mass of attack.

    B. German countermeasures complicated the offensive.

        1. General Ludendorff strengthened trench lines and withdrew to a systematically prepared line of defenses called the Siegfried Line (called the Hindenburg Line by the Allies) in February and March of 1917.

        2. The Germans subjected evacuated areas to scorched-earth policies and deported civilians.

C. The offensive began with the Battle of Arras on April 9, 1917.

    1. Vimy Ridge was taken by Canadian troops.

    2. The French attack in the Champagne region was a disaster worsened by extravagant expectations.

    3. In late April, mutinies broke out among French troops, protesting their meaningless sacrifice.

    4. General Nivelle was replaced as commander in chief by Pétain on May 15, 1917.

    5. Pétain managed to restore order, but the French army's offensive capacity was spent.

V. The Third Battle of Ypres—Passchendaele

A. In late July 1917, General Haig launched another British offensive in Flanders, the Third Battle of Ypres.

B. Hopes were heightened by the mining and explosion of Messines Ridge on June 7, 1917.

    1. Maps deceptively showed promising positions but proved otherwise.

    2. Haig had high hopes of breaking through to open Belgian territory and reaching the port of Ostend.

    3. The attack began on July 31, 1917.

    4. Rains turned the ground into seas of mud. Tanks sank in the mire.

    5. Last attacks on November 6, 1917, reached the village of Passchendaele, the British troops having gained five miles.

    6. Some staff officers later repented this venture, which cost 325,000 casualties.

VI. Outcomes

A. These battles became synonymous with the senseless mass death of the Great War.

B. The search for other ways of breaking the deadlock continued, whether through technology, opening other fronts, gaining other allies, or subverting the enemy in other ways.

Essential Reading:

John Keegan, *The First World War*, pp. 274–299.

Supplementary Reading:

John Keegan, *The Face of Battle*, pp. 204–284.

Ian Ousby, *The Road to Verdun: World War I's Most Momentous Battle and the Folly of Nationalism.*

Questions to Consider:

1. Why did other battles of attrition follow the experience of Verdun?

2. What were the lessons of Verdun, the Somme, and Passchendaele?

Lecture Nine—Transcript
The Great Battles of Attrition

In this lecture we'll be examining the great battles that dominated the Western Front from 1916–1917. Already different in their character from the attacks that had marked the opening stages of the war in the west; in part, this was as result of an evolution. Once the new and distinctive dynamics of this industrial war had slowly been recognized—including the inherent strength of the defensive side we've discussed in an early lecture due to the state of the technology of the time—there followed in 1916–1917, a series of huge battles of attrition that involved masses of men, some five million men, on a hitherto unprecedented scale on the Western Front. These battles were intended to grind down the enemy side and to tip the balance towards victory, but ultimately they, too, yielded little result beyond mass death and suffering. We'll examine in turn the months-long titanic battles of Verdun and Somme in 1916, and in 1917 the French Champagne Offensive and the British experience at the Third Battle of Ypres, also called Passchendaele. The lecture today will examine the guiding ideas behind the launching of these failed offensives, and how the battles themselves could eventually take on a life of their own, actually escaping the initial premises of their planners. The battles increasingly came to be invested with dogged irrational national pride and took on enormous symbolic significance, which made it possible to disengage at time when it might have been rational to do so.

We want to examine the commonalities, the shared features that marked the realities of these battles, both the Allies in the west—the French and the British—and the Germans had planned decisive battles on the Western Front. These turned into disasters of attrition, which is a term that we need to actually define. Attrition means a slow grinding down or draining of the enemy's forces, a wearing down of the enemy's side rather than the scoring of a decisive victory. Attrition was to be a phenomenon seen throughout total war as an experience. These mass battles that we'll be discussing in this lecture really, in a sense, had a logic of their own that soon slipped away from the rational control of the leaders, revealing their lack of control of the events on the battlefield, due both to the lack of effective communications as well as their wrestling with the problem of how a battle of this nature should be fought. In addition, back on the home front these battles became vivid symbols of national pride and assumed such significance that it was impossible to step away from them. These battles revealed again, or underlined a phenomenon that we've spoken about in an earlier lecture, the strength of the defensive side. They also revealed the generals' inability to understand how to employ new technology to break the stalemate. They eventually would be able to so late in the war, but at this stage the learning curve was still on its way up. It also revealed the growing callousness of many commanders towards the expenditure of lives. And, it also revealed another phenomenon, which was psychological—also unexpected—the ability of ordinary soldiers to somehow keep on fighting and to endure these dreadful conditions.

First let's turn to the Battle of Verdun. This titanic battle between the Germans and French in 1916, very vividly illustrated the futility and destructive power of this new war. It was a lesson that unfortunately also was slow to be learned; this lesson was repeated at the Somme soon afterwards. Verdun has taken on enormous significance in the memory of Germans and French, and the events themselves were of a scale that was truly striking. The German General Falkenhayn, who had taken over from General von Moltke at that start of war, had already started to rethink the approach towards the fighting of the war as a result of the disastrous first encounters of the first years. Falkenhayn thought in strategic terms that Britain was truly the decisive enemy, if France, the main ally of Britain, could be knocked out of the war, then Britain in a sense would have no choice but to make peace as well, and Germany would have won a decisive victory.

His key challenge then was the question of how to knock France out of the war. The answer that he arrived at was by grinding the French manpower reserves. Falkenhayn's plans aimed, as he put, to "bleed the French army white." If they could be lured into a battle, the French would have to commit their reserves again and again, and eventually, by being drawn into a blood mill, would find themselves at some point without reinforcements and unable to continue the fight. To mark the decisive nature of this battle that he hoped for, Falkenhayn named this operation, in German, *Gericht*, the word means "judgment."

Operation Judgment focused on a historic fortress city in the disputed lands on the German and French border. This was the historic fortress city of Verdun, a fortress complex that had first been established in the days of Louis XIV, the Sun King, but now had been built up into an enormous fortification to forestall a renewed German invasion such as been seen in the Franco-Prussian war of the 1870s. And Verdun was considered to be almost untakeable, almost invulnerable to enemy attack. Verdun itself was surrounded by 19 forts of the most modern fortification, and dominating these other forts was a fort named Fort Douaumont. It was precisely because of both the military as well as symbolic significance of this supposedly impregnable fortress complex that Falkenhayn chose to target Verdun above all. The entire point of this operation was to create a "salient." The definition of a salient is a territory in the front line that juts out into enemy territory; that's to say, essentially a peninsula of military territory that is confronted on three sides by enemy forces.

The whole point thus, in other words, was to draw the French into a battle for the salient of Verdun, a salient that the Germans didn't even need to actually take; they could surround it almost entirely and then expect French defenders to keep pouring in, in order to make the sure that the salient was not taken. But Falkenhayn's observation—that the point of this battle was not to capture Verdun but instead to stage a massive battle on this spot—was on occasion either not understood or forgotten by German commanders, and in some sense changed the character of the battle that he had at first planned.

On the first day of the Battle of Verdun on February 21, 1916, a massive, huge bombardment by German cannon began. German guns fired a million shells that first day, dropping 20 tons of shells per acre. The bombardments were enormous; it's estimated, at least by one estimate, some 60 million shells would fall on Verdun in the course of the entire battle; it was said that men could go mad under the impact of the long, long bombardments.

Then German forces moved forward. On February 25, German troops actually captured Fort Douaumont in a striking and sudden raid. As Falkenhayn had planned and anticipated, the French felt that they could not sacrifice Verdun. Instead, they prepared for a dogged and determined national defense of the symbolically significant spot. The man who was brought in to command the French forces was

General Philippe Pétain. Pétain was brought in to lead the defense effort, and he was in some sense the ideal man for this task, because where so many other French military leaders had become devoted disciples to the cult of the offensive, Pétain was almost alone in emphasizing the importance of the defensive side; and having thought through some of the aspects of a defense that truly could be effective, Pétain understood that this experience of the defense of Verdun would have to be handled in a way that maximally spared his soldiers.

Pétain, for this purpose, set up a rotation system which moved troops through the battle, cycling them in and out so that he would not have the same exhausted troops trying to hold the territory for weeks on end. It was estimated that soldiers would spend a maximum in what came to be called the "Hell of Verdun," and if they were able to look forward to the end of this time, they knew that at the end of that period they would be cycled out and relief would finally come. It's estimated that some three quarters of the entire French army was rotated through this meat grinder of a battle, ensuring that many French soldiers had shared in the experience of the Battle of Verdun.

From Paris, troops were moved out through the eastern railway station, the Gare de l'Est, which still, by the way, to this very day bears, under the name of the train station, the destination name of Verdun, marking this symbolically significant battle, still held in memory. They would then be moved up to Verdun and enter into its hellish experience. It was said after that soldiers who moved away from the battle after having been relieved had a particular stare, a particular abstraction, a particular lost look in their eyes that allowed veterans of Verdun ever afterwards to identify one another even without words.

The supply of Verdun, this salient, this peninsula of French territory, was ensured through a heroic effort that took place along the "Sacred Road," as it was called, a thin road where 3,000 trucks rode in and rode out daily under constant fire, one every 14 seconds, in order to provide the military and food supplies necessary for the troops. Pétain, with his own firmness of character, rallied the French defenders, vowing in a famous phrase, "They shall not pass."

The battle itself, with its enormous expenditure and its horrific conditions, soon fragmented into smaller encounters. It was in one of these in March that the young officer by the name of Charles de

Gaulle, who later in World War II had become a leader of the French Resistance, was captured by the Germans in this encounter. The battle seemed to lose coherence, no longer were there clear trench lines, but instead soldiers fought from foxholes or moved forward by jumping from bomb crater to bomb crater.

In May of the year, Georges Robert Nivelle replaced Pétain in charge of Verdun and led the effort from there on in. The battle's high point was over after June of 1916, in part because the Somme offensive, which the British were spearheading at this point opening in July, drew off German resources from Verdun and gave some relief. The battle itself, after months duration, finally drew to a close in November 1916, as the French very proudly recaptured the forts that they had lost to the Germans from October to December of 1916.

We might then ask, what was the outcome of this experience? In over ten months of inconclusive combat the casualties had been enormous. It's estimated—and the numbers are still debated and still not entirely clear to this very day, but we get at least a sense of magnitude—the casualties were 700,000 French and German casualties, nearly even. It's estimated that the French—and this is matter of debate as well—the French causalities were slightly higher than those of the German side. Of these number of casualties, that's to say men wounded as well as dead, it's estimated that about 300,000, that's to say a third-of-a-million nearly, were killed, which amounts statistically to about one death every minute for every minute of the Battle of Verdun.

The Battle of Verdun, which had been so carefully crafted and thought through at its inception, at least by Falkenhayn, the German general, was arguably the only offensive of the war where the offensive side marginally took a smaller loss than the defensive side. But in a larger sense, Falkenhayn's gamble had failed. He had succeeded in bleeding the French army white, and the French army indeed was exhausted as a result of this experience, but to a great extent so too was the German army in spite of its greater potential manpower reserves.

The toll for France was enormous, and thus it's obvious why this battle remains a touchstone of French national identity and collective memory to this very day. About 10% of all of the French—their war dead—were from the Battle of Verdun, and throughout the war, as a whole, just summing up the entire losses that this implied, one of every two Frenchmen at the age between 20 and 30 years was killed—the loss of a generation. The French army's offensive capacities were shattered as result as the experience of the defense of Verdun. This experience, the failures of the battle and the defense of Verdun, initially led to changes in military leadership positions in France; and the experience of Verdun also led to changes in military positions and leadership in Germany, as well. On August 29, 1916 in Germany, General Hindenburg, the hero of the fighting on the Eastern Front that we'll talking about in a coming lecture, replaced Falkenhayn as German commander in chief, bringing with him his talented quartermaster-general, Eric Ludendorff. We'll be speaking much more about these men who became war dictators of Germany in the years that followed.

In France, in December of 1916, General Nivelle, a new and confident officer replaced Joffre as commander in chief of the army. In all of this experience, Pétain's reputation had soared, he came to be identified with a more humane and a more caring approach to the French soldiers who had made such sacrifices in the defense of Verdun, and he was elevated to the honored position of Marshal of France. There is a bit irony yet in store in Pétain's own biography, because this man who came to be a great national hero of the French in the war against the Germans, later during World War II would head a collaborationist regime that cooperated with the Nazis, betraying the earlier national honors that he had been accorded.

I'd like to say a word about the aftermath of the battle of Verdun, because even those who visit Verdun today are still struck by the amazing traces that remain in the landscape itself, testifying to the elemental force of this battle of material. It's very difficult to describe in words, it's almost something one has to actually see to take aboard; the landscape, so many years afterwards, of the battlefield, remains to this very day still cratered and pock marked in really vivid and unnatural ways by the impact of shell explosions. Indeed, very many shells still lie, not diffused, still active, many of them in this poisoned landscape. An estimated 12 million of such unexploded shells still lay in the Verdun area; they are still being found, and hundreds of defussers have died over the decades afterwards.

Parts of Verdun where villages once stood were never rebuilt again, and trenches can still be seen in the area as well, along with tremendous and extensive graves and monuments to the battle. The Battle of Verdun also had other implications that carried on into the future. One of the French defenders of Verdun, André Maginot, later became France's Inter-War Minister of War between the World Wars. Named after him was an extensive fortification line, called the Maginot Line, which was intended to make much more determined and rational the sort of defense that Maginot himself had lived through during Verdun. But the hopes that were vested in this fortification line were in vain, as Hitler's armies would eventually simply overcome this obstacle. Verdun remains to this very day a hallowed ground, with visitors and school groups traveling to this area; and indeed, shrines that sum up its national and its human significance, shrines like the famous "Bayonet Trench" and the legends that surround it that we'll be talking about towards the end of our course when we address how the war itself was memorialized.

In quick succession, indeed before the Battle of Verdun had ended, the Battle of the Somme began. The great offensive of the Somme had been long planned as a joint Allied operation, with the French and the British cooperating together in an assault on the German lines. The defense of Verdun ended up drawing off French forces that had been intended to be committed for the Battle of the Verdun [sic Somme], and this left the British to take the lead. This was a case where earlier planning would play a fateful role now that the reality had changed. The territory that been chosen for the attack on the Somme was, in fact, chosen for a specific reason, it was an area where the British and the French could cooperate together. That was its attraction; that was the reason it had been chosen. In another sense, however, now that the French were increasingly not able to participate in the measure that earlier had been promised, this territory revealed itself as being in other ways quite unsuitable, because the Germans held the strategic heights, and thus the attack, in that sense, not as efficient as it had been hoped for before. The British forces now took the lead under the command of Sir Douglas Haig.

The first day opened with disaster. After an intense bombardment, lasting five days, of the German lines, which had been intended to cut the barbed wire and destroy the machine gun in-placements and the bunkers of German defenders, British troops were sent forward on July 1, 1916 against the German lines. The expectation of Haig and other commanders was that a breakthrough and a fast advance would follow once the lines had been broken. British soldiers often carried about 70 pounds of equipment, slowing their progress as they moved forward against the German lines. The chalky ground of this area had allowed the Germans in fact to dig far deeper fortifications and bunkers than might otherwise have been the case, and machine gunners who had simply been lying in relative safety in these deep bunkers now emerged to mow down the British as they moved forward in long lines.

On that first day of the Battle of the Somme there were 60,000 British casualties, 20,000 of them dead immediately. This was the greatest loss in one day of any army during the First World War. Four months of such battle continued. Further assaults also failed, including a quixotic Calvary charge, which soon broke down in the cratered ground and before the German guns. British tanks were put into use as well on September 15th, 1916, but they weren't there in insufficient numbers to really create a decisive result. Overall, by November of 1916, the British forces had won about seven miles at the cost of 400,000 British casualties. Throughout the battle as a whole, over a million casualties were counted for the British, French, and the Germans. Sir Douglas Haig's reputation was battered by this battle; he's remained an intensely controversial figure since, and soldiers refer to the Somme in particular as "Haig's Great Foul-Up." More bitter soldiers tended to use a stronger word also starting with "F" for the great foul-up.

The next battle that we turn our attention to came in the spring of 1917, the offensive on the Champagne. General Nivelle had planned a great French-led offensive combining force and mass of attack. He promised great and immediate results that were to follow. However, German countermeasures complicated the planned offensive; in some sense German tactical thinking in this regard got in ahead of the allied military planning. General Ludendorff strengthened trench lines and started a systematic and quiet withdrawal of German forces, about the average 25 miles back from the line that they had been occupying at this point, back to a systematically prepared and far better fortified line of defenses about 25 miles back called the Siegfried Line by the Germans after a German mythic hero of the Sagas. The Allies called this the Hindenburg Line in February and

March of 1917. This was not a retreat out of weakness; it was rather a strategic withdrawal to far better fortified and held positions. In the process, the Germans subjected the areas that they were about to give up to what is called scorched earth policies, leaving them entirely devastated—so they could be of no use to the Allies, and so that their advance would be hampered—leaving essentially a desert of destroyed villages, poisoned wells, exploded bridges, and destroyed roads; and in the process they deported some 100,000 civilians.

Nonetheless, in spite of this unexpected withdrawal of the Germans, the Nivelle offensive began with the Battle of Arras on April 9, 1917. Vimy Ridge was taken by Canadian troops, and the battle seemed to start well in this regard. But the French attack in the Champagne region was a disaster, which paradoxically was worsened by the extravagant expectations that Nivelle had created of finally achieving—by the mass and violence approach—a breakthrough at long last. As a result of these disappointments in late April, mutinies broke out among French troops. Ordinary French soldiers refused to move up to the front and refused to attack; they protested what they saw as the meaningless sacrifice of their lives for nothing. They used a very interesting phrase to describe what it was that they were doing; they called themselves "strikers," men who were striking in protest as to how the war was being conducted. We're going to speak a lot more in coming lecture when we talk about dissent about these mutinies, because they're very revealing in fact of the sentiments of ordinary soldiers who endured so long, had endured the Battle of Verdun, had endured other encounters, but now finally, as they put it, were going on strike.

General Nivelle, whose reputation was destroyed by these failures, was replaced as commander in chief by General Pétain, the hero of Verdun who had vowed that the Germans "would not pass" on May 15, 1917. Pétain now used some of the charisma, some of the image that had been built up around him as a result of the defense of Verdun, to restore order. He did so by a combination of severe discipline on occasion, as well as the assurance that policies would change and that French soldiers would not be sent to their deaths uselessly in renewed offensives of this variety. Order was restored, the mutinies and the military strike were put down, but nonetheless, very revealingly, it was clear that the French army's offensive capacity, in order to mount huge offensives of the sort that had been attempted, finally was spent.

The last of the titanic battles that we'd like to consider under the category of the great battle of attrition is the Third Battle of Ypres. The very name, the "Third Battle," suggests just how much some of this ground was fought over again and again that's known especially to the British by the evocative of Passchendaele after a village that featured prominently in this battle. In late July of 1917, General Haig, even after the failures of earlier offensives, now launched another British offensive in Flanders, the Third Battle of Ypres. The hopes for the battle were heightened by the use of unprecedented technological intensity in an event that was really quite striking. This was the quite deliberate and careful and slow mining of a strategic area that the Germans had held, the so-called Messines Ridge. British troops had undermined this ridge, which was a strategically significant location, and had packed it full of explosives, a million tons in fact, in order to prepare for a surprise explosion, a blowing up of this ridge in order to inaugurate the attack.

This explosion of Messines Ridge took place on June 7, 1917. The explosion was of such intensity that it was felt in London, far, far away. But the results of this initial breakthrough yielded only about two miles advance, and this turned out to be, while nonetheless a good omen of the possibility of breaking through, not nearly what had been hoped for as a result. In some sense military planners had been deceived by their maps. The maps, it's been argued by military historians, deceptively showed promising positions, but what was neglected was the quality of the ground, which had proved to be very wet and muddy. In fact, "seas of mud" are especially descriptive of the entire experience of Passchendaele. That's not how General Haig saw it at first. He had high hopes of breaking through to open Belgian territory, punching through the German lines, reaching the port of Ostend, and beginning an advance into Germany itself. The attack began on July 31, 1917. Rains that rained down in this period quickly turned the ground into, quite literally, oceans of mud and wet. Tanks sank that were sent forward, quite literally sank into this mud and disappeared. The last attacks of this drawn-out battle took place on November 6, 1917; they at last reached the village of Passchendaele.

The result of this battle was a British gain of five miles. Some staff officers who had been involved in the planning of the battle itself later bitterly repented the entire venture, which cost 325,000 casualties. There's one anecdote that to me sums up in a very bitter way the regret and the illusions, the lack of understanding that some of these officers had shown; one of Haig's subordinates went to the front to see the battlefield after the "British victory." He went to the front, and seeing the mud that trapped his car as they drove forward into the areas that had been fought over, he actually, with amazement, looked out over the muddy landscape and broke into tears and exclaimed, "Good God, did we really send men forward to fight in that?"

The outcomes of these battles were ambiguous; what was clear was that they were synonymous with the senseless mass death of the Great War. The search for other ways of breaking the deadlock, the stalemate, would continue, whether through technology, the opening of other fronts, gaining of other allies, or subverting the enemy in other ways. The fighting in other fronts we'll consider in our next lectures.

Lecture Ten
The Eastern Front Experience

Scope:

The war in Eastern Europe was called by Winston Churchill in his histories the "Unknown War," and the Eastern Front is still not as well understood or as familiar as the Western Front. This lecture illuminates the unfamiliar clash of empires in the East, beginning with the Russian invasion of German East Prussia and the ominous disasters of the Austro-Hungarian war effort from its very beginning, leading to growing dependence on its ally, the German Empire. After the German victory against the Russians at Tannenberg in 1914, Generals Hindenburg and Ludendorff became popular war heroes in Germany and eventually were elevated to the High Command. The German "Great Advance" of 1915 into Russian territory resulted in the conquest of vast new areas, often devastated by the conflict, which now would be occupied and administered as a new colonial empire.

Outline

I. The "Unknown War"

    A. The Eastern Front and its experience for millions has not been imprinted as deeply in the collective consciousness of Western civilization, but its impact was an important one.

        1. Winston Churchill entitled his 1931 history of the Eastern Front *The Unknown War*.

        2. The Eastern Front differed from the West in its greater mobility, its enormous scale, and in its outcome.

    B. The Eastern Front in World War II, by contrast, has been extensively studied and researched. What came before, in the First World War, has remained less familiar.

    C. The Central Powers themselves could not agree on priorities. Coordination of fighting by the Germans and Austro-Hungarian forces was spotty until the latter found themselves subordinated to German direction.

II. The Harrowing of East Prussia

    A. The war in the East opened with a traumatic event for Germans: the only sizeable incursion into the German Empire, the Russian invasion of East Prussia.

        1. Fears of an irresistible "Russian Steamroller," bearing down on Berlin, had been current before the war.

        2. Prussia had been left exposed in line with the Schlieffen Plan.

        3. Now two Russian armies approached: General Rennenkampf's Vilna army from northeast and General Samsonov's Warsaw army from the south.

        4. Russian forces had moved before they were fully ready, to aid their French ally in the hour of crisis.

    B. At the Battle of Gumbinnen of August 19–20, 1914, German troops were beaten back and officials prepared to evacuate East Prussia. Russian forces outnumbered German two to one.

    C. Russian forces occupied the eastern portions of the province.

    D. Colonel-General Paul von Hindenburg and Chief of Staff Major-General Erich Ludendorff arrived to take command.

    E. Using plans already prepared by Lieutenant Colonel Max Hoffmann, they took a calculated risk, which yielded a great victory.

III. Tannenberg

    A. German forces intercepted Russian wireless messages, giving valuable clues to Russian plans.

    B. The German forces were directed against the Warsaw army, whereas only a thin screen of cavalry troops guarded against the Vilna army. Communications between the two Russian armies were poor.

        1. German forces surrounded the Warsaw army and smashed it in the battle, which took place August 26–30, 1914.

        2. In despair, General Samsonov shot himself.

        3. The Germans took 92,000 Russian prisoners.

4. Aleksandr Solzhenitsyn's historical novel, *August 1914*, describes the events.

5. In the Battle of the Masurian Lakes of September 7–15, the Vilna army was also thrown back.

6. After the winter campaign in Masuria, East Prussia was liberated.

7. The fighting in East Prussia cost Russia a quarter-million men.

8. The Russian attack had, however, drawn two German army corps away from the Western Front.

9. After the battles, German armies were shifted to Poland and to protect Prussian Silesia.

C. Soon the Legend of Tannenberg grew up around this victory.

1. The news of the victory spread like wildfire through Germany.

2. A legend was built up around Tannenberg from the first. Its name was chosen to redeem a famous defeat of the Teutonic Knights by Lithuanian and Polish armies in 1410 (probably, the battle should have been called Frögenau).

3. It was claimed that Hindenburg had planned the battle years ago and had lured the Russians into a trap.

IV. Hindenburg and Ludendorff

A. Hindenburg and Ludendorff became war heroes in Germany at a time of reverses. On November 1, 1914, Hindenburg was appointed Supreme Commander in the East.

B. Very different in character and background, the two men formed a dynamic duo.

C. Their fame helped them rise to the position of war dictators in Germany from 1916.

V. Austrian Fortunes

A. The war began badly for the Austro-Hungarian Empire.

1. The empire fielded three army groups, one against Russia, the other confronting Serbia, with the third shuttling in between.

2. From the start of the war, Austro-Hungarian forces had shelled the Serbian capital, Belgrade.

3. On August 12, 1914, Austro-Hungarian forces crossed the Danube and Sava rivers but four days later were expelled by Serbian forces.

4. The Serbians beat off three Austro-Hungarian invasions in 1914.

5. After an initial advance onto Russian territory towards Lublin in the Polish territories, Austria-Hungary was expelled and lost Galicia.

6. In 1914, Austria-Hungary suffered more than one million casualties.

7. From December 1914 to April 1915, Russian and Austro-Hungarian forces fought in the passes of the Carpathian Mountains (the range between Galicia and Hungary). The Austro-Hungarian forces often lost more casualties from freezing than combat.

8. The Carpathian winter campaign and the fall of the Austro-Hungarian fortress of Przemysl, the main fortress in Austrian Galicia, cost more than 750,000 casualties on the Austrian side.

B. Some breakthroughs did occur for Austria-Hungary.

1. Help from German reinforcements, on which the Austro-Hungarian army would come increasingly to rely, produced the victory of Gorlice-Tarnow on May 2, 1915. A 40-mile gap was smashed in the Russian front.

2. Galicia was regained, the fortress of Przemysl retaken, Lemberg (Lvov) captured, and a quarter-million Russians captured.

VI. The Great Advance of 1915

A. After the success of Tannenberg, Hindenburg and Ludendorff, as easterners, argued for a battle of envelopment against the Russians.

1. Falkenhayn, as a westerner, believed final victory would be won in the West but went on the defensive there in 1915 and turned forces to the Eastern Front.

2. The breakthrough at Gorlice-Tarnow was even greater than had been expected, sometimes considered the only real breakthrough of the entire war.

3. A larger German offensive in the East unfolded and conquered large territories (the size of France) from the Russian Empire: present-day Poland, Lithuania, and Latvia.

4. German armies seized the fortresses of Kaunas, Grodno, Brest-Litovsk, and the cities of Warsaw and Vilnius.

5. Russian armies were pushed back 300 miles, using a scorched earth policy as they retreated.

6. The Russian forces—with 2.5 million dead, wounded, or held captive—were almost knocked out of the war.

B. In a fateful mistake, in September 1915, Tsar Nicholas II took over as Russian commander in chief from Grand Duke Nicholas Nikolayevich. Henceforth, the Tsar would be held responsible for setbacks.

C. The front stabilized by fall, running from just short of Riga on the Baltic all the way south to Romania. Falkenhayn returned his attention to the Western Front, to Verdun.

D. The large territories conquered by German troops needed to be administered, a formidable task, given their devastation and relative unfamiliarity.

1. Poland was given a civil government.

2. The lands north of Poland were consolidated into a military state called Ober Ost.

3. German soldiers were engaged in a daily encounter with Eastern Europe, its nature, and populations.

E. Ludendorff and Hindenburg worked to administer the occupied territories and conspired against Falkenhayn, their superior.

VII. Brusilov Offensive

A. Unexpectedly, in June–August 1916, General Alexei Brusilov launched an offensive (in part to draw Germans away from Verdun) that led to dramatic Russian gains.

B. Russian armies on the southern sectors of the front, Volhynia and Galicia, took a quarter-million Austro-Hungarian soldiers prisoner, as their front collapsed and their spirit was exhausted.

C. These dramatic successes convinced Romania to join the Allies.

D. However, because Brusilov did not receive support in the north, his armies took a million casualties, and this offensive would be the last real success of the Russian army.

E. Three successive offensives by Brusilov were without greater result.

VIII. Seeming Success in the East for the Central Powers

    A. By 1917, the Central Powers had scored seemingly impressive gains on the Eastern Front.

        1. Bulgaria was impressed enough to join the Central Powers on September 6, 1915.

        2. In the winter of 1915, German, Austro-Hungarian, and Bulgarian armies overran Serbia.

        3. In December of 1916, the Central Powers also conquered Romania.

    B. After the Brusilov offensive, the Russian army was in the process of disintegration. Even a new government in Russia from March 1917 could not halt this process.

    C. From July 1917, German and Austro-Hungarian forces attacked again and pushed forward the front, retaking most of Galicia and taking Riga and the Estonian islands of Saaremaa, Hiiumaa, and Muhu.

    D. At the end of 1917, Russia left the war and was forced to sign the crushing Treaty of Brest-Litovsk on March 3, 1918.

    E. To the Central Powers, it seemed that half the war had been won by their side.

Essential Reading:

John Keegan, *The First World War*, pp.143–174.

Supplementary Reading:

Vejas Gabriel Liulevicius, *War Land on the Eastern Front: Culture, National Identity, and German Occupation in World War I.*

Denis Showalter, *Tannenberg: Clash of Empires, 1914.*

Norman Stone, *The Eastern Front, 1914–1917.*

Questions to Consider:

1. If Russia had been knocked out of the war in 1915, what effects would that have had on the war as a whole?

2. In what ways did the fighting on the Eastern Front differ from that in the West?

Lecture Ten—Transcript
The Eastern Front Experience

In this lecture we consider the war on the Eastern Front. The Eastern Front is still not as well understood or as familiar as the relatively more familiar fighting on the Western Front in the world of the trenches. This lecture will seek to illuminate the unfamiliar clash of empires in Eastern Europe beginning the Russian invasion of East Prussia, and the ominous disasters of the Austro-Hungarian war effort, from its very beginning leading to growing dependence by the Austro-Hungarians on their ally the German Empire. After the German victory against the Russians at Tannenberg in 1914 that we'll be discussing in this lecture, Generals Hindenburg and Ludendorff, the victors of that battle, became popular war heroes in Germany, and eventually elevating them to the High Command—becoming essentially German dictators. The great German advance of 1915 into the vast imperial territories of the Russian Empire brought the Germans into control of vast new areas, often devastated by the conflict, which now would be occupied and administered as a new colonial empire.

When we speak of the Eastern War and its experience for millions, we really are talking to a great extent about an experience that has not been imprinted as deeply in the collective consciousness of Western Europe, of the United States, but its impact was a very important one for Eastern Europe and for world history. Winston Churchill, in his 1931 history of the Eastern Front, entitled his book *The Unknown War*. The Eastern Front certainly differed from the fighting in the West in its greater mobility, its enormous scale—it was often twice the length of the Western Front, 1,000 miles rather than 500 miles—and also in its outcome, as we'll see by the end of today's lecture. The Eastern Front and the fighting and the atrocities that took place in World War II, by contrast, have been extensively studied and researched. What came before, in the First World War, has remained less familiar, but is the subject of this lecture. The Central Powers themselves, that is to say Germany and Austria-Hungry, often could not agree on priorities in fighting on the Eastern Front. The coordination of their forces was spotty until the latter, that is to say the Austro-Hungarians, increasingly found themselves simply subordinated to German direction as they grew increasingly dependent on Germany for aid, for the war went very poorly for them.

The war however on the Eastern Front began with an event that was tremendously traumatic for German public opinion and for a sense of how the war was going. The war in the east opened for Germany with the Russian invasion. It was the only sizable incursion in the course of the war into the German territory, the Russian invasion of East Prussia. This is precisely what had been feared by many in the years before the war itself. There were nightmarish visions of an irresistible so-called "Russian Steamroller," of Russian armies made up of great, huge, peasant soldiers and of fearsome Cossack Calvary bearing down on Berlin. Such anxieties had been current before the war. But you'll recall that in the calculated risk, the gamble of the Schlieffen Plan, it had been planned to leave Germany's eastern provinces less defended in order to concentrate, as the Schlieffen Plan demanded, as much force as possible to beat France first and then to turn against the Russian Empire. However, dismaying German policy makers and military planners, Russian armies moved more quickly than had been expected. They did so, in part, at the urging of their French allies to come to the aid in the opening stages of the First World War. Now two Russian armies bore down upon East Prussia, the eastern areas of the German Empire. From the northeast came General Rennenkampf's Vilna army, and General Samsonov's Warsaw army from the south, converging on this exposed German territory. Russian forces had moved at the urging of the French before they were fully ready in this hour of crisis, and some of this disorganization that resulted would turn out to be fateful for the Russian effort. At first, things seemed to be going to well, as the Russians plunged into a lightly defended eastern province.

At the Battle of Gumbinnen of August 19–20, 1914, German troops were beaten back, and German officials prepared to evacuate East Prussia. Russian forces outnumbered the German defenders two-to-one, they had overwhelming force, and Russian forces occupied the eastern portions of the province as a whole. The German officials who had ordered retreat were now simply dismissed from their positions and new commanders were sent to the East to organize the war effort. These included Colonel-General Paul von Hindenburg, a venerable German soldier already well along in years, who was brought of retirement in order to lead this effort, and as his very able, talented—and now famous—aide was Chief of Staff Major-General

Erich Ludendorff, who had acquired fame through the taking of the Fortress of Liege on the Western Front just recently. These two men were sent out to take command and to salvage the situation in the East. In a sense they were very lucky, because an able officer was already on the scene and had prepared plans. This was Lieutenant Colonel Max Hoffmann. Using the plans that had already been prepared by Hoffman, together the military commanders took a calculated risk, which ended up yielding a great victory, what indeed is sometimes considered by sometimes by some historians as the greatest victory of the First World War, the Battle of Tannenberg, which we'll talk about now in more detail.

The Battle of Tannenberg was a calculated risk which, in some sense, the Germans were willing to take because of the role of technology at play in the opening stages of the battle. German forces had intercepted Russian wireless messages. This speaks volumes about the difficulties of communication in this war, the Russians had been sending messages uncoded, not out of stupidity, obviously, but rather because of the tremendous difficulties involved in getting a message through at all. The result was that the Germans now had in their hands valuable clues as to how the Russian armies were advancing and what their plans were. They were thus able to concentrate their forces against first one part of the advancing Russian force, and then to move them against the other.

The battle proceeded thus: German forces were directed first against the Warsaw army, concentrating against this oncoming force with their movement directed against it. Meanwhile, only a thin screen of cavalry troops was used to guard against the Vilna army, the other Russian army moving in from the east, in order to produce the impression that the Germans were there in force, as well. The poor quality of communications between these two Russian armies resulted in an unclear picture on the Russian side of what it was that the Germans were doing. The Germans now had gambled by concentrating their forces against the Warsaw army of the Russians moving in from the south and concentrating their forces upon it, they surrounded it and smashed it in a huge battle, which lasted across vast territories from August 26–31, 1914.

The result was, in this battle of encirclement, that vast numbers of Russian soldiers were taken prisoner. The Russian command collapsed; and in despair, the commander of the Russian forces,

General Samsonov, asked himself what he possibly could do at this moment. His officers recorded that he was in despair in a sense, repeating over and over again his anxiety that the emperor, that's to say that Tsar Nicholas had entrusted him with his army and he had destroyed it, and the result was that he wandered off away from his officers and shot himself, so deep was his anxiety and despair. The Germans took vast masses of Russian prisoners, 92,000, by one count. This was an enormous defeat for an entire Russian army. A great historical novel, painstakingly accurate, Aleksandr Solzhenitsyn's novel, *August 1914* describes these events both on the vast strategic scale, as well as in the experience of ordinary soldiers. In an ensuing battle, the army that proceeded from the east, the Vilna army, which had not come to the aid of the Warsaw army as it was crushed, was also beaten back in the Battle of the Masurian Lakes of September 7–15, 1914.

There followed more fighting in East Prussia, and it was only finally in the winter campaign of Masuria that East Prussia was finally liberated, as Russian troops were finally thrown back. The fighting in East Prussia had ended in disaster for the Russians. It had cost Russia a quarter-million men. The Russian attack however, had, for all of its losses, nonetheless some achievements to show. It had drawn away two German army corps that might have been used on the Western Front to aid in the defense of embattled East Prussia. In that sense, though at tremendous cost to the Russians, nonetheless they had contributed to the frustration of the Schlieffen Plan in the west. After these battles, German armies were shifted to Poland to protect Prussian Silesia. Soon a legend grew up around the Battle of Tannenberg, considered by some military historians the great victory of the First World War. The news of the victory spread like wildfire through Germany. The good news was very necessary at this moment at a time when the Schlieffen plan was failing.

A legend now grew up about Tannenberg almost immediately. It began with the naming of this battle; the name chosen for the Battle of Tannenberg was historically and symbolically significant because it had historical resonance. There had been another first Battle of Tannenberg back in 1410, and this had been a famous defeat when the Teutonic Knights, the Germanic Crusaders against the Poles and against the Baltic peoples, had been defeated by Polish and Lithuanian armies back in 1410. The name was quite deliberately chosen to in some sense redeem this earlier defeat with a far greater victory over Slavic forces. Curmudgeonly, military historians point out that the battle probably should have been called Frögenau, but obviously the name of Frögenau didn't carry these deep resonances and sounded a little bit silly, so instead quite deliberately the battle was named Tannenberg. Legends now grew up around the leadership of Hindenburg and Ludendorff. In particular, it was claimed—sort of in a conspiracy theory—that Hindenburg had in fact planned this battle years and years ago; that he had vacationed in East Prussia, that he had obsessively ridden through the areas where the battle finally took place, and had planned out in his mind years before a battle plan which eventually the Russians were lured into as a trap.

Hindenburg and Ludendorff, the architects so it was believed of this tremendous victory, became now very clearly war heroes in Germany. Such war heroes were very necessary at a time of reverses. In reflection of their increased status, on November 1, 1914, General Hindenburg appointed Supreme Commander in the East. Very clearly building on the sort of stature and charisma that his new role had given him, the commander in the East would take on an increased independence even from the commander of German forces as a whole, Falkenhayn, who was leading the war effort. Hindenburg and Ludendorff together formed what sometimes has been called a "dynamic duo," they were very different in character as well background, but together they had a certain chemistry that allowed them to, at least in the short term, be quite effective as military leaders. Hindenburg himself even called their relationship at one point, "a happy marriage."

Paul von Hindenburg, the leadership figurehead, in other words, of this dynamic duo, was a man of tremendous historical antecedents; his ancestors had been Prussian aristocrats or Junkers for centuries beforehand, and his own family was identified very much with Prussian history. He was a calm, imperturbable, icy willed and tremendously determined military leader who, it was said, could keep his calm even in the most difficult military situations. Eric Ludendorff, by contrast, was very different. He was of middle class origins, he was not of exalted aristocratic background, and he was rather a technocrat. He was, in some sense, a new breed of military man, a military professional who, through scientific planning, through ambition, through hard work, had risen through the ranks and had achieved the prominence that he now would use to the hilt.

The shared psychological chemistry of this group was supplemented by Ludendorff's nervousness, his high strung nature. It was argued sometimes that these two men, so very different psychologically as well in terms of background, perfectly complemented one another. Their shared fame helped them to rise in terms of stature as heroes to the German people, eventually becoming war dictators of Germany from 1916 on, and a war dictatorship that we'll inquire into in more detail in a later lecture.

If the Germans had scored this very welcome victory at the Battle of Tannenberg, the fortunes of their ally in the Central Powers, the Austro-Hungarians, were quite dismal. The war began badly for the Austro-Hungarian Empire, and for keen observers this was a very bad omen. The empire fielded three army groups at the start of the war, and it seemed almost as that it couldn't decide where to concentrate. One of these army groups was sent against Russia, the other was sent against the original enemy in what had turned into a larger war, Serbia, and the third one managed to shuttle indecisively in between the Russian Front and the Serbian Front. From the start of the war, Austro-Hungarian had expected an easy victory over the Serbian enemy. They started by shelling the Serbian capital of Belgrade. On August 12, 1914, Austro-Hungarian forces confidently crossed the Danube and Sava Rivers expecting victory, but four days later were expelled by Serbian forces engaged in a nationalist defense of their home land. Indeed, in the rest of 1914, the Serbian forces would two more times beat off Austro-Hungarian invasions. After an initial advance onto Russian territory towards Lublin in the Polish territories, Austro-Hungarian armies were again beaten back; Austria-Hungary was expelled and lost Galicia.

In 1914, by the end of the year, Austria-Hungary was measuring a terrible toll. It had lost more than a million casualties. In a very real sense it couldn't afford these precise casualties and these deaths because these represented the professional military, the seasoned officers and soldiers of an army that now, by contrast, was lamed. From December 1914–April 1915, horrific winter fighting took place. Russian and Austro-Hungarian forces clashed in the high passes of the snowy Carpathian Mountains—that's the range that extends between Galicia and Hungary—a mountain range in which fighting now took place. The Austro-Hungarian forces fighting in this mountain warfare often lost more casualties from men freezing than combat itself. This so-called Carpathian winter campaign and the fall of a famous Austro-Hungarian fortress, the main fortress in Austrian Galicia, Przemysl that had been surrounded by Russian besiegers, cost the Austrians more than 750,000.

Nonetheless, there were some successes that the Austrians could point to and that they were proud of. With help from German reinforcements—a sign of things to come—on which the Austro-Hungarian army would come increasingly rely in the years that followed, a victory was produced. This was the victory of Gorlice-Tarnow on May 2, 1915. A 40-mile gap was smashed in the Russian front, and the forces of the Central Powers started to pour through. This was truly a remarkable victory. Galicia, which had been lost to the Russian forces, was now regained for the Austrian Empire, the fortress of Przemysl retaken, and Lemberg—or Lvov, as it's called—was captured, and a quarter-million Russians taken prisoner. What this illustrated was that the East was more mobile in its nature and still capable of producing the sort of breakthroughs that eluded the commanders on the Western Front.

This breakthrough now opened out into a larger victory for the Central Powers, the so-called Great Advance of 1915. After their success in 1914 at the Battle of Tannenberg, Generals Hindenburg and Ludendorff had carved for themselves a position as the premier Easterners. What was meant by this was that they championed, within the debates about how strategy should evolve; the formula that victory could be won in the East and forces should be concentrated there in order to exploit the opportunity. They argued for a battle of envelopment against the Russian armies. The Battle of Tannenberg had been a great success, but it had been a tactical success; it had not strategically, in the largest sense, beaten the Russians to the point where they had to withdraw from the war. The Russians, to they contrary, had simply retreated. They pulled back and withdrew into the wide open spaces of the Russian Empire, and a final strategic victory had eluded the Germans.

General Falkenhayn, who was in charge of the entire German war effort, was a Westerner. He was convinced that final victory would have to be won on the Western Front, and viewed the East as important but not ultimately decisive. But nonetheless, Falkenhayn, humoring his subordinates, went on the defensive in 1915 on the Western Front and allowed forces to be moved to the East to win what victories might be won there. The breakthrough at Gorlice-

Tarnow was even greater than had been expected; in fact, it's sometimes considered the only real breakthrough of the entire war. Now a larger German offensive in the Eastern Europe unfolded, and it conquered vast territories, an area essentially the size of all of France, from the Russian Empire.

In the course of the so-called "Great Advance" of the summer of 1915, German armies occupied present-day Poland, Lithuania, and Latvia on the Baltic. German armies seized important fortresses that supposedly had been the impregnable defenses of the Russian Empire: the fortresses of Kaunas, of Grodno, of Brest-Litovsk, and the cities of Warsaw and Vilnius. Russian armies were pushed back an average of 300 miles, and as they did so, as they retreated they used scorched earth policies. These scorched earth policies aimed to destroy the lands that were being given up to the enemy in order to make sure that, by burning buildings, by destroying towns, by blowing up bridges, by tearing up railroads, by burning fields with crops standing in them, the enemy would not gain anything worth having.

It was very clear that what the Germans would remember as the Great Advance of 1915 would go into Russian memory as the Great Retreat of 1915. The blow was stunning. Russian forces lost two-and-a-half-million men dead, wounded, or taken prisoner as a result of this campaign. Russia was almost knocked out of the war entirely. What followed at this point was really more in the nature of a symbolic gesture, but it was enormously telling in terms of what it had to say about Russian leadership. In what turned out to be a fateful mistake, in September 1915, the Russian Emperor Tsar Nicholas II personally took over as Russian commander in chief from Grand Duke Nicholas Nikolayevich. Henceforth, the Russian Tsar would be held responsible for any setbacks to the Russian war effort. In a very real sense, he felt a deep sense of obligation and a deep sense of responsibility, which unfortunately didn't match his talents as a military commander or a political leader, had now engineered a situation in which his regime did not have plausible deniability but instead would be very personally identified with the defeats.

The Eastern Front finally stabilized by the fall of 1915, and its expanse was huge; the front ran from the Baltic Sea just short of Riga, in what today is the Republic of Latvia, all the way down south to Romania. At this point, satisfied with these gains and still convinced that victory would have to come in the West, General Falkenhayn returned his attention to the fighting on the Western Front, and to that titanic battle that he was planning, the Battle of Verdun in 1916. By contrast, now in the East, large territories had been won; this was a great contrast with the several miles of advance that might be achieved on the Western Front at great cost. Here in Eastern Europe, by contrast, huge territories had been conquered by German forces, and they now needed to be administered as occupied territory, a formidable task given their state of devastation as result both the conflict itself, the front moving through, as well as scorched earth policies and relative unfamiliarity, the strangeness of these regions to the German occupiers.

Poland was given a civil government. The lands north of Poland were consolidated into, not a civilian government of the variety that Poland had, but rather an odd sort of hybrid form, a military state, a military colony that was called Ober Ost, and we'll talk much more in a coming lecture about what the realities of occupation were like. Here it will suffice to simply mention that German soldiers, ordinary soldiers, would now in these vast wide open territories be engaged in a daily encounter, a daily confrontation with Eastern Europe; and what it was like on a daily basis, its nature, and its populations of tremendous ethnic diversity including Russians, Poles, Lithuanians, Latvians, as well as the Jews of Eastern Europe, a very important minority, even some German minorities who, living in the Baltic territories, might have been familiar to the Germans, but instead also had traits all their own that made them unfamiliar, as well. Generals Ludendorff and Hindenburg, frustrated at the fact that a total victory in Eastern Europe had still eluded them, now concentrated on administering these occupied territories, and behind the scenes were busy conspiring against General Falkenhayn, their own superior, aiming eventually to take control of the German war effort themselves.

Nonetheless, what now intervened was a surprising and, in many cases, very proud Russian success showing that the fighting on the Eastern Front most certainly still continued. This was the proud effort of the Russian army, the so-called Brusilov Offensive. Unexpectedly, in June to August of 1916, General Alexei Brusilov, a Russian General, launched an offensive. Now in part, this was intended to draw Germans forces away from the Western Front where the crisis at Verdun was playing itself out, and what this very usefully illustrates is the extent to which the fighting on the Eastern Front and the Western Front, different as it was, was nonetheless in a very real military sense linked in terms of its fortunes and its changing balance. The Brusilov offensive made dramatic Russian gains. Russian armies on the southern sectors of the front, where Brusilov's offensive took place in Volhynia and Galicia, smashed into the Austro-Hungarian forces. They took a quarter-million Austro-Hungarian soldiers prisoner, the Austro-Hungarian collapsed, and it was very clear that in a real sense their fighting spirit was exhausted. This too was a continuing, very bad omen for the fortunes of the Habsburg monarchies war efforts.

There were certainly other side effects of these dramatic successes. Succeeding on the battlefield meant that one was probably more likely to find allies willing to join one. The result of these Russian successes was that the eastern European country Rumania now settled on joining the Allies in order to share in what they expected soon would be a decisive victory. This turned out to be a miscalculation, because Brusilov offenses, successful as they had been in the south, did not receive support from other Russian commanders in the north. The result was that as the fighting continued, Brusilov's army took a million casualties, and as it turned out, this successful offensive would be the last real success of the Russian army, which was reaching exhaustion itself. Three successive following offensives by Brusilov were without greater successes.

Ultimately, in the last analysis, the fighting in the East would end with what seemed to be success for the Central Powers, with a balance of victory tipping in their favor. By 1917, the Central Powers had scored seemingly impressive gains on the Eastern Front. Bulgaria had been impressed enough with the success of the Germans to join the Central Powers on September 6, 1915. In the winter of 1915, German, Austro-Hungarian, and Bulgarian armies overran Serbia and shared in the spoils of that conquest. In December of 1916, the Central Powers also conquered Rumania, which had entered the war, as it turned out, a very bad moment. After the Brusilov offensive, the Russian army was in the process of disintegration. Even the overthrow of the Tsar that we'll be discussing much more in a later lecture about the Russian Revolution and the installation of a new government in March 1917, could not ultimately halt this process of the disintegration and undermining of the Russian armies as a whole. From July 1917, German and Austro-Hungarian forces attacked once again. They pushed forward the front forward even further, retaking most of Galicia, taking Riga and the Estonian islands of Saaremaa, Hiiumaa, and Muhu preparing for greater successes.

At the end of 1917, it was clear that Russia had reached the point of exhaustion. Russia left the war, it proclaimed its own defeat, was forced by the Germans to sign a crushing peace treaty, the Treaty of Brest-Litovsk, on March 3, 1918, which we'll discuss in more detail later. This was an enormous and crushing blow to the Allies. In the west they had lost their Russian ally, now France and Great Britain were without a weight in the East that they might use in their plans. Russia was now defeated, and to the Central Powers it seemed that half of the war, the war in the East, had been won by their side. What the fortune of fighting on other fronts was like, especially the Southern Front, we'll explore in our next lecture.

Lecture Eleven
The Southern Fronts

Scope:

This lecture examines the Southern Fronts of the First World War in Europe and the factors that made decisive victory elusive here as well. Turkish entry into the war expanded its scope. Allied landings in Gallipoli in 1915 were repulsed by the Turks in a campaign that involved one million men on all sides. Italy at first stayed out of the general war, avowing a policy of "sacred egoism." Secret diplomacy and promises of territorial gains brought Italy into the war on the Allied side in the clandestine Treaty of London of 1915. Alpine warfare and the 12 battles of the Isonzo between Italy and Austria-Hungary are surveyed. Germany and Austria-Hungary succeeded in overrunning Serbia and Romania. A 1915 Allied expedition to Salonika, Greece, proved indecisive.

Outline

I. Widening of the War: Turkish Entry

    A. The war took on a southern dimension by the addition of the Ottoman Empire (Turkey), Italy, and operations around the Mediterranean.

        1. Turkey joined the Central Powers by a secret treaty of August 2, 1914.

        2. Led by Enver Pasha, the Young Turk movement, which had controlled the empire since 1909, sympathized with Germany.

        3. Two German battleships, the *Goeben* and the *Breslau*, moved into the Black Sea and shelled the Russian port of Odessa in October 1914.

        4. In November 1914, the Allies declared war on Turkey. Operations now spread around its territories in the Mediterranean and Middle East.

    B. Britain discarded an earlier constant aim of its diplomacy and promised Russia the Dardanelles.

C. Turkey attacked Russia in the Caucasus, envisioning a great Pan-Turanian empire extending into Central Asia.

    1. The Turkish winter campaign of 1914–1915 was a disaster.

    2. Turkish soldiers froze to death, and only 13 percent of the force survived.

D. In the wake of this disaster, in spring 1915, Russian forces moved down from the Caucasus into Anatolia, welcomed by some Armenians as liberators.

E. Turkish forces made attempts to attack the Suez Canal, worrying the British.

F. On November 14, 1914, the Turkish Sultan, in his capacity as Caliph, declared holy war (Jihad), hoping to set ablaze Muslim populations under British rule in India and Egypt, and in Central Asia under Russian rule.

II. Gallipoli

A. To relieve Russia, the Allies crafted plans to knock Ottoman Turkey out of the war, beginning with a landing in Gallipoli, the peninsula at the tip of the Dardanelles Straits, and thence to occupy Constantinople to the northeast.

    1. This plan was championed by the British First Lord of the Admiralty, Winston Churchill.

    2. It has been called the only strategic idea of the war.

B. Efforts to force the straits by battleships failed, but they alerted Turkish forces, which, under the leadership of German commander Otto Liman von Sanders, began to mass to repel an assault.

C. The major landing began on April 25, 1915.

    1. Franco-British forces landed at Cape Helles and Australian and New Zealand troops (Anzacs) at Anzac Cove.

    2. An initial window of opportunity to expand beachheads was squandered.

3. Allied forces dug trenches while Turkish troops took positions atop the cliffs. Among them was a young officer, Mustafa Kemal, later Atatürk, leader of a new Turkey.

4. The advantages of the defensive were again demonstrated.

5. The British commander Sir Ian Hamilton renewed assaults in August 1915, with new landings at Suvla Bay to the north.

D. When news of disaster filtered back to Britain, Hamilton was removed and throughout December troops were withdrawn in secret. The successful evacuation was completed by January 9, 1916.

E. The outcomes were notable and long-lasting.

1. Some 200,000 Allied men died in this futile expedition. The fighting involved 1 million men on both sides.

2. Winston Churchill was disgraced, blamed for the misadventure, and lost his position.

3. The Anzac troops suffered very heavy losses. During the war, they took 62 percent of the casualties. The Gallipoli disaster came to be considered the founding experience of independent Australian identity.

4. The failure made clear that a decision would need to be reached on the Western Front.

III. Italy

A. When war broke out, Italy announced it was not bound to the Central Powers by the earlier Triple Alliance and instead would follow what Prime Minister Antonio Salandra called "sacred egoism."

B. A bidding war for Italian participation or neutrality commenced.

1. The Allies won this auction, able to promise enemy territory.

2. The Secret Treaty of London between the Allies and Italy was signed on April 26, 1915.

3. Italy was promised ethnically Italian areas under the Austro-Hungarian Empire in Trentino and Trieste, as well as larger gains in Tirol and the Dalmatian coast, and perhaps even Asia Minor.

4. Contradicting professed Allied war aims, these secret promises would later be a liability.

C. Italy prepared to enter the war.

1. On May 23, 1915, Italy declared war on Austria-Hungary.

2. Italian nationalists, the Romantic poet Gabriele D'Annunzio, and Futurist artists celebrated the war.

IV. Alpine War and Battles of the Isonzo

A. Though Italian participation was thought to be a prize, Italy in fact would require Allied assistance.

B. Italian Commander Count Luigi Cadorna threw one million men into battle against Austria-Hungary on two fronts: toward alpine areas bordering Italy in the north, such as Trentino, and also Trieste, across the Isonzo River.

1. In 11 battles of the Isonzo, Italian forces were unable to break through enemy trenches. In 1916, the Italians took half a million casualties.

2. In the high-altitude fighting in the Alps, guns had to be hauled up by pulleys.

C. The Italian war effort took a turn for the worse with the disaster of Caporetto.

1. In fall 1917, German troops were moved in to help the Austro-Hungarians. Among them was Erwin Rommel, later a famous commander in World War II.

2. In the Battle of Caporetto in October 1917, often called the Twelfth Battle of the Isonzo, Italian lines broke and a massive retreat set in to the Piave River, north of Venice.

3. Entire Italian units surrendered. The Italians lost half a million casualties, and a quarter-million Italian prisoners were taken.

4. Ernest Hemingway's *A Farewell to Arms* is about the retreat, though he arrived in Italy six months after it occurred.

5. The retreat was halted as Italian forces regrouped 90 miles west at the Piave River to defend Venice.

D. General Cadorna was replaced as commander in chief by General Armando Diaz, and the crisis passed.

V. Serbia and Romania Overrun

A. Bulgaria had joined the Central Powers on September 6, 1915, and was promised Serbian territory.

B. The conquest of Serbia would ensure lines of communication with Turkey.

C. In the winter of 1915, German, Austro-Hungarian, and Bulgarian armies overran Serbia in two months.

    1. Belgrade was captured.

    2. The Central Powers invaded Montenegro and moved into Albania in January 1916.

    3. An Allied expedition seeking to come to the aid of Serbia found themselves trapped in Salonika in Greece.

D. In a dramatic and costly retreat, the Serbian army marched across the Albanian mountains to the Adriatic and was evacuated by sea.

E. It is estimated that Serbia lost one-sixth of its population in this campaign.

F. Prematurely impressed by Russian advances in the Brusilov offensive, Romania entered the war on the Allied side on August 27, 1916, and was promised enemy territory.

G. Instead of seizing Transylvania, however, Romania was itself invaded a week later by the Central Powers.

H. By December 1916, the Central Powers, with Falkenhayn as one of the commanders, conquered Romania.

I. Romanian oil and agricultural resources now fell to the Central Powers.

VI. Salonika

A. The Allies had sought to aid Serbia by sending a military force through neutral Greece. Forces were moved to Greece by October 1915.

B. Greek politics played a part in this fiasco.

1. The Greek prime minister, Eleuthérios Venizélos, cooperated but was deposed.
2. Venizélos gathered opposition to King Constantine, who was forced to abdicate.
3. As a result of internal politics and Allied pressure, Greece joined the Allies in June 1917.

C. Unable to break the Bulgarian lines to the north, half a million Allied soldiers were trapped and idle in Salonika, which the Germans jokingly called their "largest internment camp."

D. Decision would have to come elsewhere.

Essential Reading:

John Keegan, *The First World War*, pp. 217–256.

Supplementary Reading:

Alan Moorehead, *Gallipoli*.

Norman Rose, *Churchill: The Unruly Giant*.

Questions to Consider:

1. What factors made victory elusive on the Southern Fronts?
2. Was Turkish entry into the war a mistake, as some have argued, or inevitable? Why?

Lecture Eleven—Transcript
The Southern Fronts

In this lecture we'll be examining what one might call the Southern Fronts, the battles around the Mediterranean, battles involving Turkey, Italy, and the Balkans. We'll examine the factors that made decisive victory elusive in this theater of war, as well as on the other fronts. Turkish entry into the war expanded its scope. We'll discuss the Allied landings in Gallipoli in 1915, which attempted to strategically revolutionize this situation, but which were repulsed by the Turks in a campaign that involved a million men on all sides. We'll examine the way in which Italy at first stayed out of the general war, following a policy of "sacred egoism," as it was called by Italian politicians. We'll observe how secret diplomacy and promises of territorial gains finally would bring Italy into the war on the Allied side as a result of the secret Treaty of London of 1915. We'll examine the hybrid forms of warfare that evolved as a result; the Alpine high altitude fighting in the mountain ranges between Austria-Hungary and Italy and the twelve battles of the Isonzo. We'll examine how Germany and Austria-Hungary succeeded in overrunning Serbia and Romania. We'll finally take a closer look at an attempt to find a back door in terms of the southern fronts, the 1915 Allied expedition to Salonika, Greece, and the reasons why it proved indecisive.

We'll begin by examining the widening of the war with Turkish entry. The war took on a southern dimension by the addition of operations in the Ottoman Empire, or Turkey, warfare in Italy, and operations around the Mediterranean. Turkey joined the Central Powers by a secret treaty of August 2, 1914, but was slower to join the active fighting. The Young Turk movement—the nationalist movement for inner renewal that had gained steam in the empire and had controlled it since 1909, led by Enver Pasha—had sympathized with Germany and increasingly came under the influence of German advisors and German politicians. The entry of Turkey into the war came when two German battleships—which were in essence given to the Turkish navy, and their soldiers changed out for German sailors, replacing their uniforms with Turkish ones and hoisting the Turkish flag—when these two battleships, the *Goeben* and the *Breslau*, moved into the Black Sea and begin shelling the Russian port of Odessa in October 1914.

The result confused the Allies, who still thought that diplomatically they might have a chance to keep the Ottoman Empire out of the war. But in November 1914, the Allies too declared war on Turkey. As a result, operations would now spread around the territories of the Turkish Empire in the Mediterranean and in the Middle East. A key geopolitical location, which in this regard took on tremendous importance, was the Dardanelles. The Dardanelles represents essentially where one might say Asia and Europe meet. They are the straits which join the Black Sea and the Mediterranean, and as such they're a crucial strategic location especially for the Russians. For the Russians, this was also a channel of trade; a third of Russian exports went through the Dardanelles, and the Dardanelles had been a long standing coveted place that the Russian policy makers over generations had sought to control so that they might have this crucial strategic location in their own control. In the context of this renewed war effort, Great Britain, which over generations had sought to frustrate ambitions to seize the Dardanelles, now in essence discarded this earlier constant aim of its diplomacy and promised Russia the Dardanelles as a gain of the war if it came to a successful conclusion. The stakes were thus high and growing higher.

Turkey for its part launched an attack on the Russia Empire in the Caucasus mountain range. Some Turkish politicians, especially the nationalistic Young Turks, envisioned, as a result of victory in this war and the defeat of the Russian Empire, the possibility of carving out a great new empire that might replace the rickety Ottoman Empire, a new empire on a national basis. It would be what they called a Pan-Turanian empire, meaning a Pan-Turkish empire uniting all of the different speakers of Turkish languages and extending far into territories at that point owned by the Russian Empire in Central Asia, a vast new basis of a powerful state. Nonetheless, their ambitions were frustrated because the Turkish winter campaign of 1914–1915 in the Caucasus Mountain ranges and their snowy valleys and peaks turned in huge disaster. Untold numbers of Turkish soldiers froze to death as a result of poor provisioning and communications, and it's estimated that only 13% of the attacking force survived this assault.

In the wake of this disaster, in spring 1915, Russian now forces moved over into the attack and moved down from the Caucasus into the Territories of the Turkish Empire, into the Anatolian lands.

There, in a turn of events that would be, as it turns out, quite significant later, they were welcomed by some ethnic minorities in these areas owned by the Ottoman Empire as liberators Some of these groups were Armenians. The Armenians are an ethnic group different from the Turks. They were also Christian in background, and some felt that Russian rule would finally allow them a freer exercise of their religion and their culture.

Turkish forces also opened another front by making attempts to attack the Suez Canal, which tremendously worried the British forces in Egypt. The Suez Canal, we need to recall, was essentially a lifeline for the British Empire to connect to its possession, the jewel in the crown, the Indian lands through the Suez Canal. A final attempt of a new ideological front—one might even say a religious front—came on Nov. 14, when the Turkish Sultan, in his capacity as the Caliph, as the religious protector of the holy city of Mecca and protector of Muslims, declared holy war or "Jihad." He'd announced that it was the duty of all Muslims around the world to fight against powers of Britain, France, and Russia, and his hope was to set ablaze the many Muslim populations under British rule in India and Egypt, those under French rule in Africa and Northern Africa, and in Central Asia against Russian rule. The reality was that, though this message was full of fire and of passion, it had very little resonance, in fact; but it showed that many different factors were at play in this conflict.

We need to turn now to a tremendously riveting example of an expedition which proceeded with high hopes, which could certainly have made an enormous difference in the conflict as a whole, but which ended in a disaster. This was the famous Gallipoli Campaign. The Gallipoli Campaign proceeded as a result of a tremendous ambition. Now that Ottoman Turkey had entered the war and the Dardanelles were closed as result, communication with Russia had become more difficult. It was still possible to communicate through the northern sea lane, but it had become far harder to keep up communications and trade. To relieve Russia in this more difficult position, the western Allies, the British and the French, crafted what would knock Ottoman Turkey out of the war, seize the Dardanelles, and perhaps even open up the possibility of a back door to fight the Central Powers, Germany and Austria-Hungary, by invading through the Balkans and perhaps invading Austria-Hungary—carrying the war, in other words, right into the heart of enemy territory.

The key to all of this was to gain a foothold close to the Dardanelles, and thus the plan began with a notion of a landing in Gallipoli, the peninsula at the tip of the Dardanelle Straits. Once a landing had been achieved there it was hoped that Allied armies might be able to then move up to invade the rest of Turkish territory, occupy the capitol of Constantinople to the northeast, and be in a position to strategically change the outcome of the war. This plan was championed on the part of both the British and the French by those people who were called Easterners, those who, in the debate about how best to fight the war, were convinced that there were other options in addition to slugging it out on the Western Front. And they proposed the attack upon Gallipoli, the opening up of the Dardanelles, the seizure of this territory, as perhaps the decisive key to victory in the war.

Among those champions was a man who would later play a very important role in world history, the British First Lord of the Admiralty, Winston Churchill. The Gallipoli plan might very well, if it had succeeded—in one of these great what ifs, one of the hypotheticals of the conflict—might very well have changed the outcome of this conflict. Indeed, military historians who admire this sort of breadth of vision and ambition that the Gallipoli plan represented have sometimes called the Gallipoli Campaign the only true strategic idea of the war, the only truly revolutionary notion that might have changed its outcome.

Unfortunately, bold as the plan was and high as the stakes were, the practice fell far short. Efforts to force the straits by battleships failed; and in fact, these first attacks ended up alerting Turkish forces that something larger was coming. The element of surprise was lost. Turkish forces, which earlier had not been in force in some of the areas that might have formed the target for a successful landing, were now alerted to the fact that an attack was coming. They began to fortify, to build trenches, and to mass in great numbers to repel an assault that they now understood was coming. They did so under Otto Liman von Sanders, the German commander of a Turkish army, which was defending Gallipoli.

The major landing—which unfortunately now advance warning had been given of it to the Turks—the major landing began on April 25, 1915. French and British forces, by sea, mounted an invasion and landed at Cape Helles, and Australian and New Zealand troops, popularly known as Anzac units, landed at Anzac Cove. They landed successfully, but due to confused orders and just the confusion of the situation itself—a lack of a sense of urgency on the part of commanders, we now see with perfect hindsight, an initial window of opportunity to turn these landings into expanded beachheads and to really secure a position—this opportunity was squandered. The Allied forces now discovered that Turkish troops were shooting down at them from positions atop the cliffs where they had dug in, and the Allies faced the obvious situation of having no alternative but to dig in themselves to create trenches and to fight it out. In a bizarre set of circumstance, a bizarre set of events, the result was that here at Gallipoli, one very nearly recreated the stasis, the deadlock, the trench warfare of the Western Front, but in hot miserable conditions.

Among the Turkish troops who were organizing the defense atop the cliffs and throwing back repeated attempts by the Allies to take the heights, was a young officer, a young man by the name of Mustafa Kemal—who later under the name of Atatürk would become the leader of a new, revived, nationalist Turkey that emerged after the first World War out of the ruins of the Ottoman Empire—was leading this defense. He, too, was a determined Young Turk, and he was doing his part for the national defense. The entire dynamics of the long drawn out campaign, which left Allied forces essentially stranded at their initial beachheads, unable to expand them, unable to advance, once again provided a demonstration, if such a demonstration was needed, of the advantages of the defensive side that we've already talked about in an earlier lecture on the dynamics of the Western Front. The British commander of this operation, Sir Ian Hamilton, renewed assaults in August 1915, and new landings took place Suvla Bay to the north of the initial landing spots; but these, too, did not succeed. News of disaster filtered back to Britain. When it did so, Hamilton was removed, and through December troops were withdrawn quietly and in secret. Through subterfuge, through successful attempts to fool the Turkish forces into the thinking that allied troops were still there in strength, the evacuation operation, in such complete contrasts to the landings and the invasion itself, was remarkably successful, and was finished by January 9, 1916.

But what of the outcomes? What of the results that followed upon such ambitions for what this operation was supposed to bring? It's estimated that some 200,000 Allied men died in this futile expedition. The fighting had been of enormous scale, reflecting the stakes, it had involved a million men on both sides and the question now arose: who was to blame? One man in particular who on the British side was blamed for having supported this venture to begin with was Winston Churchill. He was disgraced; he was blamed for the misadventure having supported it to begin with, and lost his position. Later, he would go on to become the determined leader of the British war effort in the Second World War, but it would take his political career a long time to recover from this fatal association with the disaster of the invasion of Gallipoli.

The Anzac troops—the Australian and New Zealand forces that had been shipped to participate in this fighting—had suffered enormous losses. This was but of a piece of their tremendous sacrifices in the war as whole. During the war, they took, it's estimated, 62% casualties. The Gallipoli disaster, however, took on a special significance in the collective memory of Australians as well as New Zealanders of their participation in the First World War. The Gallipoli disaster came to be considered the founding experience of independent Australian identity, and New Zealand identity, as well. The notion was that in this act of sacrifice, Australians and New Zealanders had shown themselves to be loyal sons of empire, yes, but also sticking together as comrades and as friends had revealed themselves to be new nations that had a right to independence and a separate identity, as well. Anzac Day, April 25th of every year, is still celebrated of precisely this searing experience in Australia. What this failure also made clear was that ultimately this had not proved to be the back door, the decisive strategic outcome. The failure made clear the decision would have to be reached elsewhere, probably on the Western Front.

We want to pursue now events happening further west in the Mediterranean and that is Italian participation in the war. When the First Word War had broken out, Italy had announced it was not bound to its obligations to the Central Powers as a result of the earlier Triple Alliance that it had participated in, and instead Prime Minister Antonio Salandra insisted that Italy would follow what he called "sacred egoism," a defense of its own interest, and a waiting to see which side it might ultimately make most sense to adhere to. What resulted was perhaps a not very noble performance, as a bidding war grew up on both sides, by the Central Powers—that's to say Germany and Austria-Hungary—and by the Allies—France, Great Britain, and Russia—for the prize Italian participation or neutrality.

In this auction for Italian participation, the Allies ultimately were the winners, and the reason for this in retrospect was quite obvious. On the one hand, precisely the Italians coveted what was held by Austria-Hungary. Austria-Hungary and Germany were not in a position to offer nearly as much, or weren't willing to offer nearly as much as the Allies could. The Allies were in this position of being able to promise enemy territory at the expense of their foes, and thus could be far more expansive, far more generous, and ultimately won this competition. But the diplomacy had proceeded in secret precisely, I think, because so many diplomats felt that the terms, if they became public, would just unseemly to too many people.

The result was the signing of the secret Treaty of London between the Allies and Italy. This was signed on April 26, 1915. The promises, while not very noble or idealistic, were extensive. Italy was promised ethnically Italian areas—those places that were considered by Italian nationalists to be *Irredenta* the unredeemed ethnic territories where Italian speakers lived that were still under the Austro-Hungarian rule in Trentino and Trieste—but also larger holdings of mixed populations where fewer Italians might live, larger gains in Tirol, in the mountainous areas, and the Dalmatian coast, and perhaps even new generous colonial gains in places like Asia Minor, currently held by the Ottoman Empire.

Many of these promises professed the more exalted Allied war aims of fighting for the civilization and for the right of small nations that we'll be discussing in a later lecture about war aims. But these secret promises would come back to haunt the Allies; they would later be a liability in public relations terms when the terms became clear. Nonetheless, with these new gains Italy now prepared to enter into the war. On May 23, 1915, Italy declared war on Austria-Hungary. Italian nationalists, and figures who praised war like the romantic poet Gabriele D'Annunzio and Futurist artists who had celebrated war as a form of necessary social hygiene and adventure, all celebrated this arrival at last of Italian participation. Not all Italians felt so, but certainly these nationalists—what one might call a delayed August Madness. The war experience of Italians that soon followed would probably quell some of that celebration.

Though Italian participation was thought to be a prize by the Allies who had bid so much for it, Italy in fact would soon discover that its fortunes in the war were not nearly so positive, and it would soon require Allied assistance. The Italian Commander, Count Luigi Cadorna, soon threw a million men into battle against Austria-Hungary on two fronts: toward alpine areas bordering Italy in the north, Trentino, and toward Trieste, across the Isonzo River to the east. In eleven battles on one spot on the Isonzo River, Italian forces attacked again and again and again, and yet were unable to break through enemy trenches. In 1916, the Italians took half-a-million casualties. A new kind of fighting also evolved in the Alps, and one of the themes of our course is the shock of the new. In this case this high-altitude fighting represented novelty in military history; guns and artillery had to be hauled up by pulleys to high vantage points dominating Alpine vistas. In this battle, glaciers could be turned into fortifications, and, in fact, fighting took place on glaciers. Trenches and tunnels were built through the ice of glaciers in what came to be called by Italian forces the "White War," up in the snowy Alps, war that for all of its modernity nonetheless could take primitive forms; when rifles froze, soldiers would be reduced to throwing rocks at one another in this high Alpine frozen fighting.

The Italian war effort took most definitely a turn for the worst with a great disaster, the defeat of Caporetto. In fall 1917, German troops had been moved in to reinforce and help the Austro-Hungarians, something that was happening with increasing frequency as the Austro-Hungarian war effort faltered. Among those special troops who were moved into to help was a soldier who would later become a famous commander in World War II, Erwin Rommel, who would become famous as the Desert Fox of the German African forces in World War II. He and other German troops, together with the Austro-Hungarians, attacked the Italian lines. In the Battle of Caporetto in October 1917, often called the Twelfth Battle of the Isonzo, Italian lines broke. A massive retreat set in and it was only halted at last some distance away at the Piave River, north of Venice. Entire Italian units simply surrendered. The Italians lost half a million casualties, and a quarter-million Italian prisoners were taken, testifying to a final breaking of morale. Ernest Hemingway's famous novel, *A Farewell to Arms*, talks precisely about this retreat, even though Hemingway himself had not experienced it—he arrived in the area six months later—it was very clear that the trauma of this experience was still present at the time. The retreat was halted as Italian forces regrouped 90 miles west of their initial position at the Piave River, to stand and defend the beautiful city of Venice. After this defeat, General Cadorna was replaced as commander in chief by General Armando Diaz, who didn't attempt any more foolhardy offensives, and instead stood, and the crisis passed.

Meanwhile, matters were turning worse it seemed for the Allied forces in other locations in the Balkans. Bulgaria had joined the Central Powers on September 6, 1915, in part because of promises made to it by Germany and Austria-Hungary of winning Serbian territory. The conquest of Serbia would not only finally settle the score that the Austro-Hungarians had initiated the conflict with, but also would ensure lines of communication open with the Turkish Ally of the Central Powers. In the winter of 1915, German, Austro-Hungarian, and Bulgarian armies finally overran Serbia in the course of two months. The capitol, Belgrade, was captured. In January 1916, the Central Powers invaded Montenegro, and moved into Albania. An Allied expedition, which tried to come to the aid of Serbia, found itself trapped in Salonika in Greece. In a dramatic and costly retreat—what's still remembered by Serbians as the Great Retreat—the Serbian army and Serbian government and the Serbian king marched across the Albanian mountains through the harsh terrain—and attacked by local forces—finally reaching the Adriatic Sea and where they evacuated by Allied navies. It is estimated that in this horrendous retreat Serbia lost tremendous casualties, and in the campaign as a whole it lost a sixth of its population.

Prematurely impressed by Russian successes in the Brusilov offensive that we had mentioned in our previous lecture on the Eastern Front, Romania had, as it turns out, with remarkably bad timing, entered the war on the Allied side in August of 1916, hoping that it might gain territory held by Austria-Hungary in Transylvania, in particular, where Romanians lived as a minority. Rather than gaining these contested territories, Romania found itself invaded a week later by the Central Powers. By December of 1916, the Central Powers, with General Falkenhayn, who earlier had commanded the entire German war effort and who now had been demoted to a regional command after General Hindenburg and Ludendorff had achieved the supreme command in Germany as a whole, vindicated his military talent by helping in the conquest of Romania. Romanian oil and agricultural resources now fell to the Central Powers, and in terms of economic warfare this turned out to be a significant gain. This is a case also where the action of secret agents turned out to be of importance as well, because British secret agents set about sabotaging the oil fields of Romania immediately before they fell into the hands of the Central Powers; they set the oil fields on fire, and the result was that at least some of these natural resources were lost for the German forces.

Finally we turn to the disappointment of Salonika. The Allies had sought to aid Serbia in its embattled position by sending in a military force through neutral Greece. Now notice please the irony of this situation, Britain and France among their war aims had denounced German violation of Belgian neutrality; in this case they weren't explicit about it and tried to veil it, another neutral country was finding its neutrality infringed upon. Allied forces were moved to Greece by October 1915, something that was quite controversial within Greece and Greek politics itself. The Greek prime minister, Eleuthérios Venizélos, cooperated with the Allies in this venture but, because of the frustration and the displeasure of his king, was soon deposed. Venizélos, however, even after he was removed as Prime Minister, gathered opposition forces around himself and set up a rival government opposed to King Constantine, who was more pro-German, who was finally forced to abdicate as a result of this pressure.

As a result of this tremendously complicated maneuvering of internal politics within Greece and Allied pressure from the outside— including something that many Greeks really resented, an Allied blockade of Greece to bring it to its senses from their political perspective—at long last Greece joined the Allies as a power, though not very enthusiastically, in June 1917. However, even as forces had been poured into Salonika in preparation for a mission to relieve Serbia, the results were disappointing.

These forces were unable to break the Bulgarian lines to the north that now were making common cause with the Central Powers. The result was that, even though many forces had been poured into to Salonika in order to aid the Balkan expedition, the result was that half-a-million Allied soldiers now found themselves trapped, idle, without a job, without an immediate military use. The Germans felt that Salonika was a grand joke, and they derisively call Salonika, in effect, the largest internment camp that the Central Powers had. The result that this promise, this lure of finding a way to open another front that might have plunged into the Central Powers from below, from what Winston Churchill would later call "the soft underbelly of Europe" on the southern front, had been frustrated. The decision would have to come elsewhere, and in part that decision would come through a clearer articulation of what was at stake in the war in terms of war aims that we'll be discussing in our next lecture.

Lecture Twelve
War Aims and Occupations

Scope:

This lecture first discusses the historical debates surrounding the war aims of the combatant powers. What goals did the Allies and the Central Powers pursue from the outset of the war? How did these goals change and evolve during the course of the conflict? We then turn to examine the experience of military occupation and how it affected civilian populations, including forced labor, deportations, ethnic manipulation, and harsh economic exploitation. The lecture surveys the brief Russian occupation of East Prussia and Galicia at the start of the war and then the longer German control of occupied Belgium and northern France and the atrocities that accompanied their initial seizure. Also surveyed is the Central Powers' rule over Eastern Europe in Poland, the Baltic region, Romania, and Serbia.

Outline

I. War Aims

   A. Prolonged warfare demanded the articulation of war aims on both sides that went beyond the initial rallying to a war of self-defense.

      1. Even among allies, individual war aims could conflict and threaten cohesion.

      2. Aims also changed under the pressure of circumstances.

   B. We start by examining the war aims of the Allied Powers.

      1. The Treaty of London of September 1914 committed France, Russia, and Britain not to sign a separate peace with the Central Powers.

      2. French war aims were seen as existential: as France had been invaded, Germany was to be expelled, the lost provinces of Alsace and Lorraine regained, and a future Germany weakened to the point that it would not again threaten France. France also envisioned colonial gains in Africa and the Middle East.

3. Russian war aims included plans for an expanded Poland (at the expense of Germany and Austria-Hungary) under Russian control and the fulfillment of a long-standing dream, the control of Constantinople and the Dardanelles, allowing unimpeded movement from the Black Sea to the Mediterranean.

4. British aims centered on restoration of the balance of power on the continent. Following British traditional strategy, leaders also hoped for colonial gains on the periphery.

5. Italy, with its policy of "sacred egoism" and signature on the Secret Treaty of London of 1915, demanded territory at the expense of Austria-Hungary along the Adriatic and in Asia Minor.

C. Let us now look at the war aims of the Central Powers.

1. As Germany dominated the Central Powers, its war aims took priority.

2. The war aims of Austria-Hungary were vague and simple survival was increasingly the overriding goal. Although Serbia was to be reduced in power, annexations were intensely problematic (as they would further increase the complexity of this diverse empire) and were resisted by the Hungarians in particular.

3. Germany's war aims included significant gains in Western and Eastern Europe.

4. Chancellor Bethmann-Hollweg's confidential September Program of 1914 outlined initial war aims (its precise intent is still debated).

5. In Eastern Europe, Poland was to come under German control, with a border strip carved from this territory to give strategic security. Russia was to be pushed back in Eastern Europe.

6. Annexationist plans called for control over the Baltic countries of Lithuania, Latvia, and Estonia.

7. In the West, annexationists demanded Luxembourg, territory in Belgium, and northern France.

8. An important concept in German war aims was the notion of constructing a unit called *"Mitteleuropa"* (central Europe), a continental economic union dominated by Germany.

9. The British naval blockade of Germany, which threatened to strangle it economically, gave added appeal to the *Mitteleuropa* concept.

10. German aims also included expanded colonial gains in Africa, establishing a *Mittelafrika* as a counterpart to domination of Europe.

11. In the 1960s, the Fischer Debate among historians also concerned questions of the continuity of German war aims in World War I and World War II. Fritz Fischer argued that there were linkages to Nazi goals.

12. However, within Germany itself, the government worried about the impact of open discussion of extreme war aims and tried to silence it.

II. Changing War Aims

A. The British and French agreed in March 1915 to Russian demands for Constantinople and the Dardanelles. This agreement represented a fundamental shift in traditional diplomacy, especially for Britain, which had long resisted this aim.

B. Germany and Austria-Hungary held conflicting views of the future of Poland.

C. In a fascinating and perverse process, some German annexationists increased their demands as the war continued, arguing that this proved the need for larger gains.

III. Occupations

A. In general, occupations of enemy territory increasingly brought total war home to civilian populations.

1. Civilians were exposed to mistreatment, deportation, forced labor, and other trends intensified in World War II.

2. In longer occupations, complex forms of social interaction could grow up between occupiers and occupied.

B. We begin with the Russian occupations of East Prussia and Galicia.

    1. The brief Russian occupation of East Prussia in 1914–1915 traumatized the population and was marked by sporadic brutalities.

    2. The Russian occupation of Galicia from 1914–1915 saw pogroms against Jews and deportations of civilians, as part of larger plans for the incorporation of the area into the Russian Empire.

    3. In both cases, scorched earth policies in retreat took a further toll.

C. Occupied Belgium was a classic case as well.

    1. The initial invasion of Belgium was marked by German atrocities.

    2. Some 800,000 Belgians fled and lived as refugees or "displaced persons" in France, Britain, or Holland.

    3. An electrified fence was erected in an attempt to close off the Dutch border.

    4. Economic exploitation through requisitions and forced labor was intense.

    5. Attempts to manipulate the Flemish or Wallonian segments of Belgian society failed.

D. France represented another area of occupation in the West.

    1. German atrocities had also taken place at the start of the invasion of 1914.

    2. Ten French departments fell under German control.

    3. Under an occupation similar to Belgium, the French suffered a double agony of foreign rule and isolation from the home country.

E. Eastern Europe under the Central Powers suffered greatly.

    1. Poles, living under three empires, found themselves forced to fight on opposite sides (1.5 million Poles served in the different armies).

    2. The conquest of Poland was accompanied by the destruction of the towns of Kalisz and Czestochowa.

    3. Poland was divided into two governments under the Germans and the Austro-Hungarians.

4. The establishment of a Polish kingdom was declared in November 1916, as the German command hoped to muster a Polish army to fight for the Central Powers, but the result was disappointing.

5. Polish political leaders were themselves divided on which side to favor in the war.

6. A socialist, Józef Piłsudski, at first cooperated with the Austro-Hungarians in creating Polish legions but later resisted growing German control and was imprisoned in 1917.

7. Roman Dmowski, leader of the National Democratic Party, favored the Allies and with the famous pianist Paderewski promoted the Polish cause in the West.

8. In the territory of the Baltic countries and Belarus, a German military colony called Ober Ost was established. In this military utopia, ambitions for control of populations and cultural and ethnic manipulation took on vast proportions.

9. German views of Eastern Europe were conditioned by the devastation of the region. The remnants of the scorched earth policy, disease, ethnic variety, and disorganization were seen as *Unkultur*, which needed to be redeemed by a German cultural mission.

10. Harsh policies of economic control and requisition alienated the native populations.

11. The Central Powers occupied most of Romania in the winter of 1916, and it became a German economic colony, yielding food and oil.

12. Serbian civilians suffered tremendously in the successive invasions by the Central Powers. The country was divided into Bulgarian and Austro-Hungarian zones, which saw armed resistance.

IV. International Relief Efforts

   A. International efforts were organized to bring relief and food to Belgium.

      1. An American engineer of great managerial talents, Herbert Hoover, coordinated the Commission for Relief in Belgium.

2. This organization aimed to feed 10 million people.

3. These and other efforts brought Belgium more than 3 million tons of food aid.

B. War-torn areas in Eastern Europe were harder to bring assistance to, but efforts were expanded there at the end of the war by the American Relief Administration under Hoover.

Essential Reading:

Stéphane Audoin-Rouzeau and Annette Becker, *14–18: Understanding the Great War*, pp. 45–69.

Supplementary Reading:

Vejas Gabriel Liulevicius, *War Land on the Eastern Front: Culture, National Identity, and German Occupation in World War I.*

Helen McPhail, *The Long Silence: Civilian Life under the German Occupation of Northern France, 1914–1918.*

Questions to Consider:

1. After Germany, which Great Power had the most extensive war aims?

2. Did military occupations differ in Western Europe and Eastern Europe? If so, how?

Lecture Twelve—Transcript
War Aims and Occupations

In this lecture, we'll be examining war aims and the experience of occupation. It might be best to start with just a brief explanation of why it makes sense to view these two larger themes in conjunction, together with one another. In short, war aims were often about occupation, whether wanting to see one's own national soil freed of foreign occupation or the coveting of territory that was seen as necessary for national sovereignty, on the other hand. We might ask, in particular, why it is that it would be appropriate in this lecture to talk about war aims when we've already been discussing a considerable narrative of the history of the war itself. The short answer to this is that the war aims themselves, changed over time. It's truly fascinating to observe precisely the dynamics by which those war aims changed in response to the needs of public relations, as it became ever more important to explain to a public why it was that such sacrifices were necessary and how the pressure of events themselves could alter war aims, as well.

This lecture first discusses the historical debates concerning the war aims of the combatant powers. What goals did the Allies and the Central Powers pursue from the outset of the war? How did these goals change and evolve during the course of the conflict? Very often, occupations were involved precisely because the experience of occupation could shape war aims. Thus, we'll next turn to examine the experience of foreign military occupation, how it affected civilian populations, how it included forced labor, deportations, attempts at ethnic manipulation, and often, very harsh economic exploitation. This lecture will survey the brief Russian occupation of German territory of East Prussia and Austro-Hungarian Galicia at the start of the war, and then it will survey the much longer German control of occupied Belgium and northern France, with a little more detail added about the atrocities that accompanied their initial seizure and the Central Powers' rule over Eastern Europe in Poland, the Baltic region, Romania, and Serbia.

Prolonged warfare, in particular, demanded that the warring powers articulate their war aims and the purpose of what it was that populations were fighting for, in a way that went beyond the initial rallying to war of self-defense. In our discussion in this course about meanings assigned to the war, you'll recall that the notion of fighting for the defense of the fatherland or of one's home country had been the initial universal motivator at the start of the war in 1914; but as the war dragged on, it would increasingly be necessary to somehow give voice to larger purposes, larger causes, some transcendent meaning that would justify the horrors of the war as they continued. Even among allies, however, even among those who were fighting side by side—either in the Central Powers or the Allied Powers—individual war aims might not always correspond, even among friendly countries, and they could threaten the cohesion and the unity of a warring side. In the second case, as we'll see in today's lecture, the war aims could also have changed under the pressure of circumstances of a dynamic process that continued, as the war itself went along, which we'll see operating almost by a logic of its own.

Let's start by examining the war aims of the Allied Powers and then later turn to those of the Central Powers. The Allied Powers had, from the very start, committed themselves to a common agenda. It would still have to be fleshed out, still have to be set down in detail, but from the very beginning, they committed themselves to a common cause. The Treaty of London of September of 1914—not to be confused with The Secret Treaty of London, which brought Italy into the war later—but the September, 1914 Treaty of London, right at the start of the war, committed the Allies—France, Russia, and Britain—not to sign a separate peace with the Central Powers. They would all work towards and fight towards that peace and would dictate it together, rather than making a separate peace, which eventually a defeated Russia finds itself forced to do.

The individual war aims of these countries were different, even though they might correspond in the larger perspective. The French war aims were seen as very basic and existential. France had been invaded. France had been invaded by Germany. Germany was to be expelled from French territory. Beyond this, the long dream of regaining the lost provinces of Alsace and Lorraine, which had been taken from a defeated France by Germany after 1871, would at long last be regained; they would return to France. Precisely because the treacherous attack of 1914 had revealed French vulnerabilities, it was essential that the French war aims ran that a future Germany should be weakened, somehow. It should be weakened to the point where it could not again threaten France as it had in two wars in quick succession. France's war aims also came to envision colonial gains in Africa or the Middle East, at the expense of Ottoman Turkey. So there were other larger territorial and geopolitical issues involved, but in the French case, it was above all the war of national defense and the regaining of national territory that took priority.

Russian war aims were distinct. They included plans for an expanded Russian Empire. They included plans for an expanded Poland. Poland had been divided up among three empires—Prussia, Austria, and Russia—at the end of the 18th century. So Poland, which had been wiped off the map, had been divided up. The war aim of Russian was now to reunite this lost unity, not out of solicitousness for Polish independence—far from it—but instead to reunite this unit at the expense of Germany and Austria-Hungary, who would lose their Polish provinces. Instead, it would all come under Russian control and Russia itself would be expanded as an empire. Then, there was the fulfillment of a long-standing dream that we've already mentioned in our previous lecture, the long standing ambition of controlling the Dardanelles, the straits that allow access between the Black Sea and the Mediterranean, essential for Russian trade as well as the projection of military power. The control, as well, of the great capital of Constantinople with all of its imperial associations was also part of this dream.

British war aims were different. British war aims centered on restoration of the balance of power on the continent. British politicians were well aware of what it would mean if Imperial Germany crushed France and retained Belgium. Germany would now be the hegemony on the continent, and was sure to threaten Britain in a geopolitical way that wouldn't have been possible before. The restoration of the balance of power on the continent, however, while a very realistic geopolitical goal, was hardly the sort of thing that would set hearts aflame. Thus, this particular goal of achieving the restoration of the balance of power was couched in more idealistic and liberal terms. The slogan went up of a defense of international law, a defense of the neutrality and the rights of small nations like Belgium. This was a way of rephrasing, though more idealistically the concept of restoring a balance of power. A small nation like Belgium across the English Channel represented security for Britain. If those territories instead were under the control of a great and aggressive power like Imperial Germany, this would represent a threat. Britain also not only pursued this long standing diplomatic goal of insuring a balance of power on the continent—Great Britain had functioned as a balancer of the balance of power in centuries previous—it also pursued another traditional strategy of British politics. The aim was to not only restore the European balance of power, but perhaps also gain colonies or an aggrandizement of imperial territory on the peripheries of this conflict, as well; a traditional long standing aim.

We've mentioned already in a previous lecture, Italy's pursuit of its war aims. These had been defined by its policy of "sacred egoism" that kept it out of the war at first and then the Secret Treaty of London of 1915 had outlined Italy's demands for territory at the expense of Austria-Hungary along the Adriatic, and ambitions expanded colonial in Asia Minor as well. Very clearly, the forces of imperialism that had reigned in the latter part of the 19th century were alive and well.

Let's turn now to an examination of the goals of the Central Powers, by contrast. As Germany increasingly dominated the unequal partnership of the Central Powers, as it increasingly was the dominant in the pair of Germany and Austria-Hungary, its war aims took priority. The war aims of Austria-Hungary, by contrast, were at times quite vague, contrary, and increasingly they became more and more basic; they were simply surviving as a state. This became increasingly the overriding goal. Certainly Austria-Hungary had entered the war with the determination to settle accounts with Serbia. Serbia was to be reduced in power, and in terms of public relations, it was to be demonstrated by Austro-Hungarian victory that Austria-Hungary as an empire, as a state, as a Hapsburg, was certainly still a going concern. Beyond this, things became very problematic. Did Austria-Hungary want more territory? Did it want, for instance, to include or annex or occupy Serbia itself and incorporate it into its empire?

On the contrary, annexations or occupations and enlargement of imperial territory, in fact, were intensely problematic, because including more people with more ethnic diversity in what already was a tremendously complex and diverse empire of 12 major ethnic groups, would simply complicate matters further and perhaps make the empire finally unworkable politically. In particular, in the Austro-Hungarian partnership, the Hungarians as a ruling elite, in particular resisted any additions of other peoples—in particular,

Slavic peoples—to an expanded empire as they felt this would only dilute their own share of power and would endanger the empire as a whole. If Austria-Hungary's war aims were ambiguous and uncertain and increasingly basic, reduced to just surviving in some fashion, Germany's war aims were quite expansive. Germany's war aims included significant gains in Western and Eastern Europe and increasingly questions turned on, how expansive? Just how large would these gains be?

In particular, historians have spent a lot of debating, ever since the Fischer debate of the 1960s that we had outlined in an earlier lecture, about the causes of the First World War, just how extensive those war aims were. Historians have focused their debate on a document, the so-called September Program of 1914, which was outlined by Chancellor Bethmann-Hollweg of Germany, which set out initial war aims and these essentially dealt with security and expanded borders for Germany in the West and in the East. Now, historians have spent a lot of time debating whether this was intended as a thought experiment of what might be possible or whether these were minimal demands that would later grow or whether this was an attempt to strike a compromise between different political factions. Ultimately, however, German war aims were elaborated, and in later years grew in size and scope. In Eastern Europe, Poland was to come under German control, with a border strip carved from this territory to give Germany strategic security as a buffer zone, in essence. This, too, for many historians, struck a very ominous note, because that border strip was to be emptied of its Polish and Jewish populations who were to be expelled, in order to provide an empty area for German settlement and ethnic redrawing of borders. In some sense, this was, one could say, of an extremely tragic trend of the wholesale movement and expulsion of peoples. Russia itself was to be politically weakened and territorially pushed back in Eastern Europe, maybe even pushed back out of Eastern Europe.

The annexationist plans of the most rabid German nationalists also called for control over the Baltic countries that belonged to the tsarist empire at this point—Lithuania, Latvia, and Estonia. The latter two had ruling classes that were ethnically German, and thus it was hoped they might more readily come under German control. In the Western Europe, nationalist annexationists demanded a whole shopping list of territories—Luxembourg, territory in Belgium, northern France, industrial areas, coal mines—all of which it was announced was necessary strategically. In some cases, some of these annexations were already thinking about the next war. An important concept in German war aims, as they were articulated, as they were debated and thought about, was the notion of constructing a unit called *Mitteleuropa*, or Central Europe, around Germany. *Mitteleuropa*, or Central Europe, would be in essence a continental economic union dominated economically and politically by a powerful Germany at its center. There are those commentators with a wicked sense of humor who like to suggest that the European Union today could be described in very similar terms, but it's obvious that Prussian militarism gave a very distinctive flavor to this particularly for German domination of Europe. The British naval blockade of Germany that was starting to bite and to threaten to strangle Germany's modern economy—and we'll talk more about that in a later lecture—gave added appeal to the notion of Germany becoming the center of a free trade area, an integrated economic area that would allow it to be self-sufficient.

The war aims of some German nationalists and some military figures went beyond this, as well, to include expanded colonial gains as well; gains in Africa, where it was suggested that for the purposes of symmetry, perhaps one could establish a *Mittelafrika*, a Central Africa, under German control as a counterpart to domination of the European continent. In some sense, the war aims were seen as a chance to make up for the omissions of the pre-war years. The way in which Germany had been left out of the scramble for colonies might now be made good by energetic policy in the present. The Fischer Debate among historians from the 1960s that we described in an earlier lecture was in part so explosive, in part so prone to great passions on the part of those who were engaged in the debate, in part because Fischer suggested that there were long-range continuities revealed in German war aims. Fritz Fischer had argued that there was a continuity of German war aims from World War I to World War II. He argued that there were linkages between the aims of World War I to those later espoused by the radical, racist Nazi, and this was very clearly a significant historical assertion. However, within Germany's government itself at the time, it was clear that these debates that took place over the aims were just that; they were debates. There was no one monolithic opinion; in fact, the German government itself worried that a far too open discussion of war aims and especially the extremist war aims of ultra nationalists might very well represent a social danger. The presenting of Germany as fighting a war no longer of defense, but of expansive territorial gains, might very well start to break down the *Burgfrieden*, the internal truce that had played such an important role in cementing German determination back in 1914, and attempts were made in the first years of the war to silence or even to censor debate over war aims.

A crucial dynamic that we'll be examining later in the course as well, is how war aims could evolve and change. One example of this was the way in which the British and the French, in part to encourage their Russian ally who had experienced such setbacks in the first years of the war, the British and French agreed in March of 1915 to Russian demands for Constantinople and the Dardanelles. Especially in the case of traditional diplomacy, this represented really an epochal shift, a truly profound change to traditional diplomatic patterns and conventions. The British as a sea power had long resisted any such control of the Dardanelles and now, under the pressure of war, under the pressure of the demands of the moment, they changed this long-standing tradition. Another example of how the pressure of war itself might change war aims came with the Central Powers and the question of what future lay ahead for Poland. Germany and Austria-Hungary could not decide among themselves readily on this question. The Germans already were articulating the notion of a German-controlled Poland. Austria-Hungary suggested that since they already had Poles, they might very well be able to incorporate more of them into a new unit with the Austro-Hungarian Empire.

At the same time, there were conservatives, especially in Germany, who worried that Poland should simply not be incorporated into an expanded German Empire and thus dilute the purity or the homogeneity of the German Imperial population, but instead should simply be given back to Russia wholesale in order to not even have to deal with this problem of multi-ethnic populations. Nations held conflicting views of the future of Poland. Under the pressure of war, however, a new plan was put into action. Some German policy-makers would urge that Poles could be won for the side of the Central Powers to fight as allies or subordinates—something that we'll explore a little bit further in a moment. Then, finally, in a fascinating and perverse process, one could see how some German annexationists—even as the war continued, and in some cases recognizably started to go against Germany—some German annexations would actually increase their demands rather than scaling them back, because they argued that precisely the fact that war was not going well or was not to be won conclusively proved the need for larger gains once the war was brought to a successful conclusion. Almost by an internal logic that had little to do with rationality anymore, war aims could grow more expansive precisely as the passions of war increased.

Let's move to a consideration of occupations as these figured often among war aims. In general, occupations of enemy territory increasingly brought home total war as a lived reality to civilian populations. In occupations, civilians were exposed to mistreatment, deportation, forced labor, atrocities, and other trends that would intensify in the next total war, in World War II. At the same time, in longer occupations, complex forms of social interaction or coexistence could also grow up between occupiers and occupied, in some cases, including what later was called "collaboration." We'll start with the brief Russian occupations of territory of the Central Powers. The brief Russian occupation of East Prussia in 1914–1915 traumatized the population and was marked by sporadic brutalities. The Russian occupation of the territory Galicia owned by the Austro-Hungarian Empire from 1914–1915, actually saw pogroms against Jews and the deportations of civilians, as Russian authorities pursued larger plans for after the war, incorporating this area into the Russian Empire. In both cases, as Russian forces withdrew, scorched earth policies in retreat would take a further toll.

A truly classic case of occupation came in occupied Belgium under German control. The initial invasion of Belgium was marked by German atrocities that we have mentioned in earlier lectures. The fear of these events and later brutality and harshness of occupation, led some 800,000 Belgians to flee their homeland and live for the rest of the war as refugees or displaced persons in France, Britain, or Holland. The new measures—some of them very harsh—that the occupiers took started with the necessity of cordoning off so that such escape no longer became possible. An electrified fence was set up, which in uncanny ways, almost anticipates the Berlin Wall later in the century. This electrified border represented a current of 2,000 volts surging across wires on the border between Belgium and Holland, and more than 2,000 people died trying to cross it out of desperation in the course of the war. Economic exploitation, through requisitions of material and forced labor of Belgians, was also intense. German attempts to manipulate and to divide the society by splitting into Flemish or Wallonian segments of Belgian society, breaking along languages lines, failed.

Occupied France represented another area of occupation in the West. Germany, their atrocities, had also taken place at the start of the invasion of 1914 and had established a pattern of brutality. Ten French "departments," as these regions were called, fell under German control. Under an occupation similar to that of Belgium in terms of its intensity and exploitation, the French under German occupation suffered what one might call a double agony; foreign rule and isolation from the home country of which they couldn't receive news or communicate with readily.

Eastern Europe under the Central Powers was also an important area of military occupation. Poles, living under three empires at the start of the war—Austria-Hungary, Germany, and Russia—found themselves at the start of the war forced to fight on opposite sides. Consider the agony that comes with thinking that one's ethnic cousins might very well be across the front lines shooting at one another. It's estimated that 1.5 million Poles served in the different armies of Eastern Europe. The conquest of Poland was accompanied by the destruction of the towns and civilian centers of Kalisz and Czestochowa. Poland under occupation had divided into two governments; one under the Germans, the other Austro-Hungarians, who finally, at long last, agreed as part of a plan to exploit Poland's manpower, to the establishment of a Polish kingdom in November, 1916. The German command, in particular Ludendorff, hoped to muster a Polish army to fight for the Central Powers, but the result was disappointing. Polish political leaders who were being invited by the Germans to fight against Russia were themselves divided. On which side to favor in the war much depended on who they thought would win. A socialist leader, later a leader of Poland itself after it regained its independence, Józef Pilsudski, at first cooperated with the Austro-Hungarians in creating Polish legions. But, once it was clear that the Germans aimed to subordinate them to their control, he resisted and was imprisoned by the Germans in 1917. A representative of a different political faction took a different view. Roman Dmowski, the leader of the National Democratic Party, a nationalist and more ethnically-based group, favored the Allies and, with the famous pianist Ignace Paderewski, promoted the Polish cause in the West and won sympathy for Polish Independence.

In the territory of the Baltic countries and Belarus, a German military colony called Ober Ost was established. In this strange military utopia, ambitions for control of ethnic populations and cultural and ethnic manipulation took on vast proportions. German views of Eastern Europe were conditioned by and changed as a result of these experiences. German soldiers saw just how devastated the region was by scorched earth policy and disease. They were often disoriented by the ethnic variety of these regions, and disorganization and backwardness, as they saw it, of this region, which they often called by the word *Unkultur*, which scarcely needs translation—an absence of culture. These areas, some German planners hoped, could be redeemed by a German cultural mission of bringing civilization. The flip side of this allegedly generous cultural cultivation was harsh policies of economic control and requisition that ultimately tended to alienate the native populations under foreign rules. The Central Powers also occupied most of Romania in the winter of 1916, after Romania had ill advisedly entered the first World War with splendidly bad timing and Romania became a German economic colony, yielding food and oil to the war effort of the Central Powers. Serbian civilians, for their part also suffered tremendously in the successive invasions by the Central Powers. The country was conquered, divided into Bulgarian and Austro-Hungarian zones, and armed resistance of guerilla groups of determined fighters was seen there in this region, as well.

We'd like to conclude by surveying a, in many ways, more positive part of the record of life under military occupation. What we mean in particular, international relief efforts that aimed to aid those civilians who were living under the rigors of military occupation and economic exploitation. International efforts focused, first of all, for neutral powers to bring relief and food to Belgium. Poor little Belgium, brave little Belgium, as it was called, a victim at the start of the First World War, had mustered tremendous sympathy as a result of its suffering. Now a volunteer effort was underway to aid the Belgian civilian populations under German military occupation. This, of course, raised very serious political and perhaps even ethical issues.

If outside food aid was to flood into Belgium at a time when Germans were exploiting Belgium, economically wouldn't this indirectly, given the realities of total war and its all-encompassing nature, indirectly help the German war effort? The result was an attempt to very carefully calibrate international aid and to be scrupulously neutral in its disbursement and very careful and sensitive, diplomatically, in allowing aid to flow in to these ravaged areas. The right man for the job was an American engineer who had trained at Stanford, who was perhaps the ultimate embodiment at this time of an American can-do attitude. He was an American engineer of great managerial talents, Herbert Hoover, who later had an unfortunate career as America's President at a time of economic crisis during the Great Depression. Herbert Hoover, at this time, was recognized for his managerial talents and put in charge of coordinating the so-called Commission for Relief in Belgium—the CRB. This organization with food aid aimed to feed 10 million people in Belgium.

These and other efforts during the course of the war brought to poor little Belgium more than 3 million tons of food aid. And while it didn't certainly obviate all hunger, it clearly made the difference in the margin of survival to a great many people. War-torn areas in Eastern Europe, by contrast, were much harder to bring assistance to given their geographic remove, but efforts of the sort that had been pioneered in Belgium were expanded there as well at the end of the war by the American Relief Administration under Hoover, too. We've seen, in this lecture, some of the human consequences of war aims, as well as the phenomenon of military occupation. We'll be turning to the question of the human dimension of soldiers suffering, whether as victims on the battlefield or whether as prisoners of war, in our next lecture.

Timeline

1871 ....German Empire founded after Franco-Prussian War

1873 ....Three Emperors' League founded, including Germany, Austria-Hungary, and Russia

1878 ....Treaty of San Stefano; Congress of Berlin

1879 ....Dual Alliance of Germany and Austria-Hungary established

1882 ....Triple Alliance of Germany, Austria-Hungary, and Italy established

1887 ....Reinsurance Treaty signed by Germany and Russia

1890 ....Resignation of Bismarck

1894 ....Russian-French military alliance

1897 ....German *Weltpolitik* launched

1904 ....*Entente Cordiale* between Britain and France established

1904–1905 ....Russo-Japanese War

1905 ....Revolution of 1905 in Russia

1905–06 ....First Moroccan Crisis

1907 ....Triple Entente of France, Russia, and Great Britain established

1908 ....Bosnian Crisis

1912 ....First Balkan War

1913 ....Second Balkan War and London Conference

June 28, 1914 ....Archduke Franz Ferdinand assassinated in Sarajevo

July 5, 1914...............................German "blank check" to Austria-Hungary

July 23, 1914.............................Austrian ultimatum to Serbia

July 28, 1914.............................Austrian declaration of war on Serbia

July 30, 1914.............................Russian general mobilization

August 1, 1914..........................German declaration of war on Russia

August 2, 1914..........................German ultimatum to Belgium

August 3, 1914..........................German declaration of war on France; British ultimatum to Germany

August 4, 1914..........................German invasion of Belgium; British declaration of war on Germany

August 15, 1914........................Russian invasion of East Prussia

August 26–30, 1914...................Battle of Tannenberg in East Prussia

August 28, 1914.........................Naval Battle of Heligoland Blight

September 5–12, 1914...............Battle of the Marne

September 7–15, 1914...............Battle of the Masurian Lakes

October–November 1914............"Race to the Sea"

October 18–November 22, 1914 First Battle of Ypres

November 1914..........................Battle of Langemarck

November 14, 1914....................Holy War declared by Ottoman Turkey

December 24–25, 1914..............Christmas fraternization on Western Front

January 1915.............................German bombing of London by Zeppelins begins

April 22, 1915...........................German gas attack at Ypres

April 25, 1915 .... Armenian massacres in Ottoman Turkey begin

April 25, 1915–January 9, 1916. Gallipoli landings

April 26, 1915 .... Secret Treaty of London to bring Italy into the war

May 2, 1915 .... Central Powers break through at Gorlice-Tarnow

May 7, 1915 .... German submarine sinks the *Lusitania*

May 23, 1915 .... Italy enters the war on the Allied side

Summer 1915 .... German "Great Advance" into the Russian Empire

September 1915 .... Tsar Nicholas II takes over as commander in chief of Russian armies

September 6, 1915 .... Bulgaria joins the Central Powers

Winter 1915 .... Serbia overrun by Central Powers

February–March 1916 .... German forces on Western Front withdraw to Hindenburg Line

February 1916 .... Sykes-Picot Agreement on Middle East

February 21–November 1916 .... Battle of Verdun

April 24, 1916 .... Irish Easter Rising

May 31, 1916 .... Naval Battle of Jutland

June–August 1916 .... Brusilov Offensive on Eastern Front

July–November 1916 .... Battle of the Somme

August 27, 1916 .... Romania joins the Allies

August 29, 1916 .... Hindenburg and Ludendorff replace Falkenhayn in German Supreme Command

December 1916 ....Romania overrun by Central Powers; Lloyd George's War Cabinet installed

Winter–Spring 1917...................Turnip winter in Germany

February 1, 1917 ....Germany declares unrestricted submarine warfare

March 8, 1917 ....Women's protest march in Petrograd sparks revolution

March 15, 1917 ....Tsar Nicholas II abdicates; Provisional Government takes power

April–May 1917.........................Nivelle offensive in Champagne region; French army mutinies

April 3, 1917 ....Lenin arrives in Russia

April 6, 1917 ....The United States enters the war

July–November 1917 ....Third Battle of Ypres (Passchendaele)

October 1917..............................Battle of Caporetto

October 31, 1917.......................Balfour Declaration

November 1917..........................Clemenceau is appointed French prime minister

November 6–7, 1917..................Bolsheviks overthrow Provisional Government in Russia and take power

December 9, 1917 ....British forces capture of Jerusalem

January 8, 1918 ....President Wilson's Fourteen Points speech

March 3, 1918 ....Treaty of Brest-Litovsk

March 21, 1918 ....German spring offensive begins on Western Front

August 8, 1918 ...."Black Day of the German Army"

September–October 1918...........Bulgaria and Turkey leave the war

October 3–4, 1918......................German government requests armistice

October 24–November 1918......Battle of Vittorio Veneto

November 3, 1918......................Austro-Hungarian armistice with Allies

November 9, 1918......................Revolution in Germany; Kaiser is overthrown

November 11, 1918....................Armistice comes into effect on the Western Front at 11 A.M.

Fall 1918 ....Influenza epidemic spreads

January 1919 ....Spartakus uprising in Berlin

January 18, 1919 ....Paris Peace Conference opens

March 1919 ....Fascist movement launched in Italy

June 28, 1919 ....Versailles Treaty signed by German representatives

March 1920 ...............................U.S. Senate refuses to ratify Versailles Treaty

1922 ....Mussolini comes to power in Italy

January 30, 1933 ....Hitler becomes chancellor of Germany

September 1, 1939 ....World War II begins

This page intentionally left blank.

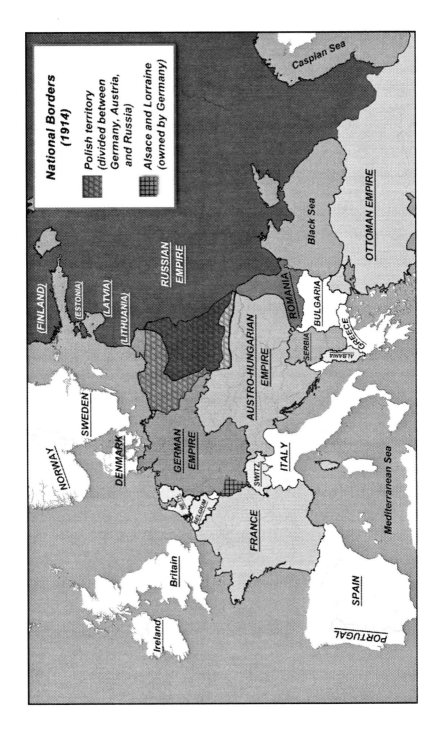

National Borders (1914)

Polish territory (divided between Germany, Austria, and Russia)

Alsace and Lorraine (owned by Germany)

©2006 The Teaching Company Limited Partnership

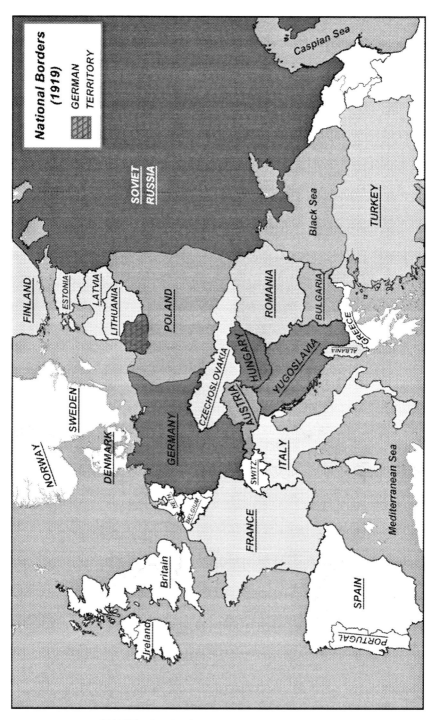

National Borders (1919)

GERMAN TERRITORY

Legend: Key Sites of World War I

Western Front

1. Amiens
2. Arras
3. Belleau Wood
4. Berlin
5. Cantigny
6. Caporetto
7. Champagne
8. Dover
9. Hamburg
10. Kiel
11. Langemarck
12. Liège
13. London
14. Louvain
15. Marne
16. Mons
17. Paris
18. Somme
19. St. Mihiel
20. Trentino
21. Trieste
22. Venice
23. Verdun
24. Ypres/Passchendaele

Other Fronts

25. Belgrade
26. Brest-Litovsk
27. Constantinople
28. Gallipoli
29. Grodno
30. Kaunas
31. Lemberg (Lvov)
32. Lublin
33. Moscow
34. Odessa
35. Prague
36. Przemysl
37. Riga
38. Salonika
39. St. Petersburg
40. Tannenberg
41. Vilnius
42. Warsaw

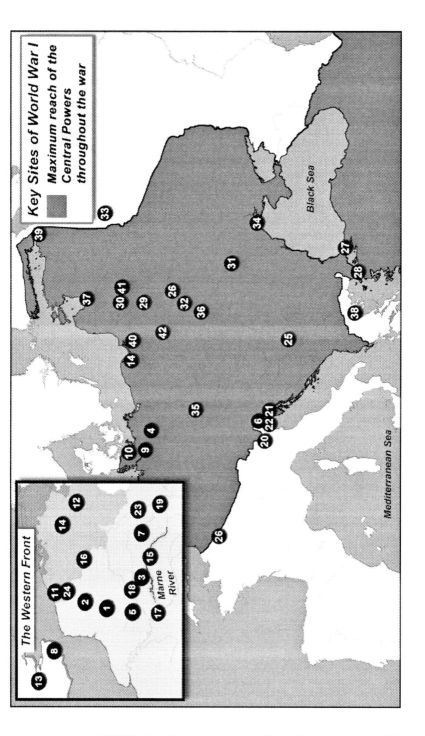

Glossary

A.E.F.: American Expeditionary Force.

Allies: At first called the *Entente* powers, Great Britain, France, and Russia (later joined by other countries) confronted the Central Powers.

Anzacs: The Australian and New Zealand Army Corps.

Arditi: Italian storm troopers; elite forces at the front.

Armistice: The ceasefire on the Western Front that came into effect on November 11, 1918, at 11 A.M.

Attrition: A key concept related to total war: the wearing down of enemy might rather than outright and decisive victory.

August Madness: Mass celebrations (though not universal) on the declaration of war in 1914.

Balfour Declaration: British declaration of October 31, 1917, offering support for the creation of a national Jewish homeland in Palestine.

Balkan Wars: Two wars in 1912 and 1913, which saw the expulsion of Ottoman Turkey from most of the Balkans, and further fighting among the Balkan states that showed the region's instability.

B.E.F.: The British Expeditionary Force, sent to the Western Front in August 1914; dramatically expanded during the course of the war.

Blockade: A crucial part of economic warfare, the British naval blockade kept raw materials from reaching Germany and exports from getting out.

Bolsheviks: Russian radical socialists led by Lenin who took power in November 1917.

Brest-Litovsk, Treaty of: Signed March 3, 1918; a harsh peace settlement imposed by Germany on defeated Russia.

Burgfrieden: The domestic truce declared in Germany at the start of the war.

Central Powers: Germany, Austria-Hungary, and Turkey, later joined by Bulgaria.

C.P.I.: Committee on Public Information; an agency established in the United States after the country entered the war; charged with producing effective and innovative internal prowar propaganda.

Cult of the Offensive: The prewar doctrines celebrating extreme attack as the moral key to victory.

Dardanelles: Narrow straits separating the Black Sea from the Mediterranean in Turkey; a coveted strategic point.

D.O.R.A.: Law passed in August 1914, giving British government expanded powers in domestic politics.

Doughboy: Archetypal name for the American soldier; its origin is unknown.

Entente Cordiale: 1904 French and British settlement of colonial conflicts.

Ersatz: German word for "substitute," denoting synthetic materials used in war economy or diet.

Fascism: Aggressive political movement founded in Italy in 1919, celebrating the state, leadership, and militarism.

Fatherland Party: German mass political movement founded in fall 1917 to call for war until total victory.

Firestep: Ledge in the trenches for marksmen.

Fourteen Points: U.S. President Woodrow Wilson's announcement of American war aims on January 8, 1918.

Freikorps: Brutal German mercenary units established in the aftermath of defeat in November 1918; they participated in civil war in Germany and adventured beyond its borders.

Frontschwein: Bitter German soldiers' self-designation, meaning "front swine."

Genocide: The extermination of a group of people because of who they are.

Hindenburg Line: Called the "Siegfried Line" by Germans, this was the fortified position to which German forces on the Western Front withdrew in February and March of 1917.

Hindenburg Program: Germany's massive economic and industrial mobilization program in fall 1916 under the wartime dictatorship of Generals Hindenburg and Ludendorff.

Irredenta: "Unredeemed territories" craved by nationalists (originally Italian, but the term later applies elsewhere).

July Crisis: The escalating political and military crisis following the assassination of the Archduke Franz Ferdinand of Austria-Hungary at Sarajevo in June 1914 that led to the outbreak of the First World War.

Kindermord: Grim German name given to the "slaughter of the innocents" at Langemarck in November 1914; celebrated in official propaganda.

"Live and let live system": Unofficial truces worked out in quieter sectors of the trenches across enemy lines to minimize combat.

Mitteleuropa: German war aim of a continental economic and political union led by Germany.

Nazism: A radical movement espousing "national socialism"; founded immediately after the war in defeated Germany and led to power in 1933 by Adolf Hitler.

No Man's Land: Blasted territory between the enemy trenches on the Western Front; the scene of raids and attacks.

Pacifism: Principled opposition to warfare for reasons of conscience.

Patriotic instruction: German propaganda campaign from summer 1917 for a "victory peace."

Peace Resolution: German parliamentary resolution of July 1917 by the Catholic and Social Democrat parties calling for peace without annexations or indemnities.

Plan XVII: French prewar military plan for invasion of Germany to recover the lost provinces of Alsace and Lorraine.

Poilu: French nickname for an ordinary soldier, meaning "the shaggy one."

Propaganda: The systematic shaping of political opinions.

Reds: Partisans of the international communism heralded by revolutionary Soviet Russia.

Reparations: Payments made by a defeated power in restitution for the damage of the war (all sides expected to make the enemy pay, but Germany ended carrying the burden).

Revolutionizing: Policy practiced on all sides of seeking to subvert enemy populations and disaffected minorities.

Schlieffen Plan: German secret plan for victory on two fronts, completed in 1905 by General Alfred von Schlieffen; it called for an attack on France through neutral territory.

Scorched earth: Policy of leaving an enemy only territory in a state of total devastation, stripped of resources.

Self-determination: The nationalist demand for independence by ethnic groups, endorsed by Woodrow Wilson's war aims.

Shell shock: Post-traumatic stress disorder; a phenomenon only slowly recognized as such during the war.

Socialism: Based on the ideas of Karl Marx; socialists (or social democrats) envisioned a world reshaped by the international supremacy of the working class.

Soviet: Russian word for "council"; such councils were democratic grassroots organizations made up of soldiers and workers and formed in revolutionary Russia.

Soviet Union: A new communist state (also U.S.S.R. for "Union of Soviet Socialist Republics") formed in 1922 from the wreckage of the Russian Empire by victorious Bolsheviks; led by Lenin.

Spanish Flu: Influenza epidemic that began at the close of the war, which killed an estimated 40 million people worldwide before fading in 1919.

Spartakus: A radical wing within the German S.P.D., later forming the German communist party in 1919 and leading a failed revolt.

S.P.D.: Germany's Social Democratic Party of Germany; founded in 1875 and a model for other socialists worldwide.

"Stab in the Back" legend: A German conspiracy theory that gained in popularity after the war, asserting that German troops had not been defeated on the battlefield but were betrayed by elements on the home front.

Storm Troopers: Elite troops (on all sides) using infiltration tactics to break through the trench stalemate.

Sykes-Picot Agreement: British and French secret agreement of February 1916, dividing the Middle East into respective spheres of influence.

Tommy Atkins: The archetypal name for the ordinary British soldier; in numbers, also called "Tommies."

Total war: A concept developed during the war to express the all-encompassing nature of the conflict, drawing in entire populations, economies, and societies.

Treaty of London: Secret agreement between the Allies and Italy, signed on April 26, 1915, bringing Italy into the war with promises of territory.

Trench community: The idea of a perfected model of comradeship allegedly evolving under fire.

Trenchocracy: The claim of front-fighters to a right to restructure politics along military lines because of their service and sacrifice.

Triple Alliance: From 1882, an alliance of Germany, Austria-Hungary, and Italy; when Italy dropped out, Germany and Austria-Hungary formed the core of the Central Powers.

Triple Entente: From 1907, the bloc of France, Russia, and Britain, which became the Allies in 1914.

U-Boats: German submarines, waging unrestricted submarine warfare from 1917.

Union Sacrée: French "sacred union" domestic truce from 1914.

Versailles: Treaty that the Allies signed with Germany on June 28, 1919, with restrictions on German armaments, loss of territory, reparations, and admission of German war guilt.

War Guilt Clause: Article 231 of the Versailles Treaty, by which Germany officially accepted responsibility for unleashing the war.

War Socialism: An ironic term to describe the movement toward increased government control and direction of wartime economies.

Weltpolitik: From 1897, aggressive German foreign policy claiming superpower status.

Whites: Antirevolutionary forces from a range of political orientations fighting against the Bolsheviks and other revolutionaries in Eastern and Central Europe from 1918.

Yellow Canaries: Young women working in British munitions factories, whose skin was discolored by chemicals.

Young Turks: Turkish nationalist revolutionaries seeking to modernize the Ottoman Empire on coming to power in 1908; increasingly coming under German influence.

Zeppelin: German airships developed in 1900 and used for bombing during the war.

Biographical Notes

Bethmann-Hollweg, Theobald von (1856–1921): Devoted Prussian civil servant and German chancellor from 1907 to 1917. His role in the outbreak of the war is strongly debated by historians, as is his September 1914 program of war aims. Any attempts at moderation he exercised were ended when the German general command had him removed from office as insufficiently committed to total victory.

Churchill, Winston (1874–1965): Descendant of a famous British political family, he began his career in politics as a member of the Conservative Party but later became a member of the Liberal Party. In 1911, he was made First Lord of the Admiralty. His support for the 1915 Gallipoli campaign ended in disaster for which he was blamed. Losing his position, he fought on the Western Front before returning to government in 1917. In World War II, Churchill would rally Britain against the Axis Powers.

Clemenceau, Georges (1841–1929): French radical politician nicknamed "The Tiger" for his determination and strength of character. Appointed prime minister of France in November 1917, Clemenceau established control over the war effort on the principle that "war is too important to be left to the generals." He rallied French morale during the war and at negotiations for the Versailles Treaty, took an uncompromisingly hard line against defeated Germany.

Conrad von Hötzendorf, Count Franz (1852–1925): Austro-Hungarian chief of staff from 1906 and a fierce advocate of preemptive war. His war plans at the start of the conflict degenerated into confusion, facing two fronts (Russia and Serbia). As Germany came to dominate the military partnership, assuming command over the Central Powers in September 1916, Conrad was increasingly sidelined and removed in March 1917.

Falkenhayn, Erich von (1861–1922): German general and Prussian minister of war from 1913, replacing General Helmuth von Moltke as German chief of staff after the failure of the Schlieffen Plan in September 1914. Discerning the outlines of the emerging war of attrition, Falkenhayn believed a decision would come on the Western Front. The 1916 Battle of Verdun did not bring the expected results, and as a consequence of this failure and the entry of Romania into the war against Germany, Falkenhayn was replaced (after extensive political intrigues and pressure) by General Paul von Hindenburg in August of 1916. Afterwards, Falkenhayn led German forces in the conquest of Romania and in Turkey and Palestine.

Foch, Ferdinand (1851–1929): Marshal of France and commander in chief of Allied armies. As a military instructor before the war, he was associated with the cult of the offensive. In March 1918, he was made the first commander in chief of Allied armies in France, guiding overall strategy. After the failure of the German spring offensive of 1918, Foch led Allied armies on the march toward Germany.

Haig, Sir Douglas (1861–1928): British field marshal. Still a controversial figure, Haig's training was in the use of cavalry, and his experience before 1914 had been in colonial wars. He was put in charge of the British Expeditionary Force from December 1915. Seeking to achieve a breakthrough, Haig led the British efforts at the Somme (July–November 1916) and at Passchendaele (July–November 1917), with vast losses for little result. Debate continues about his role and decisions.

Hindenburg, Paul von (1847–1934): German field marshal and president. Descendant of an ancient Prussian noble family, Hindenburg had retired from his military career by 1911 but in August 1914 was brought back to lead German forces at the Battle of Tannenberg. This and subsequent victories on the Eastern Front made him a war hero to Germans, who called him the "Savior of East Prussia" and "Terror of the Russians." With his associate Erich Ludendorff, he was elevated to the German high command in August 1916, taking over from Erich von Falkenhayn. Hindenburg and Ludendorff created what was essentially a military dictatorship, increasingly dominating politics and economic direction. When opposed, Hindenburg would threaten to resign. With the collapse of the German war effort in 1918, he denied any responsibility and continued to be popular among Germans. In the postwar Weimar Republic, he was elected president in 1925. Despite his abiding dislike for Hitler, Hindenburg made him chancellor in 1933.

Joffre, Joseph Jacques (1852–1931): Commander in chief of French armies. Already a soldier of long experience, Joffre commanded French forces resisting the initial onslaught of the

German armies, who were seeking to enact the Schlieffen Plan. The confrontation ended with the "Miracle on the Marne" in September 1914. Joffre's calm confidence became legendary and was very much needed at the time. Failures in the defense of Verdun led to his replacement by Nivelle in December 1916.

Kitchener, Lord Horatio (1850–1916): A famed soldier of British colonial wars who was made secretary of state for war in August 1914. After the heavy losses of the British Expeditionary Force, Kitchener appealed for a mass volunteer army. His popularity produced a massive wave of recruitments, and his person came to symbolize for many British wartime determination. Traveling to Russia in 1916, Kitchener's ship was sunk, and he drowned.

Lenin, Vladimir Ilyich (1870–1924): Russian revolutionary leader of the radical Bolshevik wing of the Social Democrats. Lenin championed the concept of a "vanguard party" of professional revolutionaries catalyzing upheaval. The outbreak of the war left him impatient in exile, until German officials intending to "revolutionize" Russia arranged to ship him back to Petrograd in April 1917. Once there, Lenin preached "revolutionary defeatism" and led the Bolshevik seizure of power in November 1917, overthrowing the fragile liberal provisional government. Expecting the imminent outbreak of worldwide revolution, Lenin negotiated peace with the Germans. Disappointed by the delay in global revolution, Lenin built up the Soviet dictatorship. After his death in 1924, his associate Stalin achieved control.

Ludendorff, Erich (1856–1937): A nervous, ambitious, and brilliant German military planner of middle-class origins who represented a new type, the military technocrat with political ambitions. He gained fame for the capture of the citadel of Liège in Belgium and was made second in command to General Paul von Hindenburg on the Eastern Front in August 1914. In the captured territories of Eastern Europe, he constructed a military utopia named "Ober Ost." Elevated to the supreme command with Hindenburg in August 1916, he directed Germany's war effort. With defeat in 1918, Ludendorff denied his responsibility and fled into exile. After the war, he spread the "Stab in the Back" legend and became an associate of Hitler's.

Lloyd George, David (1863–1945): British prime minister. Nicknamed the "Welsh Wizard," Lloyd George was a prominent leader of the radical wing of the Liberal Party in Britain. Appointed to head the new munitions ministry in May 1915, he worked to mobilize the economy for war. Lloyd George became prime minister of a coalition cabinet in December 1916. Through the war, he sparred with military leaders over the conduct of the conflict. Enjoying public popularity, he was reelected in 1918 and played an important role in the Versailles Treaty negotiations, seeking to mediate between France and the United States.

Nicholas II (House of Romanov) (1868–1918): Ill-fated Tsar of the Russian Empire. Nostalgic for the order of autocracy, Nicholas did a bad job of adjusting to the modern challenges increasingly facing his empire. When war broke out, he met it with fatalistic resignation. His royal household fell under the influence of a disreputable holy man, Rasputin. In a crucial mistake, in September 1915, Nicholas II took over personal command of the Russian armies and was afterwards held responsible for their failures. Surprised by the March 1917 revolution, Nicholas abdicated. Captured by the Bolsheviks, the Tsar and his family were executed in July 1918.

Nivelle, Georges Robert (1856–1924): French military commander. After successes at recapturing territory at Verdun, Nivelle replaced Joffre as French commander in chief in December 1916. Promising astonishing results with the Nivelle offensive of April 1917, the disappointment was cruel when these failed. When mutinies spread, the disgraced Nivelle was replaced with Pétain.

Pershing, John Joseph (1860–1948): Commander of the American Expeditionary Force from May 1917, after extensive earlier military experience in Cuba, the Philippines, and Mexico. When American forces were brought to France, Pershing rejected plans for dividing them up as reinforcements for existing Allied armies. Instead, his aim was to keep them as a coherent force, in line with American status as an "Associate Power."

Pétain, Henri-Philippe (1856–1951): French military leader who gained fame and the devotion of French troops for the defense of Verdun from February 1916. Contrary to the cult of the offensive, Pétain emphasized the role of defense and was viewed as a commander who cared for his soldiers. Made commander in chief in May 1917, after mutinies in the French army, he quelled these and reassured the troops. During World War II, Pétain headed the Vichy government in unoccupied France, collaborating with the Germans, and was tried after the war.

Trotsky, Leon (1879–1940): Revolutionary from the Russian Empire, famous for his charisma and oratory. After living in exile in the United States, Trotsky returned to Russia in 1917 and joined Lenin's Bolsheviks. He led negotiations with the Germans at the Treaty of Brest-Litovsk and became commissar of war, organizing the Red Army. In the succession struggle after Lenin's death in 1924, Trotsky lost out to his rival Josef Stalin and was killed in Mexico in 1940 by a Soviet assassin.

Wilhelm II (House of Hohenzollern) (1859–1941): *Kaiser* (Emperor) of Germany and King of Prussia. Wilhelm's bluster and militaristic posturing, likely deriving from personal insecurities, led to the dismissal of Chancellor Otto von Bismarck in 1890, an aggressive foreign policy after 1897, and Germany's growing isolation internationally. His unpredictable character was said to be the perfect symbolic embodiment of the German Empire itself. Though demonized in Allied propaganda as the diabolical "Kaiser Bill," Wilhelm II was in fact increasingly sidelined in German politics by the silent dictatorship of Hindenburg and Ludendorff. With Germany's defeat, he fled to exile in Holland in November 1918 and lived out the rest of his life there despite attempts by the Allies to bring him to trial as a war criminal.

Wilson, Woodrow (1856–1924): American academic, university president, and progressive politician who became President of the United States in 1913. At first pursuing a neutral stance for the United States, Wilson sought to mediate among the warring powers after 1914. Public outrage against Germany, especially in response to its submarine warfare and attempt to start a revolution in Mexico with the Zimmermann Telegram, led Wilson to ask Congress to declare war against Germany in April 1917. The United States joined the Allies as an "Associate Power," to underline its independence, a stance further emphasized in Wilson's Fourteen Points speech on January 8, 1918, outlining American war aims to expand democracy and build a new international politics. Wilson traveled to Versailles to share in the negotiations for the peace treaty and the establishment of the League of Nations, but domestic opposition and his own intransigence led to the failure of his plans.

Bibliography

Essential Reading:

Audoin-Rouzeau, Stéphane and Annette Becker. *14-18: Understanding the Great War*. Trans. by Catherine Temerson. New York: Hill and Wang, 2002. A brief but marvelously stimulating discussion of new insights into the war from recent scholarship.

Eksteins, Modris. *Rites of Spring: The Great War and the Birth of the Modern Age*. Boston: Houghton Mifflin, 1989. An insightful, provocative study of the cultural impact of the war. Reviewers either loved or hated it.

Ellis, John. *The Social History of the Machine Gun*. Baltimore: Johns Hopkins University Press, 1975. A classic work on the relationships among technology, society, and war.

Fritzsche, Peter. *Germans into Nazis*. Cambridge, MA: Harvard University Press, 1998. Forceful, evocative argument that German society underwent a populist mobilization beginning in 1914 that would be exploited by the Nazis to come to power.

Fussell, Paul. *The Great War and Modern Memory*. London, New York: Oxford University Press, 1975. A pioneering and indispensable work on the cultural impact of the war on Great Britain and its rich literary tradition, arguing that the war was a clear watershed.

Jünger, Ernst. *The Storm of Steel: From the Diary of a German Storm-Troop Officer on the Western Front*. New York: Howard Fertig, 1996. This diary, first published in 1919, makes for disturbing but gripping reading.

Keegan, John. *The First World War*. New York: Knopf, 1999. Authoritative study of World War I by a master of military history.

Kennedy, David M. *Over Here: The First World War and American Society*. New York: Oxford University Press, 1980. Rich overview of the war's impact on the United States.

Mack Smith, Denis. *Mussolini: A Biography*. London: Weidenfield and Nicolson, 1981. Considered one of the best political biographies ever written, a detailed record of the dictator's complicated political trajectory.

MacMillan, Margaret. *Paris 1919: Six Months That Changed the World*. New York: Random House, 2002. A wonderful combination of narrative history with diplomatic detail.

Mombauer, Annika. *The Origins of the First World War: Controversies and Consensus*. London: Longman, 2002. Useful summary of interpretations of the origins of the war and the history of the debates that followed.

Morrow, John H., Jr. "The War in the Air," in Hew Strachan, ed., *World War I: A History* (Oxford: Oxford University Press, 1998): 265–277. Brief summary of a larger field of scholarship.

Mosse, George. *Fallen Soldiers: Reshaping the Memory of the World Wars*. Oxford: Oxford University Press, 1990. A classic work by a pioneering cultural historian, analyzing how war experience and the figure of the volunteer were mythologized.

Roshwald, Aviel. *Ethnic Nationalism and the Fall of Empires: Central Europe, Russia, and the Middle East, 1914–1923*. London: Routledge, 2001. A valuable comparative study of how empires collapse.

Strachan, Hew. *The First World War*. New York: Viking, 2003. Wonderful recent one-volume treatment of the conflict.

Strachan, Hew, ed. *World War I: A History*. Oxford: Oxford University Press, 1998. A marvelous and well-illustrated collection of essays on different aspects of the war.

Taylor, A. J. P. *The First World War: An Illustrated History*. New York: Perigree Books, 1980. In Taylor's characteristically provocative style, an iconoclastic and darkly humorous brief account of the folly of the war.

Winter, Jay. *Sites of Memory, Sites of Mourning: The Great War in European Cultural History*. Cambridge: Cambridge University Press, 1995. The best book on the aftermath of the war and its cultural impact.

Supplementary Reading:

Arendt, Hannah. *The Origins of Totalitarianism*. New York: Harcourt, Brace, 1951. Classic political philosophy with theoretical explanations for totalitarian movements arising after World War I. Likely to be read centuries from now to understand the age.

Barbeau, Arthur E. *The Unknown Soldiers: Black American Troops in World War One*. Philadelphia: Temple University Press, 1974.

Study of a crucial timepoint in the evolution of American racial relations.

Barry, John M. *The Great Influenza: The Epic Story of the Deadliest Plague in History*. New York: Penguin, 2004. Gripping account of the pandemic, set against a history of science background.

Bartov, Omer. *Mirrors of Destruction: War, Genocide, and Modern Identity*. New York: Oxford University Press, 2000. Unflinching dissection of the extreme violence latent in modern industrial societies and their wars.

Bessel, Richard. *Germany after the First World War*. New York: Oxford University Press, 1993. Richly detailed and fascinating history of postwar Germany.

Bourke, Joanna. *Dismembering the Male: Men's Bodies, Britain, and the Great War*. Chicago: University of Chicago Press, 1996. Innovative study of the physical impact of the war and its implications as to how masculinity was understood.

Britain, Vera. *Testament of Youth: An Autobiographical Study of the Years 1900–1925*. New York: Penguin, 1994. One of the classic memoirs of the war by a nurse who served on numerous fronts from 1915.

Chickering, Roger. *Imperial Germany and the Great War, 1914–1918*. Cambridge: Cambridge University Press, 1998. Outstanding brief overview of German experience in the war.

Cornwall, Mark. *The Undermining of Austria-Hungary: The Battle for Hearts and Minds*. New York: St. Martin's Press, 2000. A valuable study of the disintegration of the volatile elements of the Habsburg Empire.

Davis, Belinda. *Home Fires Burning: Food, Politics, and Everyday Life in World War I Berlin*. Chapel Hill: University of North Carolina Press, 2000. Insightful examination of home-front realities in a European capital at war.

Ellis, John. *Eye-Deep in Hell: Trench Warfare in World War I*. New York: Pantheon Books, 1976. Excellent account of experience in the front lines.

Ferguson, Niall. *The Pity of War: Explaining World War I*. New York: Basic Books, 1999. Economic historian's provocative theses, revisiting continuing debates on the war.

Fitzpatrick, Sheila. "The Civil War as a Formative Experience," in Abbott Gleason, Peter Kenez, and Richard Stites, eds., *Bolshevik Culture: Experiment and Order in the Russian Revolution* (Bloomington: University of Indiana Press, 1985): 57–76. Summation of the impact of the civil war on Bolshevik self-understanding.

Gilbert, Martin. *Atlas of World War I*. New York: Oxford University Press, 1994. This very useful reference tool goes beyond maps of battlefields to depict war aims, economics, and diplomacy.

Graves, Robert. *Goodbye to All That*. Revised second edition. New York: Anchor, 1957. A great memoir of the war, capturing the mood of intense disillusion felt by so many.

Grayzel, Susan R. *Women and the First World War*. London: Longman, 2002. Concise overview of an enormous and important topic, covering women's work, daily lives, protests, and the impact of the war.

Harris, Robert and Jeremy Paxman. *A Higher Form of Killing: The Secret History of Chemical and Biological Warfare*. Second edition. New York: Random House, 2002. Broader history of chemical warfare and the origins of gas weapons.

Hasek, Jaroslav. *Good Soldier Svejk and His Fortunes in the World War*. Trans. by Cecil Parrott. New York: Penguin, 1974. A comic classic of world literature, unfortunately less known in the West, of the archetypal "little guy" (the Czech soldier Svejk) frustrating the high and mighty.

Healy, Maureen. *Vienna and the Fall of the Habsburg Empire: Total War and Everyday Life in World War I*. Cambridge: Cambridge University Press, 2004. Valuable new scholarship on the home front of a cosmopolitan capital in a disintegrating empire.

Herwig, Holger. *The First World War: Germany and Austria-Hungary 1914–1918*. New York: Arnold, 1997. Unrivalled detailed study of the war efforts of these Central Powers.

Horne, John and Alan Kramer. *German Atrocities 1914: A History of Denial*. New Haven: Yale University Press, 2001. With real historical detective work, this study pins down the facts concerning the atrocities committed in Belgium and France and their subsequent denial.

Horne, John, ed. *State, Society and Mobilization in Europe during the First World War*. Cambridge: Cambridge University Press, 1997. Important study of different aspects of how combatant societies gear up for total war.

Hovannisian, Richard G. *The Armenian Genocide in Perspective*. New Brunswick, NJ: Transaction Publishers, 1986. Interdisciplinary approaches to the debate concerning the Armenian massacres.

Howard, Michael. *The First World War*. Oxford: Oxford University Press, 2002. Though it hardly seems possible, this book provides an excellent, succinct overview of the war in a mere 143 pages.

Hynes, Samuel Lynn. *A War Imagined: The First World War and English Culture*. London: Bodley Head, 1990. Art and mythology of the war experience in the British context.

Jahn, Hubertus. *Patriotic Culture in Russia during World War I*. Ithaca: Cornell University Press, 1995. Fascinating study of a neglected topic, Russian popular mobilization for war.

Keegan, John. *The Face of Battle*. New York: Vintage Books, 1977. A classic of military history, with compelling analysis of the Battle of the Somme.

Kershaw, Ian. *Hitler: 1889–1936 Hubris*. New York: Norton, 2000. The first volume of the now standard biography of Hitler.

Kissinger, Henry. *Diplomacy*. New York: Simon and Schuster, 1994. Kissinger's personal perspective as a diplomat informs his judgments on diplomatic history.

Lawrence, T. E. *Seven Pillars of Wisdom: A Triumph*. New York: Penguin, 1982. A memoir that cemented the romantic legend of Lawrence of Arabia.

Lincoln, W. Bruce. *Red Victory: A History of the Russian Civil War*. New York: Simon and Schuster, 1989. A masterly survey of the entire sweep of Russia's civil war in all its complexity.

Link, Arthur S. *Woodrow Wilson: Revolution, War, Peace*. Arlington Heights, IL: Harlan Davidson, 1979. Fascinating brief biographical account of a complex personality and the ideas that he embodied.

Liulevicius, Vejas Gabriel. *War Land on the Eastern Front: Culture, National Identity, and German Occupation in World War I*. Cambridge: Cambridge University Press, 2000. Study of lesser-known aspects of the cultural history of war in the East.

Malia, Martin. *The Soviet Tragedy: A History of Socialism in Russia, 1917–1991*. New York: Free Press, 1994. Provocative and strongly argued narrative of the Bolshevik experiment from its beginnings to its collapse.

Marwick, Arthur. *The Deluge: British Society and the First World War*. New York: Norton, 1970. Classic work on the impact of the war on British life.

Massie, Robert K. *Castles of Steel: Britain, Germany, and the Winning of the Great War at Sea*. New York: Random House, 2003. Pulitzer Prize-winning author's account of the sea war.

McPhail, Helen. *The Long Silence: Civilian Life under the German Occupation of Northern France, 1914–1918*. London, New York: I. B. Tauris, 1999. Rich account, drawing on diaries and memoirs, of civilian experience under German occupation behind the Western Front.

Moorehead, Alan. *Gallipoli*. London: H. Hamilton, 1956. Classic account of a classic failure.

Morrow, John H., Jr. *The Great War: An Imperial History*. New York: Routledge, 2004. Recent study puts the war into a larger context of worldwide colonialism.

———, *The Great War in the Air: Military Aviation from 1909 to 1921*. Washington, D.C.: Smithsonian Institution Press, 1993. Study by a leading expert on air war of its coming of age.

Moynahan, Brian. *The Russian Century: A History of the Last Hundred Years*. New York: Random House, 1994. Vivid scenes from Russia's violent century.

Naimark, Norman. *Fires of Hatred: Ethnic Cleansing in Twentieth-Century Europe*. Cambridge, MA: Harvard University Press, 2001. Sophisticated examination of cases of ethnic cleansing in Europe, weighing similarities and contrasts.

Ousby, Ian. *The Road to Verdun: World War I's Most Momentous Battle and the Folly of Nationalism*. New York: Anchor Books, 2003. Fluently written and eloquently examined study of how the evolution of nationalism made the "hell of Verdun" possible.

Power, Samantha. *"A Problem from Hell": America and the Age of Genocide*. New York: Basic Books, 2002. A passionate and gripping assessment of American responses to atrocity from the Armenian massacres to the present day.

Rachamimov, Alon. *POWs and the Great War: Captivity on the Eastern Front*. New York: Berg, 2002. Now indispensable study of a hitherto almost unknown episode: the experience of POWs in the Russian Empire.

Razac, Olivier. *Barbed Wire: A Political History*. Trans. by Jonathan Kneight. New York: The New Press, 2002. A fascinating essay on the complicated and often brutal uses of a simple technology.

Reed, John. *Ten Days That Shook the World*. New York: International Publishers, 1919. An evocative eyewitness account of the October Revolution by an American journalist sympathetic to the Bolsheviks.

Remarque, Erich Maria. *All Quiet on the Western Front*. Trans. by A. W. Wheen. New York: Fawcett Crest, 1990. The classic literary testament of the war, in many ways ambivalent, as it captured the experiences of its author and the veterans who read it after the war.

Rose, Norman. *Churchill: The Unruly Giant*. New York: Free Press, 1994. Readable and compelling biography of a crucial personality of the century.

Service, Robert. *Lenin: A Biography*. Cambridge, MA: Harvard University Press, 2000. Insightful study of a man who shaped the 20th century, as an individual and as a political force.

Showalter, Denis. *Tannenberg: Clash of Empires, 1914*. North Haven, CT: Archon Books, 1991. A classic work of the great German victory on the Eastern Front, in its broadest context.

Snyder, Jack. *The Ideology of the Offensive: Military Decision Making and the Disasters of 1914*. Ithaca: Cornell University Press, 1984. Sober study of the intoxicating cult of the offensive dominating the outbreak of the war.

Stone, Norman. *The Eastern Front 1914–1917*. London: Penguin reprint, 1998. The classic treatment of the war in Eastern Europe.

Strachan, Hew. *The First World War. Volume 1: To Arms*. Oxford: Oxford University Press, 2001. The first volume of what will be the magisterial account of the war for our time.

Taylor, Phillip M. *Munitions of the Mind: A History of Propaganda from the Ancient World to the Present Day*. Third edition. Manchester: Manchester University Press, 2003. World War I propaganda in its broader, long-range context of political persuasion campaigns.

Verhey, Jeffrey. *The Spirit of 1914: Militarism, Myth and Mobilization in Germany*. Cambridge: Cambridge University Press, 2000. Subtle study of the crucial linkages between the August Madness of 1914 and the later venomous "Stab in the Back" legend in defeated Germany.

Ward, Candace, ed. *World War One British Poets: Brooke, Owen, Sassoon, Rosenberg and Others*. Mineola, NY: Dover, 1997. In an inexpensive edition, a collection of classic British war poets.

Weintraub, Stanley. *Silent Night: The Story of the World War I Christmas Truce*. New York: Plume, 2002. A most readable account of the dramatic and spontaneous truce of Christmas 1914.

————. *A Stillness Heard Round the World: The End of the Great War, November 1918*. Oxford: Oxford University Press, 1987. Fascinating survey of the days when the guns at last fell silent.

Welch, David. *German Propaganda and Total War, 1914–1918: The Sins of Omission*. New Brunswick, NJ: Rutgers University Press, 2000. Keen and detailed examination of Germany's often awkward propaganda effort.

Wheeler-Bennett, John W. *Brest-Litovsk: The Forgotten Peace, March 1918*. New York: Norton, 1971. Though an older history, this remains the classic account of a lesser-known but pivotal, imposed peace.

Winter, Denis. *Death's Men: Soldiers of the Great War*. London: Penguin, 1979. Classic history of the war in the trenches.

Winter, Jay. *The Experience of World War I*. New York: Oxford University Press, 1989. Marvelously illustrated with copious maps, graphs, and photographs; one of the best introductions to the history of the war.

Yourcenar, Marguerite. *Coup de Grace*. New York: The Noonday Press, 1981. A 1939 novel about the nihilistic *Freikorps*.

Zweig, Stefan. *The World of Yesterday: An Autobiography*. Lincoln, NE: University of Nebraska Press, 1964. An elegy for the world destroyed by the Great War.

Internet Resources:

The British Imperial War Museum maintains a website with links to collections of photographs and sources: http://www.iwm.org.uk.

Fordham University maintains a fascinating collection of documents and sources on World War I: http://www.fordham.edu/halsall/mod/modsbook38.html.

The Western Front Association, founded in 1980 in Britain and with branches in the United States, memorializes the experience of the First World War in Flanders and France: http://www.westernfront.co.uk.